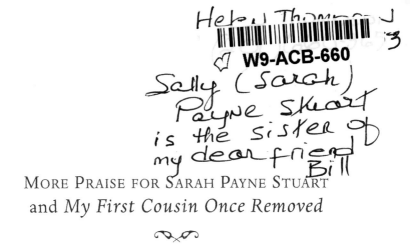

MORE PRAISE FOR SARAH PAYNE STUART
and *My First Cousin Once Removed*

ᑭ✕ᑎ

"If only more memorists could be so disarming in their condemnations, could rein themselves in and not display their ill natures or wounded vanities in an embarrassing manner, we'd all have more fun." —*Boston Sunday Globe*

"A witty, at times moving account of how the privileges of caste are counteracted by the myriad burdens of family." —*Washington Times*

"Stuart's book is as charming, peculiar and oddly unsettling as the eccentric New England clan that populates its pages." —*Elle*

"From a sometimes painful family history, Sarah Payne Stuart has created a poignant, funny, and ultimately triumphant memoir filled with great warmth and wisdom. Written in a refreshing, unforgettable voice that never falters or sentimentalizes, *My First Cousin Once Removed* is a thoroughly terrific book." —DORIS KEARNS GOODWIN

"Stuart is a deft writer who knows how to snare her audience with brilliant, bitter-black humor while touching lightly but with sure, probing fingers each of our darker fears, our least favorite wounds." —*Seattle Weekly*

MY FIRST COUSIN ONCE REMOVED

ALSO BY SARAH PAYNE STUART

Men in Trouble
The Year Roger Wasn't Well

SARAH PAYNE STUART

My First Cousin Once Removed

Money, Madness, and the
Family of Robert Lowell

HarperPerennial
A Division of HarperCollins*Publishers*

The Library of Congress has catalogued the hardcover edition as follows:

Stuart, Sarah Payne.
    My first cousin once removed : money, madness, and the family of Robert Lowell / Sarah Payne Stuart. 1st ed.
      p. cm.
    ISBN 0-06-017689-X
    1. Lowell, Robert, 1917–1977—Family. 2. Poets, American—20th century—Family relationships. 3. Aristocracy (Social class)—Massachusetts—Boston—History. 4. Mental illness—Massachusetts—Boston—History. 5. Family—Massachusetts—Boston—History. 6. Boston (Mass.)—Economic conditions. 7. Boston (Mass.)—Biography. 8. Winslow family. 9. Lowell family. I. Title.
PS3523.O89Z875 1998
811'.52—dc21
[B]   98-7787

ISBN 0-06-093036-5 (pbk.)

99 00 01 02 03 ❖RRD (H) 10 9 8 7 6 5 4 3 2 1

To Jackie, Allie, Polly, and Amory. And to Bobby.

ACKNOWLEDGMENTS

I would like to thank:

Sandy Frazier, a great writer and humorist, who, for some unknown reason, has waded through every draft of everything I have ever written, from the murky initial draft of my first novel ("That," he said, with throbbing head, leafing ahead to page 91, "that part there is *like* a novel.") to the countless drafts of this book—for shedding light, in unexpected ways, in the darkest hours, and for teaching me everything I know.

My parents, Jackie and Bill Payne, whose memories, insights and humor make up so much of this book, for sharing the stories of their lives so generously and then, after receiving in return the dubious reward of reading their daughter's interpretation of them, continuing to provide the unqualified parental support that most writers only dream about.

My brothers, Billy, Johnny, and Hunter, who early on taught me that the path through pain was humor, for providing an essential element to this book by once again demonstrating their ability to be honest, poignant, and funny in one breath.

My aunt Allie Winslow Read, a true soul mate, for her countless stories about her upbringing, so vividly rendered that they fell into my book like a dream.

My uncle Amory Sommaripa, a great raconteur, for sharing insights about his parents that enriched not only this book but this family.

My cousin Nell Devereux Joslin Styron, for her witty and perceptive stories about Bobby, his parents, and Boston society.

Lizzie Trustlow, for her beautifully rendered stories about her mother, Polly Winslow.

My Thorndike and Winslow cousins, who all my life have been open and funny about our family and supportive of my plunges into its analysis.

Fiona Hallowell for her sensitivity and smart editorial comments; Sue Llewellyn, whose sense of humor and erudition made this book better.

Liz Darhansoff, my agent, so hard to please but so worth pleasing.

My husband, Charlie Stuart, who had the unfortunate honor of seeing this book when it was a mass of unfinished, uninteresting sentences leading nowhere, for telling me with a straight face that I had a great book on my hands.

And my editor, who resisted bravely the use of his own words to save himself from the morass of my successive drafts, and whose genius as an editor nearly brought me back to the religions of my forefathers in sheer gratitude—for showing me at last the joy of writing: to watch him edit.

MY FIRST COUSIN ONCE REMOVED

Bobby and my mother, aged eleven and ten.

1

My first cousin once removed was Robert Lowell, the Pulitzer Prize–winning poet—a fact I just happened to mention on my application to Harvard College. The worst part was that I had to work this genealogical information into the essay. The application had a section for listing family members who had gone to Harvard, but it was only supposed to include immediate family members. The essay wasn't a real essay, just two little white spaces under the questions: "How have your personal experiences contributed to your intellectual growth?" and "How have your academic experiences contributed to your personal growth?" It was three o'clock in the morning, and the application was due the next day. So I started writing something moronic about my intellectual development—or was it my personal growth?—all the while saying to myself, *I can't, I can't*, when suddenly out of the blue came, "As I was having dinner last night with my first cousin once removed, Robert Lowell, the poet, I turned to him and said . . . ."

That was a long time ago, in 1969, and it is time to make a clean breast of it now. Also, I might just as well admit that I don't get poetry. In high school I was good at subjects like "the Negro" and "the Culture of Poverty," but when it came to analyzing poems, forget it. To this day, put a gun to my head and I still cannot tell you the difference between the mood of a poem and the tone of a poem. My parents were no help. When I went to them with my homework, my father would just shake his head and say he wondered how he ever got such smart kids. My father is a big bragger about us kids—a feat, considering all that has transpired. Not long ago we were at a wedding reception, and across the room I saw my father motioning to me wildly, with his fingers in his mouth, trying to get me to whistle through my teeth, a talent of mine he had obviously just bragged about. It is lucky for my father that he has four kids, because usually one of us is doing all right. One kid might be in a mental hospital, another with the Maharishi, and another with a marriage on the rocks, and my father can turn to someone and say, "My son Bill just got a raise at his job."

Still, I did not lie on the application to Harvard, technically speaking. Bobby—"Bobby" is what we called him in the family—had been over for dinner the night before. Bobby came out to visit us in Concord whenever he was teaching at Harvard. Concord, Massachusetts, is where I grew up, under the influence of the writings of Louisa May Alcott. My mother said there was an excruciating period when I called her Marmee and helped with the dishes every two seconds. Eight years ago, as a grown-up, I moved my husband and children from New York to Concord, on a wave of nostalgia. "So the kids can have swimming lessons at Walden Pond!" I cried out, though it turned out they wanted to have them at a pool.

My mother and Bobby were first cousins, which is how Bobby became "once removed" from me, meaning that he is the same relationship to me as he is to my mother, just one generation away. Understanding "once-removes" is kind of an off-putting characteristic, but it is something I grew up with. Some families discuss politics or the shortest route to I-95 or how to cook a roast chicken in a paper bag; my family has murderously hot discussions about whether Sally Pickering, a woman no more interesting dead than she was alive, is related to us by blood or marriage. (It turns out everyone is correct: She was a cousin who married a cousin.) In my family, genes are everything, so that even being a manic depressive is a kind of badge of honor, proving the family's tenacity in sticking close to Boston, where there was no one to marry but one another.

Bobby was a manic depressive. Half of my family is manic depressive; the rest is screwed up about it. I should mention that whenever I talk about my family it is usually my mother's family to whom I am referring. My father has been known to mention at funerals and other occasions that he has a family too. "The name McGuire would open any door in the South," he says, but nobody is listening.

On the maternal side of my mother's family are the Thorndikes—whose claim to fame is Israel Thorndike, the first millionaire in New England, who looted British ships during the Revolutionary War and later got his portrait hung at Harvard. On the paternal side are the Winslows, who came over on the *Mayflower*, befriended the Indians, slaughtered the Indians, governed a colony, fled to Canada during the Revolution, and sold matches on the streets. Bobby is related to my mother through the Winslows.

Bobby was an only child. He and my mother were one year apart, and when they were growing up they'd spend weeks together at their grandparents', where their mothers dropped them whenever they had a chance. Neither Bobby's mother nor my mother's mother was what you call a "baby person," although what kind of a person was left for them to be is hard to grasp since neither of them ever cooked, cleaned, earned a dime, or went to college. My mother was very beautiful—her mother used to dress her in Alice-blue velvet and have her sit at the piano with her hair flowing down her back, but sadly her talents lay elsewhere. Nor was she an intellectual. This never seemed to bother Bobby. They loved each other, though neither of them probably understood a word the other one said. My mother's goal has been to lead a normal life, and she believes in treating other people as normal, even if they're not.

Ever since the time Bobby visited when I was four years old and I said something sarcastic in front of him, my mother has been quoting Bobby back at me. Not a line from one of his poems, just: "As your cousin the famous poet once said about you, 'Sarcasm does not become one so young,'" which didn't do much to build relations between Bobby and me.

Not that I have any memory of this molding visit that was to define sarcasm as my only talent, but the frequent reference to my famous cousin certainly colored my view of poetry, making me dread the reading of each poem for school, throwing me on my knees on a

Sunday night to beseech God what in the name of Christ, our Savior, was the meaning of "The Love Song of J. Alfred Prufrock."

Most of my experiences with Bobby were at Great-Aunt Sarah's Thanksgivings, where year after year Bobby looked at me vaguely and said, "Haven't you grown taller or something?" Bobby and Elizabeth Hardwick, his second wife, would fly in from New York with their little girl, Harriet, and Elizabeth would chat away wittily while Bobby wandered around looking into the distance. At dinner Bobby was always seated between Harriet and Cousin Natalie Winslow, a great big woman (who had supposedly once been very pretty), who was forever writing a book in French about her visions of Marie Antoinette at Versailles. Bobby said he found his four-year-old daughter more intellectually stimulating.

My great-aunt Sarah was head of the family by then—everyone else of her generation had long since died. She was in her seventies in the 1960s, tall, trim, and "active"—her favorite self-description—moving with girlish confidence through her daily schedule of charity functions and ladies' luncheons, her brain untroubled by thought. "The colored people should be more active," Aunt Sarah would pronounce, settling cozily into an armchair by the fire. "*I've* been active all my life, and I've never *once* thought of protesting a thing."

My great-aunt Sarah was very rich, or rather, as was evident after he died, her husband, Uncle Cot, was very rich. Charles Edward Cotting was his full name, but Aunt Sarah called him Cot, and we called him Uncle Cot, as if the endearment might bring us closer to this reticent man, whom we never saw without a tie, even on Saturday mornings at his farm, tramping the fields in tweed jacket, vest, and cap. Being a gentleman was a concept I was brought up on, my father always carefully walking on the outside of me on the street, a custom dating back to some unspecified time when people supposedly threw their garbage out their front windows, but our standards were far lower than Uncle Cot's. (So low, in fact, that for years I assumed I had married a gentleman until, glancing out the window at the heartwarming spectacle of my husband walking our six-year-old daughter to the school bus, I saw him turn and spit on the sidewalk.) "Mr. Cotting is of historical interest as an example of the perfect Edwardian gentleman," I was told recently by the curator of the museum in Salem, Massachusetts.

Aunt Sarah and Uncle Cot were not only rich, they were childless, and although my parents considered money to be the root of all evil—*still*: Try as one might to banish the thought, one couldn't help but wonder where it was all going after they died. "Which is your favorite?" Aunt Sarah would ask me about her various houses, and, I must admit, my heart would skip a beat. The Cottings had three establishments, all within forty minutes of one another: a five-story town house on Beacon Street in Boston, overlooking the Charles River and the stream of cars on Storrow Drive ("I don't think Mrs. Storrow quite knew her money was to go toward ruining our backyards," Uncle Cot once said); a thirty-room house in Manchester overlooking an Atlantic Ocean made cozy by familiar yachts; and "the farm"—three hundred acres of apple orchards, cow barns, and Victorian houses just west of Boston.

Thanksgiving, the big family holiday, was always held at the farm. "When Cot was in his twenties he decided he needed a hobby, so he went straight out and bought himself a farm!" my aunt Sarah used to say, looking pointedly at my brother, who in his twenties was driving a taxi after a stint in the mental hospital. "*And* he bought it with his own money!" Uncle Cot had been the only child of an only child from a rich Boston family and kept inheriting money and houses all his life. When he was a young man everybody seemed to be terribly worried that he should have a hobby. His mother worried about a hobby, so he bought the farm; his father worried about a hobby, so he started collecting Currier & Ives, comfy prints about the good old days when people knew their place; his boss worried about a hobby and suggested sailing as a way to relax, so Cot bought a schooner, and then a fifty-foot yacht. I'm sure Uncle Cot was busy—at the age of twenty-six he was on the boards of at least six charities—still, *relax*? I do not think Uncle Cot ever in his life lifted his dinner plate from the table to bring it to the kitchen.

All kinds of Winslow cousins you never saw except at Thanksgiving would come to the farm, and everyone would pretend to be unabashed by the finger bowls, though they all kept an eye out to see to which side Great-Aunt Sarah placed the untouched bowl, cradled in its doily. No one ever dreamed of actually touching the water in the finger bowl, except for the youngest child, who would dutifully lift the bowl cutely to drink. (I repeated the trick as an over-the-hill eight-year-old after a much younger Harriet drank hers.) The food was good, but utterly plain as WASP food always is and always will be, as if there is something immoral in too much concentration on food. When I went to college I thought the food was heaven, because it had sauces, and was not three separate clumps of meat, rice, and vegetable. And yet now, despite indulging in a brief flurry of white sauces and crepes after I got married, I have succumbed to destiny and think really there is nothing better than a simple baked potato.

Before Thanksgiving dinner there were lots of cocktails and crackers and cheese for the grown-ups, and ginger ale for the kids in the den in front of a football game on the black-and-white TV. At dinner there were toasts, surely nothing to do with the Pilgrims and Indians, but about what I cannot remember, though I actually attempted to make one myself the fall after I got married. Passionate on the strength of three of Uncle Cot's very stiff gin and tonics, it was the one time in my life I felt moved to say something to Aunt Sarah and Uncle Cot and the assembled family. What it *was* is less clear, as I keeled over on the table in mid-sentence, dead drunk. "Poor Sally, she's a bit under the weather," everyone said as my husband carried me, out cold, upstairs. (Drinking cocktails is the one vice considered a virtue by my family, alarmed to find so many in my generation abstaining in favor of the Eastern religions or jogging. "We're so happy you drink!" my parents said when they first met my husband, Charlie, a Dartmouth man.)

After dinner, rain or shine, everyone would get into galoshes and overcoats and tramp off to the barns to look at Uncle Cot's prize cows, who lived in warm, enviably clean stalls with fresh-smelling sawdust, each with its pedigree framed and hung from the rafter above. Being one of those beloved pampered cows looked better and better as I grew older, my yearning reaching its climax the year I had to sell Time-Life books over the phone and hide from the Harvard Co-op, to which I owed three hundred dollars. In a similar way my mother might have yearned to be the chic Mrs. Hopper, with the fresh makeup and jangling gold jewelry, who was always made much of at Thanksgiving dinner. Mrs. Hopper had been the wife of Mr. Hopper, the manager of the farm, who had died rather young, at which point Uncle Cot had given Mrs. Hopper one of the large Victorian houses on the estate, even though Mr. and Mrs. Hopper were not "blessed with children in the home." As my mother's star set with the mental troubles of her children, Mrs. Hopper's rose. "Mrs. Hopper had us to dinner with *two* other couples," my aunt Sarah would marvel to my mother, who fed exactly the same number of people three times a day, "with *no help whatsoever!*"

At Thanksgiving everyone would fall into a hushed silence lest they miss Bobby saying something quotable. Bobby had created a lot of turmoil in the family before I was born, but then he had won the Pulitzer Prize and the National Book Award, and for years he could get away with anything. He could say the most outrageous thing at Great-Aunt Sarah's, and she would turn to you and say confidentially, "Bobby's a genius, you know."

This is not to say that we relatives, despite the awe in which we held him, had actually read much of Bobby's poetry, except in a rather cursory way. Not that this neglect was something any of us would necessarily have been apologetic about, on the no-nonsense New England theory that "poetry was all very well if one had the time to read it." Charlotte, Bobby's mother, had tried to foist Robert Frost on Bobby after he became interested in poetry—now, *those* were the kind of poems that would have appealed to my family, poems about practical things, like directions in the woods.

There is almost no intellectual heritage in the family at all. Bobby's mother fervently went to book club every week, but it was the club part that was fervent; Bobby said he wasn't sure if she'd ever *read* a book. The men tend to view the bookish with suspicion, not only in our family, but among the whole New England Protestant crowd. Even after Bobby won the Pulitzer, most of my parents' friends didn't know who he was. One night at one of their cocktail parties out in Concord, Mr. Brewer casually asked Bobby what he did. "I'm a poet," said Bobby in his soft voice. "No, no, no," said Mr. Brewer. "I mean what do you *really* do?"

Bobby was a genius, but then, in my family, you never know if this is good or bad. There were a lot of mixed messages about Bobby while I was growing up, except in New England we call them "conflicts." Bobby was the king of conflicts, and one of the conflicts he brought into the family was whether you wanted to be a genius and be crazy or be a dull person and be sane, as if this were a possible choice for a person to have. Even as a child of no discernible gifts, I found myself grappling with the problem of whether I wanted to be a genius when I grew up, or a librarian peacefully stamping books. On the one hand you really want to be a genius and win a prize so that the people in the family will take what you do seriously, and maybe even speak of you in hushed tones when you're not around. On the other hand, look how Bobby was always leaving his wives.

The first time I dared to glance at Bobby's poetry I was thirteen and suddenly without friends. I would come home after school and sit at the yellow Formica table to eat my snack and answer my mother, who dared to be around, in the rudest monosyllables I could get away with. My sunnier side I saved for my father, greeting him by sliding down the banister when he came whistling back from work. "Sally has just been dreadful all day," my mother would say to my father, who could only answer, "Gee, she seems fine to me." I had always been quite pro-grammatic about my snack, drinking bowls of milk while reading *Heidi*, eating flapjacks when reading *Trixie Belden*, but during that terrible year of the eighth grade, I just came home from school and ate too much, then wandered upstairs feeling vaguely greasy.

That afternoon I plunked myself down in front of the low bookcase in my parents' bedroom, and there in paperback (as opposed to the large hardback Masters and Johnson, with the jacket turned alluringly inside out) was the little row of Bobby's slim books with their violent covers, one with its golden award seal. Drawing in my breath for courage, I turned to the first poem in *Lord Weary's Castle*, hoping against hope that it might have something to do with princes and princesses—my predilection for reading about the problems of the rich having evidenced itself early on—only to be plunged into the darkness of incomprehension.

By the time I was fifteen and had experienced great suffering, in that Danny O'Dell had left me for Penny Parker, I took another peek at Bobby's poetry (while listening, under the throbbing influence of Tareyton cigarettes, to Tim Hardin on the headphones) to see if such suffering had made me any deeper, but still his poetry to me was darkness, darkness.

The truth is, growing up, I was terrified of Bobby. But that night in 1969 when he came to dinner in Concord, Bobby was so funny the tears streamed down my face. He made remarks about writers and family members I still don't dare repeat, and then we had a long discussion about Sir Thomas More. Bobby admired him and had just written a poem about him. I said I hated him, he reminded me of Thoreau who you knew was getting his laundry done at Emerson's while he was living in the woods, and Bobby laughed and said I was original, a comment I quote back to myself in troubled times. Later he read us his latest poems while my father slept on the couch and my mother and I listened attentively. I wanted so much to understand the poems, but I didn't. When Bobby got to one entitled "For Aunt Sarah," my mother said it was a lovely poem but of course he would have to change the line "Semi-illiterate, but infinitely kind." Bobby and my mother talked about the line the rest of the evening, my mother arguing that Bobby had always said he would never write about members of the family until they were dead, and Bobby arguing that changing the line would ruin the poem.

"Semi-illiterate" was pretty mild compared to what he'd written about the family before, and one of Bobby's arguments was that Aunt Sarah wouldn't be hurt by the line. But I think we convinced him she would. Or at least that's what I thought until recently a friend said, "I don't know, I think the line 'semi-illiterate, but infinitely kind' is kind of corny." Until that moment it had never occurred to me that not all of Bobby's lines were perfect. Maybe the line wasn't a hard one to lose. In fact, now that I look at it, the whole poem is too nice. It's one of the few times Bobby seemed to be writing with the family looking over his shoulder.

Whatever the reason, when the poem was published he'd changed the line to "yet infinitely kind—in short a lady . . ." And for years, my great-aunt Sarah kept the poem framed in her living room.

Aunt Sarah in 1898.

Sarah at Farmington
Mch 1912

Miss Porter's, in Farmington, Connecticut,
was a finishing school, but this did not mean
that you necessarily had to finish.

2

I NEVER READ BOBBY'S POETRY SO I CAN HAVE HIM TO DINNER," AUNT Sarah used to say, and when I think of Bobby and Aunt Sarah sipping cocktails in the front parlor on Beacon Street and eating those Ritz Cracker hors d'ouevres that were inevitably passed around by the tottering maid at exactly 7:10 P.M., it is clear that she never nestled in bed reading Bobby's poem about her father being rushed to hell by the ghost of Jesus.

Aunt Sarah was my great-aunt and Bobby's aunt—his mother's sister. She was forty-seven when she got married, though in pictures she looks twenty—her secret, she said, was to stay in bed for five days every month when she got her period. She lived at home until she got married, so she was always available to baby-sit Bobby. Bobby and Aunt Sarah adored each other, my mother says, though when Bobby writes, "We've quarreled lightly almost fifty years," it is a bit revisionist. Their arguments were not always so light, for instance when Bobby dared to write about the misery of his mother and father's marriage. "Charlotte and Bob were very, very happy together!" Aunt Sarah insisted vehemently to my mother, though I have never heard another soul agree. My mother also remembers an earlier time when Bobby and Aunt Sarah were arguing heatedly, sitting on the dock at

Aunt Sarah's house in Manchester. Bobby became so angry that he flung himself into the water and swam furiously out to sea.

Bobby told Aunt Sarah exactly what he thought—as opposed to me, who never spoke a true word in her presence—and how could they have agreed on anything? For Aunt Sarah the question wasn't whether one went to Harvard, but what club at Harvard one got into. "I prayed and prayed I would marry a Porcellian man," she told me once with a sigh, "but Cot was only in A.D." When I brought the most proper boyfriend I had ever had to dinner and he told Aunt Sarah he had gone to Yale, she blinked once and said, "Well, I suppose people have to go *somewhere*." Bobby had left Harvard of his own accord, and after that nothing he did could be understood by Aunt Sarah.

It had never occurred to me that Aunt Sarah could possibly be "semi-illiterate"—she was such a grande dame, so "well bred," whatever in the world that term means. Once when we were driving through a tollbooth, my father turned to me and said, "Now, I know you don't care, but I just want you to know that you are very well bred." When I think of the things I have done in my life, I think the phrase "well bred" has been reduced to mean "always writes thank-you notes."

Still, no evidence has ever been uncovered that Aunt Sarah ever really finished a book. Possibly she was dyslexic, or made into a dyslexic because her father forced her to change from left-handed to right-handed at Miss Porter's. Miss Porter's is the posh school in Farmington, Connecticut, the girls in my family attended two generations back, and where no one in my generation ever went. This is because there was not enough money left to send the girls and not enough snobbery left to want to. Snobbery can exist without money, but for how long? My father's family was southern and has had no money since the Civil War, but when I asked one of his aunts at age ninety-seven if she had made any friends in the nursing home, she looked at me as if I were off my head: "Why, they're just *ordinary* people."

My parents had no money, or rather, like "ordinary" people, they had to live off what my father earned—in this case, by selling Simmons Beautyrest mattresses. We went to public school, had ice cream only on Sundays, had to wait until my grandmother died to put up a stockade fence to hide the train running behind the backyard, *but* we always, always belonged to a country club. It was important to scrape the money together to join the country club—a concept completely missing in my generation.

Our parents told us that money was the root of all evil, that wanting it was morally wrong and that having it brought terrible troubles. And yet, as I was growing up, it was hard to believe that money was so bad when I saw the constant care my family took with it, weighing each dollar, so that every transaction, from the buying of a bike to the buying of dinner (a dollar limit at Howard Johnson's), was an agony of economic wizardry. In the end the perverse result of my parents' well-intentioned teaching was that I believed, and will always believe, that money spent is love bestowed—that money is love. And what I remember most about my great-aunt Sarah was that she was generous.

It is easy to be generous if you are rich, it would seem, but in New England this is not always the case, at least for the people who have not earned their money. My grandmother, who died a millionaire in 1964 despite the fact that her beautiful farm had lost money every year, gave us presents ordered from the backs of cereal boxes for Christmas, and Beeman's Chewing Gum, one stick at a time, when she visited. She did not wish her grandchildren to love her for her money, she said. My friends whose grandmothers worked for a living would get the cherished Patty Play Pal, the hideous life-size doll every girl my age coveted. But as I saw it displayed on its pedestal at Woolworth's I knew that it was never to be mine. I was taught to regard with horror the fact that my friends from "different backgrounds" received it: They were being spoiled, and spoiling was not love. But to me it was.

Sometimes there is no moral basis to New England penury: Cheapness is in itself a virtue. My father tells the story of an acquaintance, the inheritor of several millions, pondering buying a day-old "Happy Mother's Day" cake marked down at a convenience store for his wife's birthday. Other stories are not so amusing, like the uproar when my mother's cousin suggested to her friends that they each give the cleaning woman they shared a day off so that she could have a week's paid vacation—from women who had never earned a dime in their lives. As for my grandmother, when she died she left her black maid of twenty years the sum of two hundred dollars.

But not Aunt Sarah. Aunt Sarah would arrive at our shabby house with its painted-over wallpaper and its driveway of busted-up pavement, carrying armfuls of toys from FAO Schwarz. She would send my mother large checks out of the blue. Once she wandered into the Provident Institute for Savings and opened an account in my name with two thousand dollars. When my mother had a breakdown and was taken away in the middle of the night, leaving my father to cope with four kids under eight, Aunt Sarah and Uncle Cot paid a substantial part of the bill for her year-and-a-half stay at the hospital. When I was twenty-three and had a major operation and couldn't pay my rent for two months, my parents told Aunt Sarah. A thousand dollars arrived the next day in the mail.

This was the "unqualified love" one is always reading about at the hairdresser's and wishing one could get a piece of. I got a piece of it because for years Aunt Sarah poured it on me. My mother was her "favorite niece," but I was her "little princess," though sullen as a spoon and plain as a saucepan, with knobby knees and a barbershop haircut— and so unused to such effusion that I would stand straight as a stick while love was bestowed. But I will never forget what it was like.

This was the love Aunt Sarah gave to Bobby and my mother and her sisters in their youth—a kind of love they never got from their own mothers, whose love always had a motive. When Bobby's mother died in 1954, Aunt Sarah was all he had left of his past. She represented the generations that had brought him up even as he fought them all the way. She represented the "good taste" that is the mark of the Boston Brahmin, the good taste that can ruin any artistic creation.

"It is never necessary to say a disagreeable thing," my Aunt Sarah always said. Try writing a poem with that in mind.

Aunt Sarah talked of sending me to Miss Porter's, just as she talked about the coming-out party she was going to give me in the garden in Manchester (but which I declined because of the bombing in Viet-

nam, a connection that was a bit clearer to me then). Even at four-
teen, the year before I became a hippie, when I desperately wanted to
go to boarding school and make chocolate-chip cookies in the dorm
kitchen on Saturday nights, clinging to this safe vision lest I join my
depressed brothers in their despair—even then I didn't want to go to
Miss Porter's, where I envisioned girls my age going to class in mink
stoles. Later I laughed at such a vision as being very un–Boston Yan-
kee, who generally the richer they are, the more holes they have in
their clothes; but then I saw a picture of Aunt Sarah standing in front
of Miss Porter's looking like someone in a Fitzgerald story, waiting
for the chauffeur.

Miss Porter's was a finishing school back then. Still, this evidently
did not mean you had to finish. No thought was given to taking girls
out before they graduated to suit a family's convenience—so many of
my relatives were pulled out right before they would have received
their diploma—one to attend a wedding, another to go to a ranch—
that it almost seems deliberate. My great-aunt Sarah was taken out by
her father a few months before graduation because she was needed to
join a family jaunt to Europe.

Aunt Sarah lived in her father's house under his rule until he died,
and then she married Uncle Cot and moved down the street. She had
fought incessantly with her tyrannical father, but with Uncle Cot
there was no power struggle: He simply let her say anything she
wanted and quietly had his way in all things. She adopted all his rou-
tines—going to the symphony on Friday, though she hated music ("I
go to Symphony so I can see the hats"), the farm on the weekend,
Manchester in the summer. She ate the same meals, depending on the
day of the week, at the exact same time. The servants in my time had
been Uncle Cot's as a young man, even, in some cases, Uncle Cot's
mother's. (This seems impossible, but, for instance, Molly the cook
had been his mother's cook but still was younger than Uncle Cot.)
Many of them were so old you wanted to leap to your feet to help
them, especially when their hands shook as they held out a platter of
summer squash to Aunt Sarah sitting high in her chair, strong as an
ox. They ran the house the way Uncle Cot's mother had run it, and
that was that. "Oh, I *do* hate begonias," Aunt Sarah would say, look-

ing wistfully at the flowers in her Boston living room, driven in by the gardener from Manchester that morning. "They're *so* Victorian." Or to a cousin from North Carolina, "I did *so* wish to have lamb tonight, but Molly says you're southern so we must have chicken."

What I now understand is that the upper class is quite open about money. This is directly opposed to my middle-class parents, who always said you can ask what someone's father *does*, but not *how much he makes*—which I was always getting mixed up. "So, what does your father make? " I would ask a new friend casually. (For my children the issue is moot, in that none of us is able to answer *either* question about my husband, Charlie. A few years ago, when Charlie was making documentaries about Latin America, Teddy, then in kindergarten, was asked by a friend, "Who does your father work for?" Teddy paused, and then answered with a confident air, "Noriega.") In English novels the upper classes often talk in exact terms (to the pound) of what a person makes a year—Jane Austen novels sometimes begin with the precise sums being discussed. I am told she was writing about the middle class, but this is too fine a line for me. To me, anyone who is born expecting servants to cook and clean for them is upper class. When I think of the ring I inherited (which never knew a drop of dishwashing soap until it met my hand), as it is plunged past the soggy bread into the garbage disposal, I wonder what it must be thinking.

From my parents I would hear that money was not what was important. The value, they said, was in who you were, not how much you had—a noble but wishful idea—for if it was true, why was there always a little flutter around the rich? I suppose it is the most obvious thing that money is so important, the difference between whether you mop the floor for others or get the floor mopped, but for me it was a revelation, and one that came too late, in the sense that I never learned how to make money.

For my great-uncle Cot, money transcended all other values, even blood. The Boston Brahmins hated the Irish above all people, but when I asked my uncle Cot what he thought of Joe Kennedy Sr., his baseball teammate at Harvard, he said, "Well, I've got to say, he made a lot of money. "

Uncle Cot was "a genius when it came to money," although my father often said he could have been a genius too if he had started out with a million. But Uncle Cot was no intellectual—the libraries were meager in his large houses, filled with *Reader's Digest Condensed Classics* and reassuring upper-class books by authors like Marquand. Certainly I never saw any of Bobby's there. Cot's art was like wallpaper—decorative, appropriate to the house in question—portraits of ancestors and watercolors of Boston Common in the Beacon Street house, seascapes in Manchester, Currier & Ives prints on the farmhouse walls—he left all two hundred Currier & Iveses to a single museum, to keep the collection together. It's together, all right; "in storage," says the museum.

Uncle Cot's family was an old Boston family who had made their money in real estate. *Acta Non Verba* is his family motto, carved over his family crest on the brick building he gave to Harvard Business School in 1967. "Make Money, Don't Write Books," was my own particular way of paraphrasing it when I stood in front of the building last fall. Also on the building is the Winslow crest, with the family motto, *Decoptus Florio* ("Cut Down, We Flourish"). "Gluttons for Punishment," I thought.

Cotting House is located across from Harvard Stadium. I used to pass it every day in 1975 in my banged-up Subaru en route from my crummy apartment in Cambridge to my job typing transcripts at WGBH-TV. At the time Cotting House was being used to house international students. Aunt Sarah, who disliked black people, was so furious that she marched in one day and took Uncle Cot's portrait off the wall.

Uncle Cot did not like Bobby, and in the end this is what caused the trouble between Bobby and Aunt Sarah. Uncle Cot did not like artists, a prejudice that firmly cemented itself during his early one-year marriage to an actress, Constance Binney, who was always inviting artists over and trying to get Cot to invest in their plays. Constance came from a good Boston family, but, Aunt Sarah would say disdainfully, "You'd arrive at a party and there'd she'd be playing the *piano*." I never saw Uncle Cot and Bobby talk; it was Elizabeth Hardwick who argued into the night about politics with Uncle Cot, with Bobby going up to bed. "Cot is afraid you'll write about him," Aunt Sarah would say to Bobby, but Bobby never deigned to do it.

Neither did Bobby like Uncle Cot. It was Aunt Sarah he came to visit. Maybe Uncle Cot reminded Bobby of his grandfather, Arthur Winslow—whom Bobby loved (and hated) more than his own father, though they had nothing in common. Both Uncle Cot and Arthur Winslow saw money as the sign of the elect—they actually liked you *more* if you made money, and the more money you made, the better you were. Now, this concept took me quite a while to grasp. The light only began to glimmer a few years ago, after everything in the world had changed, when Aunt Sarah, approaching ninety-nine, turned to me and said, "I don't like you, you're poor." But Bobby understood it all, and he knew that in his grandfather's eyes he had failed.

Aunt Sarah at age forty-seven.
She looked twenty. Her secret, she said, was to stay in bed
five days every month when she had her period.

3

THE FIRST THING I EVER READ ABOUT BOBBY WAS THE INTRODUCTION TO one of his books. It began with the date and place he was born, followed by the simple but apparently paragraph-stopping sentence: "His mother was a Winslow." My mother was a Winslow, too, but so far, this has impressed nobody except, briefly, the principal of my high school who, after learning of my middle name when he signed my diploma, called out to me in the parking lot, "Hey, are you Winslow as in Winslow Potato Chips?" We are not the Winslows in Winslow Potato chips or, for that matter, the Winslows in anything else. If we were, I might not receive bank statements in the mail that read: "Combined checking and savings: 0."

Nevertheless we were brought up being told we were "Winslows," as if this information alone should make everything clear in our lives. What the Winslows had actually done, besides getting kicked out of England before anyone else, was never explained, despite all the privately published books on the family's shelves about the Winslows, written by the Winslows but not, necessarily, *read* by the Winslows. When Bobby wrote about the family, he had the bad taste to write something people might actually want to read. "What Bobby wrote was very disagreeable," my aunt Sarah said. "My father wrote a book, and very interesting it was too, all about how we are directly descended from Mary Chilton, the first woman to step on Plymouth Rock." Mary Chilton was the one ancestor I was ever told about, the ace in the hole, the foundation of our family pride, in honor of whom plaques were hung and family trees drawn up. Recently I learned two facts about Mary Chilton that my family never told me: She did not step on Plymouth Rock (she waded ashore); and she was completely illiterate, signing her name with a poorly formed *M* till the end of her days.

Still, the Chilton Club—a ladies' club so swank my mother, though a direct descendant of Mary Chilton, could not afford to join until she was in her seventies—still flourishes in Boston, located on a discreet side street not too far from the Ritz, its thickly draped rooms with their twenty-foot ceilings a haven for tired Newbury Street shoppers or lunchers before Friday Symphony—"the last bastion of civilization," a friend of my father calls it. Here my mother and her book club munch sandwiches on brocade sofas and have heated discussions about Salman Rushdie. Here my aunt Sarah went on maid's night off, to a place nearly identical to home, down to the grouchy family retainer who waited at table and the plain (but delicious) meat with gravy as the predominant dish. All my life whenever I have entered the Chilton Club I have felt desolate and unloved, outside the safety net of its members' lives. Recently I stood with my mother in front of the plaque in the foyer. It said: MARY CHILTON WAS THE FIRST WHITE WOMAN TO COME TO AMERICA AND SETTLE IN BOSTON. (Did this mean that a nonwhite woman had traveled to America and settled in Boston before Mary Chilton? I read it four times and still couldn't make sense of it.)

Aunt Sarah used to dress up as Mary Chilton and step ceremoniously on a rock at the Chilton Club, but I don't think she ever advanced beyond the first paragraph of her father's book. I read the book and found, in terms of damage to the family, that it is about equal to what Bobby wrote. The difference is, when Aunt Sarah's father writes about the sloth and cowardice of his own grandfather, no one is reading it.

But most of the books about the family have a different slant. When one reads, say, Kenelm Winslow's sincere, soporific *Mayflower Heritage*, with its brave theory that when the *Mayflower* main beam broke in two, *perhaps* it was the bolt from Edward Winslow's printing press that fixed the beam and saved the future nation, one can scarcely summon the courage to go forward. My cousin Mary Devereux said she threw the book down early on when she realized those Pilgrims weren't idealists at all, just a bunch of middle managers.

When Bobby wrote about the family he picked the ancestor who massacred the Indians and paraded the survivors through the streets, not the ancestor responsible for forty years of peace with the Indians. Bobby wrote "At the Indian Killer's Grave," as opposed to "Edward Winslow: Third Signer of the Mayflower Compact," and who can blame him? Poor Edward Winslow—he didn't kill anyone and nobody can bear to read about him. And yet Edward Winslow was the one true hero among my ancestors. It was he who roused into action the miserable little group of Separatists who had been languishing in Holland for eight years, getting dourer and dourer. If you've forgotten, as I had, the Separatists were Puritans who wanted to separate from the Church of England and worship their own way, which was all the time and with no priests around. They were Calvinists, and the basic idea was that you were born good or bad, one of the elect or one of the damned, and no amount of ritualistic nonsense was going to make a difference. No forgiveness or second chance for the Puritan, who is always desperately proving to himself that he is good, and plunging into the depths when he is not—a discomforting trait of no known benefit that has traveled through the generations like a kidney stone. "You are a good boy but you did a bad thing," I carefully told my young children, trying to break the cycle of guilt, only to return home one day to a broken vase and my father's affable assurance, "I told Hunter and Teddy they were bad boys. I thought they should know."

In England the government threw the Separatists into prison, and their fellow countrymen ridiculed them; in Holland, to which they fled, they got to pray all they wanted, but they were paranoid and quarrelsome and poor, with green-card problems, and their kids got more and more annoyed about not being able to have fun on Sundays and dance like the Dutch, who knew how to have a good time. Life in Holland was such a drag that some of the Separatists went back to England, preferring to risk prison; the rest sat around glumly watching their children turning into "little Hollanders."

When my son Teddy dutifully writes in his fourth-grade assignment, WRITE A LETTER TO YOUR PARENTS FROM THE MAYFLOWER: "Dear Mom and Dad, We don't want to change our English ways. sincerly Ted," he is absolutely correct, although not, perhaps, fully cognizant of the reason why.

(As I rush out to my car at nine in the morning, having risen at five-thirty to put a roast chicken in the oven for the kindergarten "Pilgrim Feast," only to pour the entire bird down the front of my silk blouse as I try to open the car door, a certain weariness with the Pilgrims and their silly hats enters my heart, and I think, Why the Pilgrims? Why does not the glory fall on John Cabot or the Jamestown crowd, who came first? Instead, from kindergarten to fourth grade in the Concord public schools, the colonial period is celebrated by the grinding of the corn into meal, with various square-dancing visits to the Concord Museum. Why they never play to a boy's love of violence with stocks and pillories and a carnage-envisioning trip to the battleground at the Old North Bridge, I don't know. I suppose it is because most of the elementary school teachers are young women who still have ideals because they are not yet mothers.)

Jammed together on one boat instead of the originally planned two, the Pilgrims on the *Mayflower* were so pious, throwing themselves into paroxysms of religious exercise every two minutes, that no one could stand them. Half the hundred-odd passengers on the *Mayflower* were going to America for plain old freedom, not the religious freedom of the Pilgrims, which probably looked even less alluring at close quarters. But the real bullies were the sailors, who threatened and jibed at the Pilgrims without mercy, until a fierce storm at sea cracked the main beam. And when the beam was repaired with the Pilgrims' large iron screw, the other passengers must have viewed their connections in heaven in a more favorable light. Or perhaps it was the sight of the savage and savage-filled American shore that persuaded those with ideas of independence to sign the *Mayflower* Compact, pledging to live under Puritan rule.

It was a bleak November day when the *Mayflower* arrived in New England to a "hideous and desolate wilderness, full of wild beasts and wild men," wrote William Bradford, though I notice that the women were ferried across alone to do the wash. Everybody had a hacking cough, and by spring half of the hundred were dead, including Edward's wife of three years, as well as the mother of twelve-year-old Mary Chilton. At one point only six people were left standing who could tend the sick. The dead were buried at night to hide the graves, so the Indians would not know how few of them were left. Yet when the ship finally set sail to return to England in April, not one of the *Mayflower* passengers elected to return.

Bobby wrote that the Pilgrims were carpenters, ". . . English overflow . . . who farmed, bred, multiplied, and had little time for introspection . . . " ("New England and Further")—well, when you think of them arriving in that wilderness, freezing, starving, dying, listening to Indian whoops in the distance, you can see why they might have been attending to their survival.

The Pilgrims were very hard on themselves, in an admirable yet annoying way; even when, starving, they happened on a store of Indian corn, they stopped to make a vow to repay the Indians before they ate it, and I'm sure, if my genes tell me correctly, they worried about settling the debt until the day they did, six months later. When five Indians arrived with beaver pelts to trade for the first time that winter, before peace was established, the Pilgrims refused to trade because it was *a Sunday*.

Life with the Indians was a bit tricky in the beginning, a little friendly sign here, a hostile package of arrows delivered there. Even nonfamily histories give Edward Winslow credit for establishing peace with the Indians. Squanto, an Indian who knew some English and was a sort of freelance negotiator, tried to agent a peacemaking meeting between the Pilgrims and the Wampanoags. Still, I don't think that when Massasoit, chief of the Wampanoags, suddenly appeared one sunny March day, standing on the hill overlooking the Pilgrim settlement with sixty armed and painted men, that it was a calming sight. Massasoit refused to come down the hill, and Governor Carver refused to go up. Edward broke the stalemate by walking up the hill alone in his sweltering armor, carrying a jeweled copper chair and knife for Massasoit's brother. For several hours Edward served as a hostage, drinking liquor, sweating, and eating with the Indians (and repeatedly refusing to sell them his sword and armor); meanwhile, below, Carver and Massasoit were tying one on while negotiating a peace settlement.

When Massasoit lay dying two years after this treaty, it was Edward Winslow who traveled miles through the snow to his side and for two days nursed him, feeding him a broth of cornmeal boiled with sassafras root and strawberry leaves, which seemed to have an immediate effect. Up to then Massasoit had been having his doubts about the treaty. When he recovered he said, "Now I see the English are my friends, and love me; and whilst I live I never will forget this kindness they have showed me." And he never did.

For forty years Edward and Massasoit kept the peace. Edward served as governor, undertaker, minister, and ambassador to England (he *was* sort of a middle manager), where he got thrown into prison by the great Puritan-hater Archbishop Laud on his first visit, and was made Oliver Cromwell's chief pamphleteer on his next. Edward was brave and adventurous and fair, but what made him great was the respect he showed the Indians. The Indians were "loving and desirous of peace," Edward wrote, and he maintained a close friendship with Massasoit his entire life. When visiting Massasoit, Edward noted that the Indian chief was amazed that the English king could go so long without a wife and, after sleeping in a bed containing Massasoit, his wife, and two aides, joked that he was "more weary of my lodging than my journey."

Massasoit and Edward trusted each other; their children grew up together. Then Edward died, Massasoit died, and Edward's son, Josiah, rounded up the women and children of the Narragansett tribe, trapped them in their wigwams so they couldn't escape, and burned them alive.

Even the tasteful family books admit that "it is only fair to say that he [Josiah] was quite a different sort of man than his father." And yet there had once been high hopes for Josiah. He went to Harvard, inherited a huge estate from his father, and became the first native-born general and governor of the colony.

Whereas his father had begun his time in America sleeping in sod huts, sharing beds with Indians, and giving nonfreemen the right to vote, Josiah, who was born in the hut across the street from Myles Standish, was determined to make himself into an aristocrat. By the second generation, snobbism was alive and well in the New World. It was all very well for the First Comers (as the Pilgrims were called then) to band together in a democratic need for survival, but the last thing their children wanted to hear about was all their hardship and humble beginnings. Instead, every opportunity was grabbed by the more successful to create class division.

Josiah was at the head of the pack, the harbinger of what would be called "Old Colony Tories," a class who made as much money as they could in an effort to hold themselves above the majority. Josiah had "patrician" tastes: He ordered ornate moldings for his house (a genetic trait, I was chilled to note, as I, in a similar fit of ostentation, ordered elaborate moldings for the large but plain house we bought in Concord); he insisted that his father have his portrait painted in England (Edward was the only Pilgrim who was painted); Josiah held his own wedding in England, crossing the seas for the sake of preten-tiousness though he'd met his wife in America. His wife, Penelope Pelham, was quite grand, descended from Lord Delaware, governor of Virginia—she was a great hostess, says a family book, at a loss for a more exciting boast. As governor, Josiah insisted on having his car-riage accompanied by four halberdiers (liveried guards), carrying, as a symbol of office, spear–battle axes modeled after those used in the fifteenth and sixteenth centuries. But "Josiah Winslow differed from his father most sharply in Indian relations," another family book qui-etly understates.

He hated the Indians. Or maybe who he really hated was his father—or at least, the plain simple ways of his father. He had grown up as an equal with Massasoit's sons, and he was desperate to dissociate himself from them. Perhaps he thought it made him aristocratic to hate the Indians—certainly it made him seem more English. In French territory Indians could grow corn or pitch tents right up to the fences surrounding French forts. In English territory there was a fine of twenty shillings for shooting anything at night but "a wolf or an Indian."

Edward had saved Massasoit's life; Josiah was blamed for the death of Massasoit's son Alexander (the English version, by an amazing stretch, of "Wamsutta"). Josiah had called on Alexander, his childhood pal, to appear before Plymouth authorities to account for his actions—one of the worst injustices inflicted on the Indians at this time was severe punishment for infractions of colonial laws they had not known about or did not understand. It was humiliating treatment for friends who in the past had negotiated over drinks. Though enraged by his treatment, Alexander spent the night at Careswell, Josiah's estate, where he became ill. When he was found dead on the shores of the Titicut River, the Wampanoags claimed that Josiah had poisoned him (which I don't think he did, though even in the movie *The Last of the Mohicans*, a bitter mention of Winslow is made at the river shore). It began to be clear to Alexander's brother King Philip (aka Chief Metacom) that the English settlers were no longer their friends, extermination not coexistence their goal. Philip planned for several years; then, when three tribesmen were executed for murder, war began.

At the outset the Indians had the upper hand. It was a fight for survival. "The bloodiest in American colonial history . . . four towns in Rhode Island and sixteen in Massachusetts were razed . . . white casualties numbered about one sixteenth of the New England population," says *Colonial America*, a book given to my father in the mid-1960s when he was thinking of leaving the Simmons Mattress Company to teach high school history. In one of its more politically incorrect moments the book continues, "On the brighter side of the picture, King Philip's War did remove the Indian menace in southern

New England. Thus a vast area of the frontier was opened to undisputed white settlement and a barrier to the subsequent growth and expansion of New England removed."

As commander in chief of the New England forces, Josiah was a weak, indecisive general—except when it came to cruelties to Indians. There he had a sure hand. His first action, which reversed the war in the colonists' favor, was to wipe out nearly all the older men and the women and children of the Narragansett tribe. The warriors fled the area; the Indians began to starve, retreat, and surrender; King Philip, betrayed by one of his own men, was captured and killed. Little more than a year after the start of the war, most of the Indians had surrendered. Despite pleadings for mercy from his top subordinate, Col. Benjamin Church, Josiah insisted that the severed head of Annawon, Philip's chief aide, be paraded through the streets of Plymouth, along with the Indian survivors, who, after this display, were executed or sold into slavery, to be shipped to the West Indies. Philip's own son and wife were sold as slaves.

A few months ago by accident I found, lying in a box in the basement of my house, an old book called *In King Philip's War*, a historical novel by Frederic A. Ober. Near the end of the book a young white boy, promising safety at the colonists' hands, brings his friend, King Philip's son, through the wilderness and fighting to the Plymouth authorities. Governor Josiah Winslow holds a solemn tribunal and finds he has no choice but to sell the Indian boy and his mother into slavery—the carnage and slaughter from the Indians has been too great not to make an example of them, even though Winslow was once their friend and knows they are innocent. The white boy decides to accompany the Indians as they are taken under guard to the ship bound for the West Indies. On the way the boy hears the sound of a horse pursuing them. It is Josiah, torn by pity and remorse, who thrusts a bag of gold coins at them, embracing the boy and saying, "But, man and magistrate, are two separate and several persons, sooth, so that what I feel constrained to do as a magistrate, I loath and condemn as a man!" And suddenly I believe it, believe that Josiah did evil because he thought it was the right thing to do—sad, terrible, but the right thing to do.

After the Indians' defeat, Josiah grew depressed, debilitated in body and spirit. He sent his wife and family away, fearing for their safety and, fearing for his own, mounted a guard of twenty around Careswell, the home he had once been so proud of. He was relieved of his command and died not long after, at the age of fifty-two.

After reading the family histories I went to my one-volume *Columbia Encyclopedia*, as a check on family exuberance. But it is all there. Under two separate entries are Edward Winslow and Josiah Winslow, negating each other in achievements. The next night at dinner with my parents, I started talking about Edward Winslow, and how he was responsible for forty years of peace with the Indians, and my mother turned to me, politely interested. "The Winslows were really something once," she said. Then we turned to the more gripping subject of how many were coming to Sunday lunch.

Winslow Coat of Arms.
"Cut Down, We Flourish"
("Gluttons for Punishment," I say).

The Pilgrim Father.
Edward Winslow: Responsible for forty
years of peace with the Indians.

The Pilgrim Son.
Josiah Winslow:
Slaughtered the Indians.

Bobby and his grandfather Arthur Winslow.
"He was my Father. I was his son."

———

4

THE FAMILY BURIAL PLOT IN DUNBARTON, NEW HAMPSHIRE, HAS BEEN around since before the Revolution. In 1960 they had to move all the bodies and markers when a flood threatened. Some of the family, like Aunt Sarah and my mother, wanted to leave the bodies where they were; others, like Cousin Emily Winslow, who in middle age had just gotten a degree in landscape architecture, felt strongly that the bodies should be moved to a new site, which the state of New Hampshire agreed to pay for. With great care the hallowed remains were moved. But after all the fuss the flood never happened, and now everybody is buried in the new plot while the old one sits abandoned. Aunt Sarah wanted me to have my wedding reception at the old plot and dance on the empty graves. The new plot is quite small. Once, when I was eighteen, I got a frantic phone call from my mother at 7:30 A.M. saying if I wanted to be buried in Dunbarton, I'd better decide soon; they were running out of room.

Dunbarton has been made much of by my family for generations. In family scrapbooks dating from 1895, there is picture after picture of the old burial plot, each photograph carefully marked with different dates but looking exactly the same. The pictures of the new cemetery in my parents' album look identical to the ones of the old cemetery, except here and there are shots of my parents, Aunt Sarah, Uncle Cot, and Bobby, slouching and smiling sheepishly in an old canvas coat, posed around the gravestones.

"It's where we're buried," Bobby said about Dunbarton. Well, it's where the family members who fought on the right side of the American Revolution are buried. Not buried in Dunbarton are the Winslows who chose the wrong side and had to flee to Canada and England. Before that they had pretty much succeeded in Josiah's mission to turn themselves into aristocrats—even, with the greatest of fortitude, managing to surmount Edward Winslow's aversion to slavery. Josiah's son, Isaac, became famous for building the most "pretentious house in the colony," brags a family book, with slave quarters for blacks and Indians. Before the Revolution, Winslows prospered in Boston and in Plymouth as merchants, government officials, and members of the establishment. One Winslow, continues the family book, made silver "better than Paul Revere." But he didn't make the midnight ride, unless it was toward Halifax. During the Vietnam War, when my brothers and I gloatingly mentioned that our ancestors had fled to Canada during the Revolution, Aunt Sarah, never a captive of truth, simply denied it.

Growing up in Concord, from whence "the shot [was] heard round the world," it took me a while to realize that the Tories weren't the outlaws. In actuality my ancestors were simply supporting their government (some of them *were* the government). A look at the Boston Tea Party, for instance, finds Winslows all over the place, but, unfortunately, in the *wrong* place—in the customs office, behind a desk at a British tea company, master of the boat bringing in the tea. They even fought for the British, under General Gage—their loyalty a strategic mistake from which they never recovered. After the war the Winslows were unable to reclaim their confiscated American lands. To condense Kenelm Winslow: The fourth Edward Winslow was back in a sodded hut. It is a sign of New England "stick-to-it-iveness" that we have managed to hang on to the shreds of our Winslow glory, despite the fact that it vanished more than two hundred years ago.

The Winslows would have been a family in decline, if they had ever been long in the ascendancy. "Cut Down, We flourish" had been the Winslow motto since they were sheep raiders in England in the 1400s—

unfortunately the second half of the motto hasn't quite panned out. "Cut down," on the other hand, has worked out pretty well, fitting us like a glove to this very day—recently my cousin Mary Devereux said that she wants to get a family seal made in the shape of a tree stump.

The Winslows were cut down so early that they missed out on the great merchant fortunes that established other Boston Brahmin families. After the Revolution the Winslows endured a pitiful century of sad but valiant men dying young and strong mothers tramping around with fatherless children, reading the Bible at night and selling matches by day, inheriting their stubbornness from the seventeenth-century religious termagant, Anne Hutchinson, who was kicked out of the Massachusetts Bay Colony by John Winthrop and was later massacred by Indians along with every member of her household (except for my ancestor, who was out doing errands). There was no merchant-pirate, as there was on the other side of my family, who stole British goods and got his portrait painted by Gilbert Stuart. There was no nothing— unless you count the shot of sunshine in 1817, when a weak remaining twig of the broken and impoverished Winslow family tree married into the Stark family of Dunbarton, New Hampshire.

The Starks became the Winslows' one salvation because the Starks had been on the *right* side of the American Revolution. Gen. John Stark had ridden all night to fight the Battle of Bunker Hill and later turned the tide of the war in the Battle of Bennington. Though I heard quite a bit about General Stark from my great-aunt Sarah over the years, none of it was illuminated by factual information. "John Stark was a strong and unforgiving man," she would say firmly at some point during an evening—as if it were a show-stopping compliment. Well, he was strong all right, ruling the roost in Dunbarton until he was ninety-four, and certainly he was unforgiving. He couldn't have been too thrilled when his granddaughter married Joshua, the sniveling son of a Winslow Tory. When she died five months after the birth of a son, the sniveling Winslow husband abandoned the baby to go lounge in the Caribbean, never to return (except metaphorically, in missives written home begging for money). The strong general refused to take in his great-grandson, who was brought up in boardinghouses by a poor Winslow aunt, though eventually he was permitted to spend holidays in Dunbarton.

The boy, Francis, pathetically remembered these visits to the scene of his early rejection as his happiest times. He would long for Dunbarton when he was away, which was most of the time, writing wistfully of the day when he would be laid to rest there, by his mother's grave. He preceded his great-grandson Bobby in writing poetry about the plot at Dunbarton, Francis penning at nineteen the lugubrious but heartfelt "Farewell to Home, as written at the Family Cemetery at Dunbarton in September, 1839"—proving, sadly, that just feeling something deeply does not mean you should write about it:

> My Boyhood's well remembered Spot!
> Sweet Place! thou ne'er may'st be forgot
> Tho' thro' long years I see thee not,
> Long years of gloom and woe . . .

and so forth.

Well, the kid was depressed. How could he not have been? At age fifteen, motherless, fatherless, without prospect, he had signed up as a midshipman, spending the rest of his life at sea, though he hated the sea, getting homesick, seasick, and just plain sick. He was frail and miserably sensitive, every second of his days a trial—reading his letters to his aunt, and later to his wife (who used his old uniforms to make their four children clothes and traveled about with them in order to see him on his short leaves), one feels the Protestant admonition "Buck up!" rising in one's throat. But then I read a letter one of the men who served under his naval command during the Civil War wrote to Francis's son years later: "Your father was one of the coolest and bravest men in action I ever knew. Standing by him during an engagement when the bullets were whistling thick and fast about us, I, being somewhat new to fire, was constantly jumping and ducking. 'Why do you do that?' said your father, 'you cannot dodge them, and it is just as well to stand straight and face the music.'" When word of his death at sea at age forty-four came to his wife from the newsboys on the street, his son, Arthur Winslow, was two.

Arthur Winslow was my mother and Bobby's grandfather, and there was nothing frail or sensitive about him. Arthur was tall, strongly built, and no-nonsense. He too longed for Dunbarton, but instead of writing poems about the Stark burial grounds, he simply bought up Stark lands and funded the cemetery and the farmer who took care of it. Arthur's dream was to bring back the family glory, and in order to do so, he went out and made a million dollars. He was one of those people who knew how to make money—the type one wishes one could marry until one attempts a conversation—the opposite of his melancholic father and the line of weak, depressive Winslow men that preceded him. He was also the opposite of his grandson, Bobby. But it didn't seem to matter; Bobby would crave his approval all his life, writing about him in almost every book. "He was my Father. I was his son."

Family lore claims that Arthur went out West and discovered a silver mine when he was twenty-one; but I have a letter he wrote saying he was "a poor man" until he made his million at age forty-four. He was a mining engineer who traveled from site to site. When he struck it rich it was not by luck, as the family always implied, but after years of hard work and risk taking. Bobby seemed to know it was not luck, writing that his grandfather was "proud of being self-made." After he made his fortune, Arthur bought a large, brown-pillared house on the top of Beacon Hill, and a seven-chimneyed farm near Plymouth Rock. "Grandpa liked being near Plymouth Rock," my mother says, "because it was where the family began."

Arthur was handsome, his profile as strong as a face on a coin, and intimidating, stamping his foot when angry at his teasing southern wife. Everyone who knew Arthur talks of the gold-headed cane he wielded, with names of the Alps he had climbed inscribed on it, "more a weapon than a crutch," wrote Bobby in "Dunbarton." Arthur had met his wife, Mary (whom, for simplicity's sake I will call by the childish nickname Gaga, as both my mother and Bobby did) on a mining project in North Carolina. Gaga was pretty and diminutive, compared to the tall rangy Winslows, just five feet tall, one of nine children of the Devereux, an impoverished but genteel southern family—"genteel" meaning they had once owned sixteen hundred slaves.

My father always told me what gentlemen the Confederates were, and how the northerners were much worse to their factory workers than the southern whites were to their slaves. In the fifth grade, to the northern chill of my Concord, Massachusetts, classroom, I explained in detail the Confederate victory at Chancellorsville, following which battle my paternal ancestor Hunter Holmes McGuire amputated Stonewall Jackson's arm (Jackson died afterward, but never mind). I used to say I was five-eighths southern. But then I read the privately published book *Plantation Sketches,* by Gaga's mother, Margaret Devereux, extolling the peace and abundance of a great plantation (if you happened to be the owner, and not one of the sixteen hundred slaves), and learned how, as a young girl, Gaga's mother sat to meals at which the tablecloth was changed between courses, and walked to school with one slave carrying her cold water and the other carrying her hot lunch. Now, I say I am a northerner. Whether the Winslows were ever quite Abolitionist, however, is a question upon which I have found no light to shine. "Why did we fight the Civil War?" the nurse asked ninety-nine-year-old Aunt Sarah. "Because," said Aunt Sarah, "the South didn't want us to have a front parlor *and* a back parlor."

Gaga's mother's maiden name had been Mordecai, though one notices that the name that gets used over and over again in the family is Devereux. "I always thought Gaga had a Jewish look," said my cousin Nell Devereux Styron, Bobby's contemporary, "but you know, nobody ever brought it up." Our Jewishness was never hidden, but it was not talked about, Nell said, until it came out in an article about Bobby. Bobby was one-eighth Jewish ("at least one-eighth Jewish," Bobby said, wishing it were more). What is confusing is that Bobby was Jewish on both the Lowell and the Winslow sides of his family, and both ancestors were named Mordecai (the Winslow as a first name and the Lowell as the last). For years I thought our Jewishness came from the Mordecai Myers Bobby wrote about in *Life Studies,* but of course if one just *reads* the book, one sees that Mordecai Myers was a Lowell. Like the Lowell Mordecai, our Mordecai was hardly a romantic figure, marrying one daughter of a wealthy plantation family (and, when she died, prudently marrying her sister) and converting to Protestantism.

The genteel but impoverished Devereux were not wild about Arthur Winslow—"he was so *northern,*" was the complaint—bridling when he swept down with his family, no expense spared, for a visit. The Devereux all loved little Gaga, but they never got a chance to enjoy her because Arthur Winslow was so dominating. Though he was the guest, it was he who made all the plans. He would hold court in the living room, surrounded by the female relatives, answering their admiring questions about his mining experiences. In middle age he was still youthful and striking in appearance, Nell remembers, and "you got the feeling he knew a thing or two about trollops and the shenanigans of his friends, of which he did not approve."

Arthur had a suspicious mind about sex; he would sit in the room with his daughters when suitors came to call, separated by a screen, coughing whenever he disagreed with a comment. The story goes that his three children fell in love the summer he went away: his daughter Charlotte got engaged to Bob Lowell Sr., his son, Devereux, fell in love with my grandmother, and my great-aunt Sarah had a romance with young Hepburn out in Concord and was whisked away to Europe on her father's return to get over him. (When I broke up with my boyfriend in college, I remember wishing my parents would whisk me off to Europe so I wouldn't have to keep seeing him going off to play squash with the girl with the thin legs.)

My mother never saw more than a cold good-morning kiss pass between her grandparents. Arthur and Gaga had separate bedrooms and met only at mealtimes. Gaga refused to step into her husband's den—the long, cold, narrow room where Arthur spent his time in the house on Chestnut Street—a dark, hard-chaired room with a fireplace at one end. Though it had begun as a love match, it was clear that their marriage was a failure. Arthur was athletic, disciplined, and exact. Gaga was soft, relaxed, and pointedly uninterested in Arthur's diatribes about the efficiency of the Germans. She loved everything French—literature, history—she even decorated her house in French provincial. She wouldn't have dreamed of climbing a mountain with her husband. When Arthur went on pilgrimages to Dunbarton, taking his young grandchildren to stay at the farmer's house and tend the graves of his Revolutionary ancestors, Gaga refused to go. She hated Dunbarton.

Eventually Gaga stopped accompanying Arthur on his travels altogether—Charlotte, Bobby's mother (at the age of forty), took her mother's place on at least one extended European trip. Even in the days when she had accompanied him, Gaga never pretended to be interested in his activities, drinking tea in the chalet while Arthur climbed the Alps in knickerbockers and a great cape along with Mrs. Elizabeth Winfrey, a distant relation who always seemed to be around.

Recently I was given a stack of the booklets Arthur painstakingly wrote about his travels, perfectly preserved. I opened one, *The Lure of Mont Blanc*, to find "First Edition. Limited 6 copies. This Copy No. 1" typed and centered on the title page. I wouldn't have been too worried about plagiarism if I were he. They are the most boring things I have ever read: page after page of "arrived 6:00, breathtaking view," or, if I may quote from the resounding climax of *Journey in Norway* (Limited Revised Edition): "In conclusion, Norway, as I saw it, is a pleasant place to visit." I suppose the books are crimes of enthusiasm, like those photos of the sunset my husband, Charlie, takes on every vacation, that later get stuck to the bottom of a kitchen drawer. Or, maybe, as I look at the dates, there is another explanation for such passionate busywork. The booklets begin not long after the death of Arthur and Gaga's son, Devereux, at age thirty.

Devereux was my mother's father, the middle child of Arthur and Gaga. He was thin and tall and studious looking, with blue-black hair and wire-rimmed glasses over brown eyes. He was quiet, as opposed to the rest of his family, and nature loving, removing himself from the fray of his father's household whenever possible. Bobby wrote a poem about him called "My Last Afternoon with Uncle Devereux Winslow." Literary criticisms of Bobby's work often claim that Devereux was weak (one even said "emotionally stunted"), in order to make him a symbol for the decline of the Winslows, but Devereux was not weak. During World War I, when he was refused four times by the army for bad eyesight, Devereux went north to join the Canadian army, serving as a private in the Tank Corps. But he did not die in the war; he came back to his wife and children and got cancer when he was twenty-nine.

Bobby said his mother was "her father's favorite," but Devereux was Arthur's only son. To Devereux on his marriage had gone the Ohio lands bequeathed to General Stark by the government for his services in the war. All Arthur's hopes for the family were pinned on Devereux, the last male bearer of the Winslow name. As if in quiet defiance, Devereux had fathered three children, all girls. Then he died, and Arthur turned to his five-year-old grandson, Robert Lowell, to be the savior of the family.

Bobby's grandmother Winslow.
Mary "Gaga" Devereux.
From an impoverished, genteel
southern family—"genteel"
meaning they had once owned
sixteen hundred slaves.

Bobby's grandfather Winslow.
Arthur Winslow.
One of those people who knows
how to make money—the type
one wishes to marry, until one
attempts conversation.

Devereux Winslow.
Books about Bobby always say
his Uncle Devereux was weak,
but Devereux was not weak.

Bob senior and Bobby.
My cousin Nell: "No one liked [Bob senior]
and he knew it and it was sad."

5

After Devereux died Arthur couldn't stand to be around anyone but Bobby: "My Grandfather found / his grandchild's fogbound solitudes / sweeter than human society. / When Uncle Devereux died . . ." In the poem "Dunbarton," Arthur takes the five-year-old Bobby up for a fall weekend at Dunbarton, to rough it in the farmer's cottage. "Grandpa would drag Bobby up to Dunbarton to rake the leaves at the cemetery," my mother says, "but I think Bobby was glad to get out of his house and away from his family." With Bobby's father away in the navy, Bobby wrote in "Dunbarton,"

> it seemed spontaneous and proper
> for Mr. MacDonald, the farmer,
> Karl, the chauffeur, and even my Grandmother
> to say, "your Father." They meant my Grandfather . . .

I don't know if Bobby loved his father, Bob senior, who, absent and shy, receded behind Bobby's domineering mother. Certainly he didn't respect him, learning early from his mother's disdain. The only thing Charlotte didn't disdain about her husband was the blood that ran in his veins. The Lowells were a prominent Boston family, mill owning and far richer than the Winslows. Unfortunately for Charlotte, Bob senior came from a relatively poor branch (which included James Russell Lowell and his nephew, Charles Russell Lowell, the suicidally brave Civil War soldier nicknamed "Beau Sabreur," but not the fat Amy, known more for her cigar smoking than her poetry, who came from a richer branch); he was also, despite his pedigree, something of an outsider in Boston circles. His father had died when his mother was still pregnant with him, and after his birth she had stayed on with her only child at her mother's house on Staten Island.

Aunt Sarah said that Bob Lowell Sr. met Charlotte at a dinner party one night and turned to Aunt Sarah and said, "I'm going to marry your sister," and the next day sent a huge bouquet of roses, about which Charlotte couldn't have cared less. My mother's theory is that Charlotte married Bob senior because at twenty-six she was beginning to be an old maid and there was nobody else around courting her.

I never knew Bobby's mother, my great-aunt Charlotte; I was a baby when she died. She was six years older than her sister, my great-aunt Sarah, and very put together, just *so*. Aunt Sarah admired her greatly. She always wished she could get her hat to sit like Charlotte's. It is difficult for me to imagine anyone being more of a grande dame than Aunt Sarah, but I will say this: I think Aunt Sarah was vulnerable where Aunt Charlotte was hard.

The truth is, the sisters didn't get along and seldom played together. In childhood photographs Charlotte usually sits on the lawn by herself, while Sarah sits close to Devereux, on a swing, in a wagon, as she smiles at the camera, unabashedly holding his hand. In a photograph taken on a family trip to Europe before she married, Charlotte stands far to the front, nearly blocking out Sarah, her large hair swept up under a large hat, squinting crossly into the camera, looking exactly like Bobby in feature, but with none of his shy, slouching manner. Charlotte held herself beautifully, she was very proud, my mother said. Even in her forties Charlotte looked good in a bathing suit; she was handsome as opposed to pretty, with black eyes and naturally rosy cheeks.

Bob senior was smart, in a scientific way, but it was not a way anybody in the family appreciated—certainly not Charlotte, who loved to gossip. He was painfully polite, with a set smile; he was also vacuous and cold. I was told that when he spoke to you, it was totally impersonal. He could have been speaking to anyone, he was just saying what ought to be said. "No one liked him and he knew it and it was sad," said my cousin Nell. My mother says it is true what Bobby claimed, that he always smiled and smiled while his wife practically— but not quite—called him stupid to his face. Still, he was head of the house. Just as prime ministers used to adhere to the belief in divine right, even when they thought the monarch was an idiot, so Charlotte respected the office of man but not the man himself. The emotion I most imagine Charlotte evincing is irritation—irritation at the man she married and at herself for marrying him. But she would have stopped short of expressing her dislike directly. (How did one stay married in those days without ever expressing one's hatred of one's spouse? "*One* of the reasons I hate you," Charlie began the other day after I let the tub overflow, ruining the living room ceiling; ten minutes later he was happily getting me a cup of coffee.)

During the first year of their marriage, Bob senior was sent to Guantanamo by the navy, and Charlotte, pregnant, was forced to stay on Staten Island with her girlishly sentimental mother-in-law and grandmother-in-law. Mrs. Lowell and her mother had looked forward to Charlotte's visit, but if she had envisioned cozy feminine nights chatting about babies, she'd picked the wrong daughter-in-law. Charlotte, lacking an ounce of baby-shower mentality, was miserable stuck in this widowed society, away from Boston. Boston was the only place where she felt like *someone*—she was a Winslow and a Lowell, and nowhere else in the whole wide world would anyone care. "My mother's true lover was Boston," Bobby wrote, "or living in Boston, or perhaps *not* living away from Boston . . . " (from the essay "Antebellum Boston"). She left Staten Island to have Bobby in her father's house.

In *Day by Day*, Bobby's last book of poems, which he described as containing memories suppressed from *Life Studies,* he writes of his mother pregnant with him on Staten Island, looking out to sea:

... Mother,
I must not blame you for carrying me in you
on your brisk winter lunges across
the desperate, refusey Staten Island beaches,
their good view skyscrapers on Wall Street ...
for yearning seaward, far from any home, and saying,
'I wish I were dead, I wish I were dead.'
Unforgivable for a mother to tell her child—
("Unwanted")

After her marriage, Bobby wrote (in "Antebellum Boston"), his "[m]other sighed for her father, whose urgent domination she had long been accustomed to and been sustained by." No effort seems to have been made to keep these feelings from Bobby, who knew the details down to the penny of how Arthur Winslow had paid for his daughter and son-in-law's first house, with all kinds of forgiven loans and mortgages. For a brief moment as a very little boy Bobby had admired his father for his uniform, but by the time he was three he had caught on to his mother's scorching contempt and made it his own. Three is a bit young to be contemptuous, and yet I'm sure he managed it—if sarcasm is the shield of the weak, who is weaker than a three-year-old child? Bobby's prose essay in *Life Studies*, "91 Revere Street," is funny because it is a child's defense against pain.

In "91 Revere Street" Bobby's mother proclaims, "I have always believed carving to be *the* gentlemanly talent." Ever anxious to please his wife, Bob senior enrolls in a carving "college." "Each Sunday from then on he would sit silent and erudite before his roast. He blinked, grew white, looked winded, and wiped beads of perspiration from his eyebrows. His purpose was to reproduce stroke by stroke his last carving lesson ...." After his father jokes, "I am just a plebe at this guillotine," and his naval buddy Commander Billy blusteringly recites a carving poem, Bobby "... furious for no immediate reason, blurted out, 'Mother, how much does Grandfather Winslow have to fork up to pay for Daddy's carving school?'"

Charlotte derided Bob senior's naval career, insisting that he take a lesser naval job so she could live in Boston, then refused to live with him at the Boston naval base, like the other wives, because the navy was not socially acceptable in her book. In "91 Revere Street," Bobby writes how each night he watched his father exchange his tuxedo for his uniform, then take a trolley back to the navy yard to sleep. When finally Charlotte makes him quit the navy altogether, Bobby's father explains in pathetic fatuity to Commander Billy about his new civilian job at Lever Brothers Soap in Cambridge: ". . . I guess for *cits* [citizens], Billy, they've really got something on the ball, because they tell me they want me on their team.'" In "Commander Lowell," Bobby continues this sad history by poem:

> He was soon fired. Year after year,
> he still hummed "Anchors aweigh" in the tub—
> whenever he left a job,
> he bought a smarter car.
> . . . In three years
> he squandered sixty thousand dollars.

No, there was nothing happy in the marriage, not for a moment. Charlotte didn't even get to be rich. And Charlotte, who had been nearly an adult before her father made his money, wanted desperately to be rich. Like her father, she worshipped money, for the beautiful things it would buy and for what it signified. Finally even her father would fail her by losing his fortune, and in the end it was Aunt Sarah, her baby sister, sweet, silly Aunt Sarah, who became rich.

His father weak, Bobby became a bully. In "91 Revere Street" Bobby describes himself as "thick-witted, narcissistic, thuggish" as an eight-and-a-half-year-old boy at the Brimmer School, a girls' school in Boston that allowed boys in the lower grades, second-class citizens under the oxen headmistress, "an extension of my mother's [regime]." At Brimmer Bobby "was distracted in my studies, assented to whatever I was told, picked my nose whenever no one was watching, and worried our third-grade teacher by organizing creepy little gangs of boys at recess." One spring day in the park Bobby bloodied one boy's nose against a statue of George Washington, bloodied another nose, then "stood in the center of a sundial tulip bed and pelted a little enemy ring of third-graders with wet fertilizer." The next thing he knew he was being ceremoniously expelled from the Public Garden as his mother and thirty nurses and their charges watched.

With Bobby's graduation from Brimmer in the fourth grade, he and his father were sent by Charlotte to look at suburban boys' schools, middle class in Charlotte's opinion, but a "respectable stop-gap" for the three years before Bobby could enter Saint Mark's. "Saint Mark's was the boarding school for which I had been enrolled at birth," Bobby wrote. "These expeditions were stratagems designed to give me a chance to get to know my father; Mother noisily stayed behind and amazed me by pretending that I had forbidden her to embark on 'men's work.'" But even at the boys' schools his father doesn't cut muster, somehow never getting in to see the headmaster, too busy chatting up janitors.

"A ray of hope in the far future was my white-haired Grandfather Winslow, whose unchecked commands and demands were always upsetting people for their own good—he was all I could ever want to be: the bad boy, the problem child, the commodore of his household."

Frank Parker, another of Bobby's childhood friends, told one biographer that he remembered Grandfather Winslow as "a dreadful, self-centered old tyrant," but for my mother and Bobby he was their earliest male love. In the beginning he loved them totally, simply because they were his grandchildren. He knew how to relate to little children. Both my mother's mother and Bobby's mother couldn't wait to get their children out the door, but Arthur spent all day, sometimes all night, with his grandchildren, taking them on hikes and overnight trips. He also was generous, giving them gold coins at Christmas and sending them brand-new radios out of the blue. Even the strictness of his rules gave a kind of sense to the universe not found at home. My mother and Bobby spent Christmases, Easters, and Thanksgivings together at their Winslow grandparents' at 18 Chestnut Street, where the pillars were the color of chocolate ice cream and the food was delicious—sausage at breakfast kept hot over flames on the sideboard; at dinner, brick ice cream sliced from the block for dessert, or vanilla with chocolate sauce. In the summer the grandchildren spent weeks on end at Chardesa, Arthur Winslow's summer estate, named for his three children, Charlotte, Devereux, and Sarah, in the cloying WASP tradition. Not only was the big white rambling "farmhouse" near Plymouth Rock, the town was even called Rock. Charedesa was on two hundred acres, with the original farmers still working it, the house filled with Adirondack furniture. "Like my Grandfather, the décor/was manly, comfortable,/overbearing, disproportioned," wrote Bobby in his poem about his uncle Devereux.

Installed at Chardesa, amid her crumbling snacks and stacks of novels, was my mother and Bobby's maiden great-aunt, Sarah Stark Winslow, the only one of Arthur's siblings Bobby would ever write about, the one artist of the family. She had studied piano with Liszt and had a career for one brief shining moment, until her good breeding interfered. "Forty years earlier/twenty, auburn headed," Bobby wrote in his poem about Devereux, she had been scheduled to solo at Symphony Hall. "On the recital day, she failed to appear." By the time Bobby and my mother were children, Great-Aunt Sarah Stark, charming but vague, was reduced to spending the summer at her brother's house, where Arthur and Gaga complained of her piano playing, until a solution was found. "Up in the air/by the lakeview window in the billards-room,/lurid in the doldrums of the sunset hour," Bobby wrote, "She thundered on the keyboard of her dummy piano," which had been "... bought to spare the nerves/of my Grandmother ..." My mother said it was Arthur who insisted the piano be soundless.

Chardesa is where Devereux had his duck blind on the island in the lake, and his cabin, which he built with his college friends. Here he would play guitar and rough it with his friends for days, now and then appearing at the house for a hot meal. Even after his marriage, Devereux seemed to prefer the cabin to his parents' house; it is there Bobby remembers him, at twenty-nine, a few months before he died, among his guns and old college posters, away from the domination of his father, wearing on his diminished frame the Canadian army uniform of "his engagement picture" as he closed up the cabin for winter, and for life.

Devereux had avoided his father's wild exploratory trips, but Bobby lived for them, preferring the fields of Chardesa to all other vacation spots. "Nowhere was anywhere after a summer/at my Grandfather's farm," Bobby wrote, with ". . . [its] paths forever pioneering." The atmosphere was secure, affectionate, the opposite of home. Bobby would refuse to leave Chardesa when his parents came to pick him up.

My mother spent an entire summer at Chardesa with Bobby when she was ten and Bobby was eleven, ages when the sexes, suddenly attracted, often hurl themselves into enemy camps. Though my mother and Bobby were always friendly, a photograph of them that summer shows them sitting at opposite ends of a bench looking embarrassedly straight ahead. Bobby's parents were beginning to go crazy with him, and so they left him for two whole months with his grandparents and a tutor. It was very fashionable for a boy to have a tutor in the summer, not so much for academic reasons but to do "boy things" together. My mother would spend the day with Aunt Sarah, while Bobby spent the day with his tutor and grandfather on the trails. Bobby had a menagerie outside the house, all fenced in, with snakes in one place, skunks in another, and toads, frogs, and turtles (turtles are always uxoriously cropping up in Bobby's poems: "A man without a wife/is like a turtle without a shell—" he wrote in "Shadow"). "You never saw so many creatures," my mother said. "Bobby was always out fixing those animal cages" and sneaking their inhabitants inside. At home his mother would have thrown the horrible creatures out, but at Chardesa the atmosphere was more relaxed. His tutor, who was prim and proper, disapproved of the menagerie, but Arthur didn't mind. In fact he rather liked it. My mother and Bobby met only at breakfast and at dinner. Before bed Bobby would go about in his nightshirt, joking around and saying goodnight at each bedroom door—as if happily counting the bodies, as an only child might.

That summer Bobby was growing into adolescence, and for the first time Arthur Winslow began to criticize him. Certainly Arthur

Winslow didn't attach the same reverence to adolescent angst as my generation has, coming of age in the 1960s, revered at our worst by our own parents. ("The younger generation is the hope of the country," my mother once said, as I lounged in my dorm room smoking cigarettes and refusing to go to classes unless Harvard sold its stock in Gulf Oil.) But Arthur Winslow didn't tolerate any veering from the norm. He simply got up in the morning and went about his business, whereas Bobby—well, he once said he thought his popularity was due to the problems he had with "ordinary living." When Arthur's grandchildren became teenagers with minds of their own, he didn't understand why they couldn't all just toe the line, why Bobby wouldn't join a club at Harvard, or the girls do Red Cross, instead of all these artistic things they insisted on doing. He couldn't understand why the grandchildren who had once revered him couldn't be made to listen. He felt betrayed—just as he had by his wife, whom he had loved for her soft, teasing ways, until he discovered the strong will that lay beneath them; just as he had by Devereux, who had ignored him; and by Sarah, who, though she lived in her father's house for almost fifty years, took everyone's side but his own. His stubborn insistence that he was always right had lost him his wife and his children, and now it lost him his grandchildren. Then, worst of all, he lost what his sense of rectitude had been based on—the money he had made.

Arthur had invested his fortune in Boston real estate. He had owned numerous properties in the Back Bay. He had no partners in his business enterprises, only lackeys. When the Great Depression came, he was forced to sell almost everything, even the house at 18 Chestnut, moving to "the four rooms" at Otis Place that Bobby writes about in his poem about Gaga, "Mary Winslow." My cousin Nell says they were the most elegant rooms, a large living room and dining room, a bedroom, a kitchen, and one maid's room, overlooking the Esplanade and the Charles River. Reduced circumstances for Arthur Winslow, but not for anyone else I know.

A few years later, still rock-climbing-strong at seventy-five (his health was another sign of his being among the elect), Arthur was diagnosed with prostate cancer. When it was clear that he was dying, my mother came to see him, up from New York, where she was attending an acting school with the future stars Gregory Peck and Tony Randall. Though he was in terrible pain, her grandfather forced himself up in the chair to register his disapproval of his nineteen-year-old granddaughter. "I want you to give up the theater," he commanded over my mother's protests. "It's all immoral women, fallen women." He died a few days later.

"To my children and grandchildren I bequeath the gift of life in New England and the heritage of our ancestry dating back to early times," Arthur Winslow wrote in his last will and testament. It was just about all he had left to bequeath. The *Boston Globe* found his will so singular that they ran an article about it under the headline: BOSTON ENGINEER WILLS LIFE IN N.E. TO CHILDREN.

Gaga lived for four more years at 10 Otis Place. Then one day she came home and announced that she was not going to play bridge anymore. My mother doesn't remember her speaking again after that, except once when my mother was arguing politics at dinner. Gaga turned to her and said, "Jacksie, don't be so good that it's boring"; she died a few weeks later. That's my mother's version. Bobby's version in his first book is somewhat different.

Several years after his grandmother's death, Bobby took Elizabeth Hardwick down South to meet the Devereux cousins. They all went out to dinner, and he and Elizabeth were a big hit; the Devereux relatives just loved Bobby. Later they went home and read "Mary Winslow" in *Lord Weary's Castle*, about how their sweet little Gaga went blitheringly senile, dribbling the mush spooned by her Irish maids. "Nobody would ever have said anything," my cousin Nell said, "but the feeling after that was, no one wanted to see him."

In *Lord Weary's Castle* Bobby also has a poem about his grandfather: "In Memory of Arthur Winslow," a title that is bitterly sarcastic. The poem is an anti-eulogy, inspired by Bobby's anger at his grandfather, the first but not last stage in his emotions about Arthur Winslow. In the poem Bobby's condemnation is so great that he dissociates himself from his family, saying, "Your people set you up in Phillips' House" (the rich section of Massachusetts General Hospital, and then he describes Arthur's cancer as a crab whose ". . . claws drop flesh upon your yachting blouse. . . ." In the end Arthur Winslow is rushed to hell.

As a young man, Bobby would rage against his grandfather and everything he stood for, but I think what he really couldn't bear was his grandfather's disappointment in him. Arthur had looked to Bobby to bring back the family glory. In the end, of course, Bobby *did* bring back the family glory (though he had to do it over his relatives' bodies), but it was too late, and it was not glory in the way his grandfather would have understood.

By the time Bobby wrote *Life Studies*, his anger against his grandfather had changed to a yearning for the love and safety Arthur's money and his confidence had once provided. "The farm's my own!" he says twice in the poem "Grandparents" (my mother is not quite sure what he is referring to, since Chardesa got taken over by the state and was under several feet of water), but nothing is the same without his grandfather there, chalking the cues, playing pool for both of them. "Grandpa! Have me, hold me, cherish me!" he cries out.

By the time Bobby was writing his last book, *Day by Day*, he was only in his late fifties but yearning for death. Bobby said that he didn't know whether what he wrote was sad or happy, that sometimes you are sad and what you write comes out happy and vice versa. But nothing is sadder than this last book, in which he writes of learning that he was an unwanted child, that his mother wished she were dead rather than pregnant. He felt that he was weak, not strong like his grandfather, unworthy to live. In his despair he at last seems to have bought into the Protestant ethic that money made you one of the elect.

> He needed more to live than I,
> his foot could catch hold anywhere
> and dynamite his way to the gold again—
> for the world is generous to the opportune,
> its constantly self-renewing teams of favorites.
> ("Phillips House Revisited")

Charlotte and Sarah, 1898.
In the end it was Aunt Sarah, Charlotte's baby sister,
sweet, silly Aunt Sarah, who became rich.

Boston Engineer Wills
Life in N.E. to Children

Arthur Winslow Bequeaths 'Heritage of Ancestry Dating Back to Early Times'

To the children who survived him at his death a week ago, Arthur Winslow of Boston, once an outstanding mining engineer, left "The gift of life in New England, and the heritage of our ancestry dating back to New England's early times." His will was filed for probate today.

"I am proud to be of New England and happy to have completed my life there," the testament read. "Its antecedents I count among the most valuable legacies to my children.

"My fortune," he wrote, "is a sad, small residue after four years of continued depression, of what was acquired by many years of persistent work."

Mr. Winslow specifically eliminated all bequests to public institutions.

"They are excluded from my will," he wrote, "for the reason that inheritance and other taxation of our citizens already is excessive, and the wastefulness and inefficiency accompanying public expenditure discourages any donation.

Mr. Winslow, who lived at 10 Otis place, Beacon Hill, left his entire estate in trust for his family after making a few donations to friends, employees and private funds. Other bequests were made to friends and servants and $1000 to the Phillips Brooks Memorial Endowment Fund of Trinity Church.

The heirs are his widow, Mrs. Mary L. Winslow; two daughters, Mrs. Charlotte W. Lowell of Boston, wife of Robert T. S. Lowell, and Sarah H. Winslow, and three granddaughters, Jacqueline, Alice A. and Mary Chilton Winslow, daughters of a son, the late John D. Winslow of New York city.

Chardesa.
Now under several feet of water.

Devereux and his cabin at Chardesa—
closing it up for winter, and for life . . .

Devereux and Alice.

The last honeymoon.

6

My Uncle was dying at twenty-nine.
"You are behaving like children,"
said my Grandfather,
when my Uncle and Aunt left their three baby daughters,
and sailed for Europe on a last honeymoon . . .

In "My Last Afternoon with Uncle Devereux Winslow," five-year-old Bobby watches as Devereux and Arthur argue, his grandfather failing to impose his will on his dying son:

> I cowered in terror.
> I wasn't a child at all—
> unseen and all-seeing, I was Agrippina
> in the Golden House of Nero . . .

The poem is set at Chardesa. But my mother, almost four, the eldest of the three baby daughters in the poem, remembers the argument between her grandfather and father having begun during a telephone call at their house on Mt. Vernon Street. Her father was getting over the flu, she remembers, or what they told her was the flu. Arthur said he would love to send his son away for a rest, and when Devereux replied that his wife, Alice, and he would love to go on a vacation, his father had said, "Oh no, I'm not sending Alice, she should stay home with the children." Then my mother remembers Devereux rising from his sickbed—he never said a cross word to anyone, but she could tell he was angry—and putting on his hat and coat and walking up the Hill to 18 Chestnut Street. "I'm not going away unless Alice goes," he said, which resulted in the fight Bobby wrote about, with Aunt Sarah siding with her brother. "Don't worry, Dev, I'll take care of the children. I'll move right into the house—you and Alice *must* go." "Alice's place is at home with the children!" Arthur furiously insisted, but Aunt Sarah was unrelenting—she would be punished for it later. Devereux and Alice went to Europe; Arthur Winslow paid.

It seems strange to me that my grandfather, knowing he was dying, could go away for three months without his children, but leaving small children behind was common among these wealthy families. The Thorndikes, my grandmother's family, were always leaving the children home with nurserymaids, for months, even years, at a time. Sometimes it seems a bit more than a genetic accident that my ancestors produced so many manic depressives. Even before her husband was dying, my grandmother, Devereux's wife, thought nothing of dropping my six-week-old mother, whom she was nursing, to follow Devereux to Canada, returning home three months later, pregnant with her second daughter. Possibly Arthur was not being such an ogre when he argued that his rather neglectful daughter-in-law should stay home with the children. The Winslows had never abandoned their children.

My mother remembers her mother as very happy before Devereux got sick, but at a distance, always off riding her horses. Each of the little girls, Jackie, my mother ("Jahk—LEAN," her mother called her), Alice (Allie), and Mary Chilton (Polly) had her own nurse; by the time my mother was four she had her own French governess to teach her French. My mother and Allie, thirteen months apart in age, kicked and screamed and bit each other all day long, frantic for maternal attention.

My mother remembers that Aunt Sarah moved into the Mt. Vernon Street house with them while their parents were in Europe, three little girls under four, squabbling constantly. Aunt Sarah was my mother and her sisters' favorite aunt; she would get right down on the floor with them in her tidy, elegant clothes and play games for hours, as opposed to their mother, who would hug them madly once and then dash off to spend the rest of the day without them. Alice played Beethoven on the piano and took singing lessons, though she sang rather terribly, and when she went out at night she sometimes wore red hose with a dress that was short in the front and long in the back. She was the opposite of Aunt Sarah, and though they had been at Miss Porter's together (Alice was also pulled out before graduation, in her case to be sent out West so as not to get in the way of her sister's coming-out party), they had never been close—until the year Alice fell in love with Devereux, Aunt Sarah's brother. Sarah, Sarah, Sarah—the name fills almost every journal entry in the desperate little diary Alice kept that year, 1916, "Cheerful Days" embossed on its leather cover. After she married Devereux she wrote one guilt-ridden letter from her honeymoon about how next year they planned to repeat the trip with Sarah along, and then, though they would remain friends, Alice wrote no more to Sarah.

Devereux never forgot his little sister. When he became engaged he sent her flowers. "Dear Sally," says the card which she kept for more than seventy years, "you silly little girl. To write of yourself as an *outsider* in the *secret*. Don't you suppose that I love you still even if I do love Alice too?" When Sarah took care of my mother and her sisters, it was Devereux who wrote from abroad, never Alice, even when they learned that three-year-old Allie had gotten very sick with scarlet fever.

The night they came back, my mother remembers her parents tiptoeing in to kiss them. It was summer, and for a little while her father seemed better; "in bully condition," Devereux wrote Sarah.

But that fall brought the following exchange of letters:

Devereux dear,

Papa has just told me that you have had a return of your old trouble. Isn't it the devil? I think the All Mighty has decided that no one can be absolutely happy in this world and when he sees two people like you and Alice who really love one another and have three darling children he decides that it is too much of a good thing and puts a damper on it all. However it is beyond me to explain the reasons for things in this world and perhaps they reach out beyond any of our understanding and certainly our power to control. But we're going to fight this, old man, and get you fixed up for after all it is simply a question of finding out the root of the trouble and what helps you and then sticking to it until you are well. I am afraid last spring we didn't give you enough time. I am wondering now if you and Alice are planning on going away for a while, if so please, please, remember your idle sister who is waiting to go back and have some of the fun she had last spring. For you know how I loved it and the feeling that I was being of some use in this world . . .

   Devereux dear don't be unhappy that this horrid old trouble seems to hang on for I have a feeling if you only give yourself time it will be well soon and all we have to do is simply not let it get fastened on you as it did last spring. With much love to Alice and the children.

Lovingly Sarah

Darling old Sally:

You certainly are most wonderfully a friend in need and every other time too. I got your letter in the office this morning and have felt better for it all day. Although I am afraid that you have given me much more sympathy than I deserve. I had my last treatment this morning for at least a week and within two or three days I expect to be feeling very different, in fact all ready for most anything. But it helped a lot to get your letter and to always realize that you know as well as I do how much I have to be thankful for. Also having been through this sort of thing before it does not worry me in the least. After all, whatever happens will have plenty of "silver linings" and of these "Sally" will always be one of the very brightest.

Your affectionate
Devie.

It became clear to my mother that something was wrong with her father, and the word "Hodgkin's" was finally spoken, a disease which was always fatal in those days, though it was possible to survive for years. But her father was desperately sick, and her mother took him out to the country thinking the fresh air would help him. Nothing did. Soon people began coming to see her father, to pay their last respects, and her mother would not let them up the stairs. One day Grandfather Winslow took my mother and her sisters walking in the snow. They had run out of coal, my mother remembers, and the house was so cold and her father so sick and her grandfather was desperately trying to get everything fixed for them. Finally they returned to Boston, to her Thorndike grandparents' house so they could be near the hospital.

In Bobby's poem his uncle Devereux stands behind him as he plays in the dirt:

His face was putty.
His blue coat and white trousers
grew sharper and straighter.
His coat was a blue jay's tail,
his trousers were solid cream from the top of the bottle.
He was animated, hierarchical,
like a ginger snap man in a clothes-press.
He was dying of the incurable Hodgkin's disease . . .
My hands were warm, then cool, on the piles
of earth and lime,
a black pile and a white pile . . .
Come winter,
Uncle Devereux would blend to the one color.

"What did Aunt Sarah do when her brother died?" I asked my mother.

"She loved *us*."

My mother and her sister Allie were four and three when their father died, ages when children seem to think constantly about death (and its logical companion, God), a circumstance that passes in a year, only to crop up again in the middle of the night when they are forty. My sons Hunter and Teddy at age four and three couldn't be gotten off the subject. "Mommy," I would hear tearfully, out of the blue, from the backseat of the car, "I don't *want* to die!" At which point I would go on at length about heaven and God (called Guy by Teddy), to a snuffling silence, until again came another wail from the backseat, "We *still* don't want to die." Yet I have noticed that it is their own deaths they fear; another's death when it happens they simply can't take in. My mother-in-law was murdered in 1989 in her own house in the middle of the afternoon. We still do not know by whom or why. Because there was a great deal of press, I was forced to tell the boys, who, five and four years old, seemed to have no reaction to the news. Charlie and I worried and worried, but the months passed, and still there was no reaction. Then one day I heard the boys on the front porch listening to a friend describe in graphic detail a gory death he had heard about on the highway. Four times I listened, frozen, as Hunter tried breathlessly to interrupt with "My grandmother—" until finally he had the others' attention. "My grandmother," he said drawing in air for the pronouncement, "has the *same exact* name as my sister."

My mother and Allie have little memory of their father. Allie only remembers him smiling at her, at a birthday party after he learned he was sick, and later, lying bare-chested on her mother's bed. My mother was the only one of the children to have any memory of her father before he was sick. She remembers him as always loving and kind, not strict like her mother, who would be loving and indulgent one moment, extremely negligent another, and moralistic and punishing the next. My mother threw tantrums nearly every day when she was little, probably to get attention, and whenever these occurred, her mother would lock her in the closet (as her own parents had done to punish *her*) for what seemed like forever, and just let my mother scream.

One afternoon, when her father was dying, lying in the bedroom below, and my mother was screaming and kicking in the attic closet, she heard him slowly hobble up the stairs to let her out. "I'm sorry, Alice," he said to his wife after he had released his daughter. "Don't put Jackie in the closet."

Then one day Alice appeared dressed entirely in black, with an enormous black hat, and, weeping, told the girls, "Your father is dead." The next thing the girls remembered was not being able to bathe, which was nice, because they'd had smallpox vaccinations and their arms were swollen and they each had a bandage over this great wound filled with pus. They were going abroad for a year.

Allie, Polly, and Jackie.
The three baby daughters left behind.

7

Alice was twenty-eight when she set out for Europe with her baby daughters. She had grown up with every luxury but the one that seems to count the most—the luxury of early parental love. Her parents, the Thorndikes, are remembered by their grandchildren as big jolly Victorians, merrily dispensing creams and sauces (the signature dessert being chocolate cake with hot chocolate sauce) and inviting stray relatives to stay with them at their lavish houses. "Twenty-five to breakfast!" Alice's mother would say happily to her assembled family, while Alice's father had so much empathy for the children he operated on as an orthopedist that he founded a school for them—the first free day school for disabled children in the country. To their own young children, however, Alice's parents had been strict and moralistic. Alice, growing up in the shadow of a prettier (and, as it would turn out, manic-depressive) sister, had looked to food for comfort, tipping the scales at 180 by the time she was a teenager. She lost weight, but she was never trim like Aunt Sarah and her family. For the Thorndikes food was anesthesia, for the Winslows fuel.

Alice was a widow at an age when most of us are still talking hopefully about our potential. And yet, she was not grown up. She loved her children, but she loved them as a child loves a pet. When I was pregnant with my first child I read the introduction to *Doctor Spock,* in which he said, Ask yourself why you are having children—to be loved or to love? It never occurred to me that the former was an option, looking at the wretched return my brothers and I had given our parents, but my grandmother would have been amazed to consider the latter. She was too desperately in need of the love she was denied as a child: She didn't want to *be* a mother—she wanted to *have* a mother. And she looked to each of her children, in their turn, to fill the role.

It was a bleak midwinter when Alice, sheathed in widow's veils, sailed to Italy in 1923 with Jackie, Allie, and Polly, dressed in matching jerseys with elfin caps. There was a Miss Brown in attendance, although she seemed to evaporate later, to be replaced by a sporadic stream of nurses. Alice caused quite a sensation on the boat, romantic in her deep mourning and so tragically young with her stunning though less than perfectly behaved girls: my mother and Allie in violent dispute, and Polly, at one and a half, the serene angel. "Polly's my comfort," Alice would say, and as if in response, Polly would grow into a soft, melancholic, blue-eyed girl who emanated warmth, attracting everyone in need.

When the boat arrived in Venice, Alice began searching, through her veils and quarrelsome children, for the gondolier who had been hired for her. She'd written ahead requesting one who sang. "Look at that one over there, " she said pointing to a gondola garishly decorated with an American flag. "Isn't that funny?" Then the gondolier oared up. " For you, Mrs. Wilson, the American president's widow," he said gallantly, launching horribly into song. Also in Venice to meet Alice was her brother Gus and his wife. Gus, the eldest of my greatuncles and father of five children, was perceived by all as a paragon of virtue. But when he and his wife met Alice's boat they had settled in Europe for a two-year stay without their very young children. Gus had been offered a Guggenheim fellowship and had left the children at home with the help.

Alice and her daughters wintered in Rome, where the girls were often ill and Alice drank with royalty. She was pursued by at least one prince—or at least she ended up with a lot of gold jewelry someone gave her, as well as a beautiful cape and some Italian furniture. From time to time the nurse would quit, and Alice would announce that she could manage the girls perfectly well, which she couldn't at all, and when the battles got out of control, she would simply walk out, leaving them alone in the hotel room. At night she would come home and sob inconsolably about her dead husband and make my mother get into bed with her, where Alice would tell her she was the only one who could make her feel better, and that she, Jackie, was just like her father, a statement my mother knew to be absolutely untrue, with her daily tantrums, her wickedness, and the fact of her father being a saint. Her mother had developed an angelic and godlike vision of who her husband had been. They *never* fought, she said.

Alice returned in late August, moving back into the Mt. Vernon Street house she had shared with Devereux, and proceeded to become the belle of Boston. She was beautiful in her way, I'm told. Sometimes I get a little suspicious when everyone generations removed from me is always described as having been beautiful. That my mother was beautiful is a fact, with the fine features and high cheekbones that even age can't diminish. At seventy-nine she is still beautiful, more beautiful than most of my friends of forty. (Of course, as her daughter, growing up, I thought she looked like Bozo the Clown, inspired by a remark a friend made in reference to her hair. In those days one did not pass such remarks on to one's mother; nowadays a mother goes dolled up to help in the first-grade classroom, only to learn on the child's return from school, "Donna Debrock thinks you have a nose like a triangle.") In the pictures I have of Alice she looks square and chunky, with crow's-feet at twenty-four, much older than her beloved Devereux in his jodhpurs and spectacles, like a boy in a Ralph Lauren advertisement. It was the life in my grandmother's face, I'm told, her smile, that attracted you. By the time I knew my grandmother, in her early sixties, her white cheek was so creased that it was as soft as a dog's ear. But even then, my mother says, "the men loved Mother."

In the Mt. Vernon Street house, the girls were on a separate floor from their mother, who had a whole floor to herself, with a great, platformed bay window and blue velvet curtains. Here the girls acted plays, dragging up the maids and cooks from below as their audience. They were allowed to see their mother at tea. Looking after them was Louise, a sad widow hired in Switzerland, who read them long stories. For two years she would be their mother. The girls were so happy. Besides Louise, the girls befriended Margaret, an enormous woman who cooked, and they spent a lot of time with both of them down in the cellar kitchen. My mother was old enough for school but wasn't allowed to go because Alice didn't believe in kindergarten.

Meanwhile Alice—out of widow's weeds by now—received a constant stream of callers in her tiny upstairs living room, with a little fireplace and a big table and two chairs. The girls would be summoned every day at five dressed in their best dresses to say "How do you do." By then they had realized that most of the visitors were men, and that one of them might marry their mother.

"I always thought teatime meant your mother's beaux came to call," my mother said. The girls favored familiars like Cousin Cameron Winslow, their father's first cousin, who was courting Alice fervently, and who had the same last name, which made it especially wonderful, and Harold Hoskins, who got down on the floor and let them ride on his back, and took them to the circus, though their mother was too busy with her other beaux to come. And then there was a Mr. Sommaripa, who had an accent. One day he would come with a bald head and glasses and be very handsome, the girls thought, and the next day he arrived with dark, thick curly hair and very dark skin. The girls couldn't figure out how he managed it; of course it turned out that there were two Mr. Sommaripas, brothers who had escaped from Communist Russia and were on the lookout for heiresses to marry.

One day the girls felt a great romance in the air. "Why can't you marry Mr. Hoskins, or Cousin Cameron?" they wailed, but it was Mr. Sommaripa their mother had chosen, the one with the curly hair, who was so rude to the servants. You could imagine him flogging serfs, Allie said later.

Alexis Sommaripa's parents had been great aristocrats in Russia. Their ancestors had originally come from Italy (hence the name, pronounced "Sum-ma-REEPA") and had been ennobled and given lands by Catherine the Great, for whom they had privateered. At seventeen Alexis escaped from the Red Army, which was going to shoot him, and, according to Aunt Sarah, swam the Bosphorus with a stamp collection in his mouth—the sale of which took him through Harvard Business School. It was at the business school that he had met Alice's youngest brother, Amory, and been brought to tea. Sommaripa was nineteen when he arrived in the United States, twenty-three when Alice accepted him, five years her junior. He had already been refused by at least one Boston heiress, a younger cousin of Alice's, with whom Sommaripa had been violently in love. In the beginning Sommaripa had only visited Alice in order to talk about her cousin. When Sommaripa and Alice got engaged, the cousin said, "Alice, you're a making a great mistake." Alice's parents thoroughly disapproved of the match as well, but they couldn't forbid it—their daughter was nearly thirty, and she had her own share of the trust.

Sommaripa was small; "brilliant, handsome, and autocratic," is the phrase used to describe him in the family. Somnaripa, my Aunt Sarah called him, as if the name were too un-Boston to get right. He had a boldness and a direct sexuality that my Aunt Sarah would have hated, her girlish flirtatious manner having nothing whatsoever to do with actual *sex*, and then he was, after all, replacing her brother, Devereux. Aunt Sarah always maintained to me that Sommaripa had fathered a number of children among the Boston elite. When we went to Singing Beach Club, Aunt Sarah would point out some dark-haired child playing in the sand and say, triumphantly, "Look, Russian blood."

After Alice accepted Sommaripa, her Winslow in-laws invited the couple and the three girls to lunch at 18 Chestnut Street. Devereux had not been dead three years. Gaga, who often took the girls by limousine to their father's grave, was still in deep mourning; she would remain in mourning for the twenty-two years she survived her son, although the black would change to lavender sometimes and, in the summer, white. She never wore any other colors that my mother can remember.

After a rather uncomfortable lunch, Sommaripa asked to see his hosts alone in the parlor. "I assume if I marry Alice, you will take the girls," he said, meaning adopt them, so that he and Alice could start a new family. The Winslows never spoke to him again.

Alice.
Alice weds Alexis Sommaripa, a White Russian who, according to Aunt Sarah,
swam the Bosphorus with a stamp collection in his mouth.

Jackie at age ten.

8

My mother and her sisters would always know, without being told, that their mother had been willing to give them up for Alexis Sommaripa. "I wish we *had* gone to live with our grandparents," my mother told me. "We would have been better off." But at the time my mother must have been terrified at the thought of losing her mother. When I think of my small children clinging to me piteously as I tried to go grocery shop ("But I'm not *used* to Daddy!" was four-year-old Teddy's last-ditch ploy), I cannot imagine what my mother and her sisters must have felt with a father dead and a mother so dangerously in love.

Alice was tremendously, embarrassingly in love. Even the girls saw that the enthrallment was obviously just sex, whatever sex was. "Dahlings!" their mother had said after Devereux died, gathering her little girls into the bed with her. "I had such a grand sex life with your father!" She then proceeded to talk to them all about how babies were made in details graphic enough to disgust them, but euphemistic enough that though they knew it was the most wonderful thing in the world and that you positively *fainted* from joy, they didn't know what "it" was.

After the wedding Alice swept up the girls to follow Sommaripa to Buffalo (where he had just gotten a job), on the romantic notion of putting aside the income from her trust and living from her husband's earnings. Alice had a fairy-tale vision of being a poor little bride, which was awkward with three daughters, and not so much like a fairy tale once they moved into the cramped third-floor apartment in Buffalo. There was no room or money for nurses and governess, and Louise, the Swiss nurse, who had been the girls' only anchor, was fired—Louise, who had read them their favorite story, "Les Vacances," in bed every morning, and taught them one French word a day, leaving them even today, nearing eighty, with a vocabulary of infant French, remembering *dodo* as the word for nap. The loss of Louise caused more lasting sorrow than did the death of their father.

Without the usual coterie of servants, the move to Buffalo exhausted Alice. She had one servant, Della, who did all the work and who fascinated the girls because she didn't shave under her arms. This is a bit like reading Jane Austen and trying to drum up some sorrow for the heroine because she and her sisters are down to two servants, but for my grandmother, whose parents had had one servant assigned simply to the towels, it was a deprivation.

Alice always said that she lost two babies changing beds in Buffalo, though my mother doubts that she ever made a bed. What she did was *stay* in bed, while my mother and Allie, seven and six, did the chores before Della arrived. My grandmother said she wanted her daughters to be better than she was, to learn to do the things she wished she had been taught. Allie was too brilliant to need school, was Alice's excuse for keeping her at home. Every time Alice was sick or had a miscarriage, Allie emptied bedpans and cooked breakfast and made beds. When she was well, Alice would take off for weekends with Beaupère—"Beautiful Father," the name the girls called their stepfather in the French tradition—carelessly leaving the girls with a nasty baby-sitter who took them to adult movies.

The girls despised Beaupère, though many years later they gained sympathy for him. He had had a terrible time adjusting to American ways, and he didn't know how to act with children; he came from a feudalistic background in which young children were bundled off with servants, and suddenly, at age twenty-four, he was in a small, chaotic apartment trying to maneuver between stacks of unopened boxes and three squabbling girls and a mother who could not control them. He tried to be nice. He admired Allie's brains and my mother's looks (from then on Alice's view of the girls would be etched in stone: Jackie, pretty and dumb; Allie, brilliant and fat; Polly, the saint.) As his stepdaughters grew older, Sommaripa grew more interested in their character development, enjoying their increasing but more cleverly expressed rudeness to him. But he was a Russian aristocrat, and he wanted complete obedience.

One time Alice was trying to hurry Allie along to go out somewhere, and Allie said: "Haven't you got eyes? Can't you see I'm tying my shoes?" At which point Beaupère picked up the other shoe and began hitting Allie with it while her mother watched helplessly. That night when her mother came to say goodnight to her, Allie turned her head away and faced the wall. Alice began to cry. "Oh, please forgive me," she said to her little daughter, but Allie would not turn her head. She had lost all respect for her mother. She was seven.

For two years my grandmother chose to live without the benefit of her unearned income, and the experience must have dampened her ardor for poverty, because when Sommaripa was transferred to Manhattan, the unearned income was back on display. Suddenly life was rather grand, with a butler named Basil who wore spats and a bowler hat when he walked the girls to school. My mother prayed that the other children would think Basil was their father. "Your father is *so* good-looking," the other girls would say, to my mother's modest smile. Basil's wife, Natalie, was the cook; Beaupère was very particular about his food, which was beautiful, rich Russian food with lots of caviar. They lived at 1165 Fifth Avenue, a cooperative apartment, not particularly smashing, my mother said, just a living room, dining room, three bedrooms, two tiny maid's rooms, and a bath, overlooking the park—well, if you *strained*, overlooking the park. The cross street was Ninety-eighth Street, and in those days one never went above Ninetieth.

In Manhattan, Alice and Sommaripa were very fashionable and entertained lavishly. They held musical evenings, and once the dancer Anita Zong came and danced around the tiny living room. Alice was friends with opera singers and took singing lessons in the afternoon, and Russian lessons in the morning from Mrs. Mogulot, who wore very thick powder and had very dark circles around her eyes and a dark spot on her cheek and smelled terrifically of smoke. Alice never did learn to speak Russian.

Sommaripa was bright and opinionated, and the guests loved to argue with him; Alice had an effusive charm, a kind of flair for drama, though all of her entertaining was done in the most terrible taste. She had no sense of decor, the furniture was clunky, and the dining room was painted a sort of hospital green. But Alice prided herself on having rather advanced ideas: The dining room had a long refectory table on which she put enormous Italian candlesticks, and once she made the unusual addition of tall pear-shaped vases with live goldfish swimming in the candlelight. It was a quite a sight, for about ten minutes. By the time the guests came into the dining room, all the goldfish were floating dead on the surface.

By the time I knew her, my grandmother wore synthetic print dresses ordered from the Sears catalog, topped off with huge leopard hats. But back then she took great time and pride over what she considered high fashion. She always had a terrible figure; she had lost so much weight so quickly as a teenager that she had flaps of slack skin hanging from every limb for the rest of her life. Not that she ever let it get in the way of wearing the most extravagant costumes. Allie remembered her horror one summer at the sight of her mother in a sort of cowgirl outfit, short pants with flab hanging from her knees. Another time Alice met her at a train station, rushing toward her gaily in a miner's cap with a patent leather brim.

In Manhattan, Alice had baths and massages and high-colonic irrigations and took taxis down to the dressmaker to supervise the directions of the stripes on her zebra coat. When the zebra coat finally emerged, it had monkey fur collar and cuffs, of long black hair. With it she wore an outlandish peaked hat, to her daughters' chagrin. Her hair was always messy and unfashionable. She tried cutting it once, in the hope that its girlish look would please her young husband, who seemed to be losing interest in her. "Act your age, Alice," he said at dinner.

Even during the summer my grandmother would make overnight trips from their rented summer house in Connecticut for her high-colonic irrigations; when she returned the girls would strew armloads of wildflowers at her feet. The bowel movement was very fashionable in those days; it was part of the era. Life began with the nanny holding you over the potty. Everything else about the bodily functions was off limits, except for the bowel movement, which could be discussed quite openly in graphic detail. The girls might be jumbled off to school a mess, hair uncombed, but every morning their mother asked after their bowel movements. You could not make it out the door without "Did you have your bowel movement today?" Of course the girls always said yes; it turned out to be an early lesson in lying.

In Manhattan, money was spent freely, but not on the girls. Jackie and Allie were sent to a third-rate school, where the students happened to be Jewish, because it was the cheapest private school around (a hundred dollars a year). Then they were told they could not invite friends back to the house because they were Jewish. I always knew that my grandmother, who tried to be so avant-garde, was really a snob; "I don't care who anybody is," she used to tell her daughters about prospective beaux, and then run home to look up the person in question in the Social Register. Only recently did I learn she was anti-Semitic, despite the fact her first husband was part Jewish. I don't know why my grandmother disliked the Jews, unless she was trying to please her Russian husband, who had been poisoned by his parents' prejudice. "I can smell a Jew," Beaupère used to say.

One terrible time, Alice went to Europe with Sommaripa for several months and arranged for the girls to board at the school, though it did not take boarders. Then the girls got sick, and Aunt Sarah had to rush down to New York to take care of them. She was appalled by the school and even more appalled that Alice had left the girls there. Throughout their childhood Aunt Sarah was always coming down to see her brother's children. She would arrive with all sorts of presents and say, "Now, Jackie, I want you to close your eyes," and then this lovely fabric would go over my mother's head, and it would be a beautiful sweater knitted by Sarah. (The one domestic chore allowed women in the upper class, for some reason, was any kind of needlework).

Alice forbade her daughters to eat candy, yet allowed them to run free in New York. She was never at home when they returned from school, and Jackie and Allie would smoke her elegant Melacrino ciga-rettes, and then go off to Lipschitz Drugstore to buy magazines and the forbidden candy with their bus money. Afterward they would roam Central Park. Often they went to the movie house above One-hundredth Street and Madison (then considered the ghetto), which was filled with screaming, bedraggled children. The movies were five cents and played continuously, like an old cowboy serial with different installments every Saturday. They especially liked an adults-only movie called *Bad Girl*, pulling down their hats at ages ten and eleven to look old enough to be admitted. *Now we'll finally find out all about sex*, they thought. In the movie the heroine was kissed once and had a baby. This was the dirtiest movie they had ever seen, and when their mother found out, the punishment was no movies for a month, which in the end punished their mother. Even Polly, who was so young, was allowed to wander the streets of New York alone. Once when Aunt Sarah was visiting, to her horror she found seven-year-old Polly, all dressed up, headed out for Bloomingdale's, where she often spent Saturday mornings.

Polly felt the burden of living up to her mother's image of her. Sometimes she wouldn't talk to Jackie or Allie for two days because she felt they hadn't treated their mother well. "Oh my darling Polly," Alice would say, "How could I live without you, you're just like your father, and he was so sweet." Yet Alice loved to boast about Jackie and Allie's adventures. "*Guess* what those girls did?!" she would say to her friends.

Once Alice left Allie alone all day at the Metropolitan Museum because she thought the guards would take better care of her than her older sister would. The guards did all right until the museum closed, and Allie spent two hours waiting in the dark for her mother, who had completely forgotten her and arrived stricken, begging forgiveness.

In the evenings my grandmother often took the girls to the opera, keeping them out till after midnight to hear Wagner in Mrs. Morgan's box. They also went to the ballet, particularly the Ballets Russes de Monte Carlo, in which George Balanchine danced, and also Alexandra Danilova, who had been a ward of Beaupère's family in Moscow, and probably, my mother and her sisters later surmised, their stepfather's mistress.

.   .   .

My mother was twelve when her mother gave birth to a long-awaited son, Amory, except he wasn't called Amory for several years, but rather Mstislav Alexeivich Sommaripa. My mother was to be his godmother. Although she disapproved of the name, Alice and Beaupère didn't listen. The boy was to be named after Beaupère's brother, who had died in the war. Mstislav's nickname was Dushka. When Dushka started being called "Douche" in school, he became Amory Mstislav Sommaripa, after Alice's favorite brother.

My mother had been made godmother for a reason; it was she, not her mother, who slept in her brother's room when he was an infant to tend him during the night. Amory was made to wear metal gloves so as not to suck his thumb, and his ears were pinned back so they would not stick out. The girls had been sent to a third-rate school, but Amory was sent to St. Bernard's, the lovely school next door to the apartment, and they could look down on the yard where the children played from my mother's room. Alice had a mad crush on Amory, because he was a boy, my mother remembered. Yet Amory's childhood memory is of yearning for his mother, who was often away on long vacations with his father. Sommaripa was a tough father, once slapping his son to stop him from throwing up, and although Alice tried to protect Amory from him, she was also neglectful. When she went out with the girls and Sommaripa at night, she left Amory in the care of the doorman, who was to check in on him periodically. One night when he was about two, Amory awoke to find no one home. When Alice and the girls returned, they found him standing up asleep against a sofa, its arm drenched in tears.

After Amory was born, my grandmother went to Doctor Shields, the gynecologist who treated all her friends, to find out why her husband was no longer interested in her. "What is he doing on his own time?" asked the doctor. "He's only thirty years old; is he faithful?" It had never occurred to Alice that her husband would be unfaithful; it was not something that was common in her family. But then she started to look about her, and she found out that a lot was going on. There was, for instance, his secretary, who suddenly had a child after years in a childless marriage. Sommaripa did not deny the affairs.

When one mistress got in trouble with the law on an unrelated matter, Sommaripa went to my grandmother and said, "Alissss, I have given up having affairs for two years."

Meanwhile my mother and Allie were fighting with Beaupère, refusing to obey him, and made to stand in the corner since the closets in the New York apartment were not big enough to hold them. When their stepfather would permit them to leave the corner, Allie, never missing a chance to provoke him, would say, "Oh, don't take me out, I'm having a good time."

My mother hated her stepfather. Sommaripa tickled the girls and stroked my mother's arm during nightly prayers, and told his wife he admired Jackie's figure. She had started menstruating and her complexion was bad and her body was developing and she felt strange and unhappy. At night she would pace the floor sleepwalking, moaning and crying, keeping the household awake. Her mother would beg her to stop so she wouldn't wake her husband. After a fight with Beaupère, my mother would often pack a pillowcase to run away from home, though she never quite managed to get the courage to ring the elevator bell.

One day in the middle of a fight, Jackie ran out to the balcony and threatened to jump. She was thirteen. The next day her mother picked her up after school and told her she was taking her to a special place—to a psychiatrist—and my mother started to cry. Going to a psychiatrist was a stigma, one compounded by the fear of becoming like her mother's sister Mary, the manic depressive, who would kick the girls when she was high and tell them that it was disgusting for them to look in the mirror. Alice and my mother arrived at the funny little house of Olga Canuff, a fat German therapist. My mother cried the whole visit, and Olga said, "We are not going to talk when your mother is here. You must come see me yourself." My mother returned two times alone. She told Olga her dream that she turned on the faucets and fishes came out. Olga told my grandmother: "Your daughter is in love with your husband." In that era it was the girl, not the husband, who was blamed.

Suddenly the money was found to send the girls away to boarding school.

. . .

It is confusing to me that my grandmother, Alice, who was a great reader and lover of the arts, was so against formal education for women, but it seems to have been a common concept of this era, culled from the English upper class, who even today would find a college degree a bit tacky in a Princess of Wales. Alice was fierce on this subject, making my mother's enrollment at Milton Academy contingent on her not taking a course of study that would earn her a high school diploma. She instructed the headmistress that my mother was to take piano instead of Latin—she had a vision of her daughter as a great pianist, based solely on her romantic looks. "Jahk-LEAN is not going to college, I can't afford it," she told the headmistress. But it wasn't only the money; later, when Allie earned full scholarships to Bennington and Mount Holyoke, my grandmother still refused to let her attend. "I want you to go to the college of life, " Alice told her daughters, signing her letters to them at boarding school, "Your Adoring Mother."

Despite everything, my mother loved Milton, acting in plays opposite Elliot Richardson (later attorney general under Richard Nixon), and living at the house of her distant cousin Clippie (Cleveland Amory), with whom she was great friends but who was not often around, leaving my mother at the mercy of his mother. Mrs. Amory had a certain coldness about her; she was quite grand, but the Great Depression had forced her to accept money from Alice for my mother's room and board. One time my mother was put in charge of the younger children and told them that she, as the eldest, would be responsible for pouring the tea. "You must never do that again," Mrs. Amory reprimanded her later, and forever after my mother knew she was not to be an equal in the house. (I must say I was not too sad to hear that when Cleveland Amory's great, funny book, *The Proper Bostonians*, was published, his parents were so embarrassed they had to move away from Milton.)

At her Milton graduation the other girls got diplomas, my mother only a certificate of attendance, because she had been forbidden to study Latin. "But I've worked so hard," she said. "I've earned a diploma!" Finally, they made an exception, and my mother could say something her mother never could: She had graduated from high school.

Hats like wedding cakes.
Charlotte (far left), *Gaga* (far right), *Sarah* (center).

9

As a mother Charlotte Lowell wasn't very "nurturing," to use the popular term. "Take him, take him," she had greeted a Devereux cousin she had not seen for years, thrusting the infant Bobby into the cousin's arms. "He's as squirmy as a worm." She had an aversion to little children and didn't care who knew it. Even Alice had hugged her children. But Charlotte never allowed Bobby in her lap lest it crease her dress. Charlotte was ruthless and strong, my cousin Nell said—malignant. "But she would have hated to have been thought of as strong—it wasn't the fashion. She would have preferred to be called, perhaps, steadfast, Puritan."

No one ever seems to have a nice thing to say about Charlotte Lowell—except that she was very chic, if that's a good thing to say about anybody. In my family it decidedly is, although by my generation there is no fashion left. Even I, who am very vain, have to make an enormous effort when I visit my children's teacher not to appear as a member of the homeless (my day-to-day look) or a (aged) hooker (my husband Charlie's style for me).

The time my grandmother and Aunt Sarah and Aunt Charlotte spent on clothes—the fittings, the materials ("pink and blue chiffon peacock colored bodice," describes Alice in her diary), the hats like wedding cakes! Even for the next generation appearances were everything. In their seventies and eighties, my parents still buy clothes as if they were teenagers. The best, most wonderful compliment you can get from my parents is that you look good. They care so much, they ask so little, and then I arrive for dinner having rubbed the stains off old wool pants with a shedding Kleenex.

My mother said that as opposed to most Boston ladies who had no style, Charlotte and Aunt Sarah were always very chic, not frumpy or little girlish, but expensively elegant. The Boston ladies wore their suits for twenty years and drove their cars into the ground. They had what they called "banana wagons," station wagons, but open on the sides, which were enclosed in the winter with old-fashioned isinglass. Everyone froze to death, my mother said, and all the Boston ladies chugged around in these ten-year-old cars, as a sort of reverse snobbism. If you had a very shiny new car, people said, "Nouveau."

The Winslow girls were chauffeured about in a limousine. Nell, who was often taken in for meals at the Winslows and the Lowells, said Charlotte always wore a navy blue suit with simple lines and pearls, and the most elaborate hats. Once Nell arrived at Charlotte's for lunch and threw her old tam on Charlotte's perfect white bed—Charlotte's room was very stylish as well, all white, down the hall from her husband's—only to walk into the dining room to discover the ladies seated at the luncheon table still burdened by their monstrous hats—except for Charlotte. Evidently the hostess, by the obscure rules of their society, was the only one allowed to dine light-headed.

Charlotte loved Bobby in her way, my mother said, reading him book after book on Napoleon and fretting about him constantly, but she was cold and proper, the opposite of Bobby who was hotheaded and wild. The seams of Charlotte's stockings were always perfectly straight, while Bobby, even in his twenties, by his own admission, had to be instructed to tie his shoes. At St. Mark's School, where he wore the same dirty clothes day after day and beat up friends and enemies, he was nicknamed Cal—for Caliban, I was told, but later I heard it was for Caligula.

Bobby was thirteen when he entered St. Mark's. "St. Mark's was the beginning of the trouble," my mother said. "It was a very strict Episcopal school—they restrained him, and he hated that." Even at school Bobby had not yet found an intellectual outlet (he was near the bottom of the class his first year) or a place among his classmates. Several years later, in his valedictory at Kenyon College, Bobby sneered at St. Mark's, before launching into an attack on Kenyon. But in adolescence, when all that matters is being accepted, Bobby was an outcast, and in his last book, *Day by Day*, he describes the pain of his first two years at St. Mark's. "A boy next to me breathed my shoes,/and lay choking on the bench," Bobby wrote. In the dining hall they sang "Noel, Noel," substituting "Lo-well, Lo-well."

> I was fifteen;
> they made me cry in public.
> Chicken?
>
> Perhaps they had reason . . .
> even now
> my callous unconscious drives me
> to torture my closest friend.
> ("St. Mark's, 1933")

In his last two years at St. Mark's, Bobby plunged into a lifelong friendship with Frank Parker and Blair Clark. "When Cal was ordaining the lives of his two acolytes," Blair Clark remembered, "he decreed that Frank was to be the artist, and tone-deaf Cal thought the three of us would cover the arts if he assigned me as the musician. He based that ukase on the fact that I'd been in the school choir for a while." The three read Homer and pondered "truth" and the meaning of life, questions asked only by the young because only they believe they can be answered. "We looked in the face of the other/for what we were," Bobby wrote in the poem "To Frank Parker":

> . . . we sat by the school pool
> talking out the soul-lit night
> and listened to the annual
> unsuffering voice of the tree frogs,
> green, aimless and wakened:
> "I want to write." "I want to paint."

Many years later, in the mid-1950s, when Bobby was working on
a prose autobiography, much of which would ultimately become *Life
Studies*, he envisioned the work as a "sort of immense bandage of
grace and ambergris for my hurt nerves. Therefore, this book will
stop with the summer of 1934. A few months after the end of this
book, I *found* myself" ("Near the Unbalanced Aquarium").

My mother never saw the side of Bobby he describes in *Life Studies*,
but she did know that his parents considered him "impossible." My
mother didn't think there was anything so unusual about Bobby
when he was at college. "He was getting to be rather hippie-like, but
then a lot of people were bohemians in college that I knew and went
out with. By the time he was at Harvard, though, his family was hav-
ing a fit. He wasn't doing the regular thing." My mother knew boys
who hid in the cloakroom at deb dances, but Bobby simply didn't go.
He didn't join a club at Harvard, and he was going around with "an
older woman."

Anne Dick was all of twenty-four and came from a very good
Boston family on Beacon Hill. (Anne was the cousin of Frank Parker,
who had introduced her to Bobby.) Anne was quick and blond and
very pretty. "Sort of a pretty Jean Stafford," my mother said. But she
also remembered Anne as a mixed-up girl, over at Bobby's rooms all
the time. "It was a very hot and heavy romance, and everyone just
assumed they were sleeping together," my mother said. "It was a great
release for Bobby. She was very much in love with him, sincerely so."

Bobby had met Anne the spring of his freshman year and pro-
posed to her almost immediately—even at nineteen he was a "mar-
rier," unlike most men. Charlotte and Bob senior were rigidly
opposed to the engagement and did not welcome Anne to the house,
but Aunt Sarah had Anne and Bobby to tea often, despite her sister's
protests, or maybe because of them. When Bob senior wrote Anne
Dick's father implying that they were sleeping together, Bobby
knocked his father down in the hallway of their house. Bobby was
horribly guilt stricken about hitting his father, still writing about it
more than thirty years later in the poem, "Mother and Father I":
". . . I hit my father. My apology/scratched the surface of his

invisible/coronary . . . never to be effaced." But, soon after, his passion for Anne became indifference.

Charlotte and Bob could not understand why Bobby couldn't just "toe the line." Of course all parents want their children to toe the line; certainly my parents weren't ecstatic when the sixties and manic depression and drugs and divorce came into our lives, but eventually we broke them in, and now they stalwartly brag about whatever morsel they can pick up. Of course it is never the morsel one wishes. "You know," my mother says bashfully to me, "if you ever get tired of writing, you could be an interior decorator, or even, a real estate agent."

Bobby had to win the Pulitzer Prize before Charlotte began to be broken in. Luckily he won it at age thirty. When *Life* magazine came to interview "Mrs. R. T. S. Lowell of Boston and Manchester-by-the-Sea" (the latter being a cottage loaned to her by Aunt Sarah), she was quite gracious. But in the years before, she was tearing her hair out about him, and when Bobby knocked his father down, she exploded in fury, shutting her door to him for months and exploring the possibility of committing him to a psychiatric hospital. Meanwhile, that spring, his sophomore year, Bobby was refused by the *Harvard Advocate*, the undergraduate literary journal. Harvard was a disaster—he was writing like crazy, but it was incoherent. ". . . I rolled out Spenserian stanzas on Job and Jonah surrounded by recently seen Nantucket scenery. Everything I did was grand, ungrammatical, and had a timeless hackneyed quality," Bobby wrote in his essay, "Dr. Williams." When he showed a long, handwritten epic poem about the Crusades to Robert Frost, who was teaching at Harvard, Frost famously remarked that it did go on a bit.

Then, by luck or possibly by brilliance, Charlotte sent Bobby to a psychiatrist she had been seeing, Merrill Moore. Moore was also a poet; he had a book of a thousand poems published, called *M*. I can't help but think of a shrink who publishes poems in such volume as being a self-satisfied, quasi-Renaissance man, scribbling poems in the ten minutes before the next psychiatric wreck wanders in to be confronted by his blinding confidence. Possibly I am influenced by Nell's description of Moore arriving for lunch, bragging that only an hour before he had swum out to the lighthouse in Boston Harbor, then dashed off a sonnet to Gaga on a napkin, *supposedly* off the top of his head, and smarmily showing it all around. And also by Bobby's poem mentioning Moore, "Unwanted":

> . . . in his conversation or letters,
> each phrase a new
> paragraph,
> implausible as the million
> sonnets he rhymed into his dictaphone,
> or dashed on windshield writing-pads . . .

All the hoopla over Bobby and Anne Dick visiting his rooms is a little hypocritical if it was true, as everyone in the family seemed to believe (except Aunt Sarah) that Charlotte was sleeping with her son's psychiatrist. "Did he become mother's lover/and prey/by rescuing her from me?" Bobby continues in "Unwanted."

Bob senior, passive as always, had *no* idea of this affair, my cousin Nell said. She would be invited to lunch at the Lowells as a kind of companion to Moore's pretty southern wife, who was insulated and unsophisticated and very made-up—the idea being that since Nell was also southern, she could take care of the dull wife while Charlotte and Merrill flirted.

Charlotte sparkled when Moore was around. "Oh, when you go off on medical trips with Merrill you *never* know when you're going to have dinner!" Charlotte would cry delightedly, having eaten dinner all her life at exactly the same hour. Charlotte had seen Moore originally to talk about Bobby, and Moore had been so impressed with Charlotte's intelligence and self-control that he hired her to work with him on his alcoholic cases. The recovering alcoholics were not from society, and Bob senior, even snobbier than his wife, did not like the sight of them sitting on his parlor couch. But the work invigorated Charlotte—she was "full of it," happily excited by her mission, as my mother had never seen her before. Moore probably saved Charlotte's life. He certainly saved Bobby's (although he also blighted it by telling him he was an unwanted child). It was Moore who arranged for Bobby to leave Harvard to study with Allen Tate and John Crowe Ransom, who had started the *Fugitive* magazine at Vanderbilt, along with Robert Penn Warren. Moore even traveled to Nashville with Bobby, who within days had pitched his tent on the lawn of Allen Tate and his wife, novelist Caroline Gordon. At the Tates' Bobby wrote furiously all summer and congregated with other writers, such as Ford Madox Ford. Ford made Bobby feel "I was far too provincial, genteel, and puritanical to understand what I was saying. And why not? Wasn't I, as Ford assumed, the grandson or something of James Russell Lowell and the cousin of Lawrence Lowell, a young man doomed to trifle with poetry and end up as president of Harvard or ambassador to England?" (from "Dr. Williams").

"When Bobby went down south and met these people, he saw the carrot," my mother said. "The reason to work."

Sarah, Bobby (age fifteen), Charlotte, Gaga, Arthur Winslow at Chardesa.
As a teenager Bobby was nicknamed "Cal"—for Caliban I was told—
but later I heard it was for Caligula.

10

However bad your life, meet it, live it, it's not as bad as you are . . .
— Bobby, quoting Thoreau, the original guilt-tripper
("Thoreau 2")

No one in my family has ever had the slightest sympathy for Jean Stafford or her nose, which Bobby broke in a car accident (and later, allegedly, in a fight). She was a whiner, they believed, and in my family the answer to "How are you?" must always be "Fine."

My family was shocked and indignant when a biography came out maintaining that Bobby had hit Jean Stafford, as if such barbarism was unimaginable in someone from our background. But Bobby *did* hit his father, and, by his own account, was violent in his youth, and later in his manic states. Whether it was part of his sickness, his drinking, or his rebellion, I can't say. I never witnessed any of it. By the time I knew him, his violence had turned into an intense warmth.

I read Jean's first novel, *Boston Adventure*, which Charlotte told Nell she was a character in, but Nell couldn't find her. I also read *The Mountain Lion*, but I just couldn't bring myself to read *The Catherine Wheel*—not with that title—though I bought it once and kept it near my bedside for several months. She's obviously a very good writer, and yet I don't like reading the novels. There's something dreary about them. When I went back to *Boston Adventure* recently and read again about the little girl's cold dingy shack and then remembered how her father leaves her, I took a glance through the many pages remaining and slunk back to Dickens. I mean, if I'm going to read about something depressing I'm going straight to the top.

Of course, I am the most prejudiced person in the world. To this day I continue a pathetic vendetta against Thoreau (like the mouse beating the paw of the lion), whom I have disparaged in everything I have ever published, and yet, I must admit, except for that ant fight in *Walden*, I have never actually *read* Thoreau. Growing up in Concord, he was shoved down my throat. "Simplify, simplify," the teachers would breathe softly as my classmates and I stood shivering in the damp leaves at Walden Pond, staring at the four bricks marking the site of Thoreau's hut. To quote Otto von Bismarck: "Hatred is as great an incentive to me as love."

I talk against Thoreau so much that a friend found himself proclaiming that Thoreau was a "mooch" when he won a literary prize and Elizabeth Hardwick handed him a copy of *Walden*—a remark that was in dubious taste as an expression of thanks, he realized later in a sober moment. Now my friend, the traitor, tells me that Thoreau is actually a great writer. He even asked me to locate a copy of *Two Weeks on the* Assabet. When I was walking around the Concord Book Shop gingerly holding the book, two guys with beards actually tried to pick me up—until I assured them I had *no* intention of ever opening the book.

All right, I said to myself recently when I was somewhere in Concord where a book by Thoreau happened to be lying about. (You can't move in this town without bumping into Thoreau: Thoreau Street, Walden Street, even a rather run-of-the-mill restaurant sporting the name "A Different Drummer.") So I turned to Thoreau's essay on walking, thinking, *All right, give it a whirl.* "I think that I cannot preserve my health and spirits," says Thoreau, "unless I spend four hours a day at least,—and it is commonly more than that,—sauntering through the woods . . ." and once again I threw the book down.

And yet, I loved Louisa May Alcott, even though I realize she is the lesser writer of the two. Six times in a single year I traveled to

Orchard House to view Amy's golden curl enshrined in its glass case, and courageously rose above the fact that in photographs Meg looks as if she needs a shave. To this day I still grapple with whether I want to be Jo or Amy, or on a bad day, Beth. No amount of psychiatric work can undo the damage of comparing myself to these paragons of virtue. Whenever I have a nonaltruistic thought, a vision springs to mind of the March girls in their darned gloves and old, burn-spotted tarlatan dresses, munching on apples, having just given their Christmas breakfast to the poor, struggling (*always* successfully, even the perfume-buying Amy) against every selfish desire. And when I have really sinned, the alluring vision of becoming Beth creeps into my consciousness, wasting away, perhaps, but with a conscience as clear as the air in spring, beloved by the very sparrows in the trees.

And still, even in Concord, where Orchard House, which Louisa called Apple Slump and fled whenever possible, is so breathlessly busy with back-to-back bus tours that it can barely close its doors, I look for the man or boy who has the slightest inkling what *Little Women* is about.

Recently I was at a party for new neighbors, where, as a parlor game, on our backs were stuck the names of "famous" Concordians, which read rather more like the names of roads unless you have children in the school system. There I met an interesting guy who mentioned that his daughter had been one of the leads in the most recent Concord Players production of *Little Women*. Which part did she play, I asked, thrilled at last to find a man who had sat through an entire performance. He looked at me as if I had struck him a fatal blow. "Uh, one of the young ones," he bluffed. "But they're all young," I said, as he gazed at me helplessly. "She wasn't Beth, was she? She didn't *die*, did she?" "Well, you know," he said, brightening a little, "I think she might have!"

Men are immune to *Little Women* because it is a guilt-grounded book, in which any triumph over selfishness is rewarded by a kiss from Marmee. For, contrary to all their claims, the guilt men suffer passes only as twinges, clouds over the summer sun—whereas I am still guilty for peeking under the blindfold in Pin the Tail on the Donkey. (My daughter, Emily, at age four already knew the cling of guilt, I realized, when, following a week of inexplicable misery, she burst out: "I was supposed to practice my cartwheels for gymnastics!") I need go no farther for an example than Bronson Alcott, the cause of all the trouble in that family, who nearly starved everyone to death on apples and flour and his staunch belief that for him to earn a wage was "unrighteous;" Bronson Alcott, who sent his wife and daughters out to work; Bronson Alcott, who reading in his deceased wife's journal about the terrible exhaustion and depression that plagued her life, allows that he *"almost* repents" of the suffering he caused her. Even Thoreau remarked in a letter to Emerson that Alcott was, as usual, "nowhere doing nothing." The Alcott women, hardworking and philanthropic, died off like flies, save for "Meg" (but who ever wanted to be Meg?). But Bronson lived to a ripe eighty-eight, cared for by Louisa who, ill and toiling to make money in addition to cleaning and cooking for the family, asked in her journal, "Shall I ever find time to die?" only allowing herself that privilege two days after her father's death.

I love Louisa May Alcott because while she may have fought pettiness, unlike Thoreau she really understood it. She wasn't holier than thou, and yet to me she lived a far, far more noble life than Thoreau, working around the clock in sickness to keep her family alive. Give Thoreau a batch of children and no free meals, and let's have a look, I say. Somehow I can imagine my sons quoting Thoreau to me with a superior air some drug-dazed summer in the not-too-distant future, as I serve them dinner, while Emily, wanting to make peace, thinks hopefully to herself Beth's horrific line: "Birds in their little nests agree."

Men are immune to *Little Women*—except for Bobby, who read not only *Little Women* but *Little Men*. But, then, Bobby's guilt was so deep and so wide it spanned the centuries.

Even as a woman, I look in my heart and find no sympathy for Jean Stafford, as hardworking and wrenched with guilt as they come. I know this is wrong. When I think of what Bobby put her through, how she had to type at a terrible job so he could write, and perform thanklessly every single domestic chore, how his religious conversion to Catholicism early in the marriage turned him into an ascetic ("I fell in love with Caligula and am living with Calvin," is Jean's famous quote to Eileen Simpson), I believe every word Jean wrote in "An Influx of Poets" about megalomaniac poets staying up all night and reading their poetry aloud while she did the cooking and cleaning up. Perhaps meanest of all was when Bobby gave up drinking and turned on her a self-righteous eye—the final blow! He was crazy without being fun; she nagged and drank and fixed up the house. Yet I seem to forgive him.

Jean's fame never affected Aunt Sarah, who refused to refer to her by name, merely as "that girl Bobby married just because he broke her nose," implying that Bobby had only done the gentlemanly thing. But there had been nothing gentlemanly about it. Bobby had engaged himself to Jean long before he drunkenly drove them into a wall; he had relentlessly been pursuing Jean all through his years at Kenyon College, where, after his summer at the Tates', he'd followed his mentor, John Crowe Ransom. Jean was a few years older, had studied in Europe, and was on the verge of being published when Bobby met her at a writers' conference in 1937. In his short story "1939," Peter Taylor, Bobby's roommate at Kenyon, described a fictional Jean as "a real novelist," with long, loose golden hair and more interest in the book she had just sold to a publisher than in Bobby. The courtship was tumultuous; much of it conducted at long distance, with Jean harboring a secret fiancé, and at short distance, with a great deal of drinking and fighting. The car accident, which occurred one night in Cambridge, smashed Jean's nose so badly that even after five operations her face looked cockeyed and her eyes always watered. Bobby met her in secret while her insurance company sued for medical expenses, and then married her against his parents' wishes (though I notice that Bobby and Jean are always visiting his parents before and after the marriage, and never once Jean's).

In pictures Jean looks very pretty, although no one in the family thought so. Charlotte thought she was "common," meaning that she did not come from a good family. Her mother had run a boarding-house and her father had written western novels and they came from some place out west, the name of which Charlotte pretended never to remember. Jean hated Charlotte and made fun of her grandness, but she also wanted some of it for herself. Even after her own name was well known, one biographer noted, she continued to write "Mrs. Robert T. S. Lowell" on her return address.

Jean had her own pretensions, intellectual ones, her conversations endowed with German phrases and references, which had charmed Bobby at twenty, though later he was brutal about it. *"Towmahss Mahnn:* that's how you said it . . ." Bobby wrote; ". . . Roget's synonyms studded your spoken and written word. / . . . your confessions had such a vocabulary / you were congratulated by the priests— . . ." ("Jean Stafford, a Letter"). Her pretentiousness only grew more desperate around Bobby's family, who felt that schoolroom conversation was in poor taste at the dinner table. Even Nell, who didn't share Charlotte's prejudices, found Jean off-putting. At Easter dinner at Gaga's in 1940, she remembered Jean rudely monopolizing the conversation, talking about Joyce's *Finnegans Wake,* which no one there had read, and wouldn't have understood if they had. Jean made it very clear that she considered them a bunch of Philistines. Nell remembered that Jean and Bobby looked pretty hung over that Easter dinner; for all their passion about religion, it was clear that neither of them had been to church that morning. They were married the following Tuesday in New York.

When Bobby and Jean were living in New York, working at the Catholic publishing house Sheed & Ward, my mother and Allie were invited over for tea (meaning drinks) to meet Jean. "There was never a time when Bobby was not fond of us," my mother said; he always wanted to keep up with family. Jean and Bobby had a very nice apartment in Greenwich Village. When Allie and Jackie arrived, they found Jean and Bobby drinking heavily. It was all very awkward, the two debutantes and a sodden Jean and Bobby, who announced dramatically that he was going into the navy (this was during World War II). He had decided: He was going to fight. It was a just war. He prattled on about his decision while my mother and Allie sat politely, and Jean, obviously bored beyond belief, blew smoke at them, making no effort to disguise her yawns.

I asked my mother recently why the family was so against Jean. "She was common," says my mother. But, as opposed to Charlotte, what my mother means is that she was rude.

When the draft board actually did call him up in August 1943 (having previously examined him six times and refused him for bad eyesight), Bobby did what my children would call a one-eighty, deciding to become a conscientious objector—not because he was against taking human life but because he was against collaborating with one totalitarian regime (Russia) to destroy another (Germany). He wrote a letter to President Roosevelt, referring to his ancestors more than once, and calling his decision "painful" in light of their tradition of service to America. At his sentencing the judge told him he had "marred" his family name.

While Bobby was in jail, "Charlotte Hideous" (Jean's nickname for her) wrote Jean saying how generous Bobby was to let her have the income from his trust (about a hundred dollars a month) as "this is all the money that he has in the world, and he will be completely penniless when he is released from prison, if you care to impose on his generosity" (as quoted in Ian Hamilton's biography). When Bobby was paroled, he got a job mopping latrine floors. His first book, *Land of Unlikeness*, was quietly (a euphemism for privately) published, with a small first printing of 250 copies and reviews from a few colleagues. Soon after, Jean's first book, *Boston Adventure*, became an instant bestseller. This must have been great for the marriage. Certainly it did nothing for Jean's relationship with her mother-in-law, in the company of whom, Jean wrote in a letter, she still found herself "more thoroughly, more icily, more deeply disliked than ever on account of my book" (as quoted in Hamilton).

With the earnings from the sales of Jean's novel, Jean and Bobby bought a house in Maine, which Jean redecorated with a homemaker-ish fervor that irritated Bobby. At the end of the summer of 1946, Bobby left her, having fallen for a guest, Gertrude Buckman, the former wife of poet Delmore Schwartz. Soon after, Jean was admitted to Payne Whitney mental hospital, where she wrote a barrage of desperate, accusatory, lovesick letters to Bobby, who responded with an infuriating calm, seemingly indifferent. The letters later became the basis for "The Mills of the Kavanaughs," a poem he labored on for years.

Like some of my best male friends, Bobby seems to have needed women who knew how to give him hell. The women berate and berate, like the surf breaking over his head, Bobby wrote. "Look at other men who marry their secretaries," Bobby said. "Don't I get credit for marrying three writers?" But Elizabeth and Caroline Blackwood (the third wife) were different from Jean Stafford. They were devoted to Bobby, I think, whereas Jean was completely self-absorbed.

Bobby and Jean were married for seven years. All I ever heard Bobby say on the subject was, "We got married and drank all summer in Maine and broke up." ("All winter too," adds my mother. "They were just never sober.") He said it softly and affectionately and then he added, as if his mother's disdain for Jean's background had been his own, "The curtains she put up were awfully tacky."

Suddenly, for a moment, I had sympathy for Jean Stafford.

Allie and Jackie.
Alice was very enthusiastic about her daughters' coming-out,
once her youngest brother offered to pay for it.

11

DURING THESE YEARS MY MOTHER AND HER SISTER ALLIE HAD COME OUT.
Alice was very enthusiastic about her daughters' coming-out, once her youngest brother, Amory, offered to pay for it. She moved up from New York to Boston for the season, into her parents' house, hired a cook and a maid, and got herself listed in the Social Register. Then she refused to buy her daughters dresses or give them a dinner party—the custom before the dances, which were held almost every night. The girls' grandmother Thorndike bought them each one dress at Driscoll's for the season. Allie had a *tulle de lamé*; my mother, a white satin dress that looks exactly like a negligee in the glamorous, languorous photograph I have of her. Alice had told my mother definitively, "That's the kind of dress you don't wear a bra with," so my mother had dutifully danced, shimmering and braless, night after night.

Alice's parents lived in a great pillared double house on Commonwealth Avenue in the Back Bay. The house, which had six floors, was so big it actually had two separate addresses and two front doors, which stood side by side. When you opened the doors you would find two other doors, which, when opened, put you on a landing with double staircases ascending, with a wall in between. A wide door between the two living rooms could slide open to make one enormous room. At this time there were at least three families living in the house: Alice and her daughters on one side; her parents in the large apartment on the top floor; Alice's manic-depressive sister Mary (between hospitalizations), with her husband and four children, on the other side. At twenty-nine Mary had had a hysterectomy; these were often done at the time to cure "hysteria" (the two words actually have the same root), after which she proceeded to have a breakdown every nine months. Ferociously moralistic when high, poor Aunt Mary was not a favorite with the girls, but they loved her husband, Uncle Lyman. How they wished they had a father like him—though, hard as he tried, he did not have much success with his own daughters, who were apathetic, as might be expected with their mother in an asylum. One daughter was my mother's age, and her father included my mother's and Allie's names on the invitation to her spectacularly expensive coming-out party, which included a hired train and the rental of the entire Trapp Family Lodge in Vermont, with dirndls and lederhosen for 150 people.

When Alice returned to New York, Aunt Sarah moved into the Thorndikes' house to chaperone my mother through the rest of her debutante season. Aunt Sarah was still single, though fresh as a girl, in her mid-forties, still living with her parents in the Otis Street apartment, where she had a tiny studio. It was the winter of 1936–37, the period in which Bobby knocked his father down and decided to leave Harvard, and Aunt Sarah was probably not too unhappy to move out of her parents' apartment, where Arthur, stricken with cancer, was vociferous in his disapproval of his grandson. Even after her marriage to Uncle Cot a few years later, Aunt Sarah's houses were a haven for Bobby, always warm and cozy (the trick was to have one shabby thing in every room, she said), as opposed to his mother's, which were repellently elegant. My mother said you were afraid to sit down at Charlotte's lest you rumple the chair.

It was at the Thorndikes' that my mother remembered Aunt Sarah having Anne Dick and Bobby to tea after they were barred from his parents' house. It was not a happy period for Bobby, but it was one of my mother's happiest. She and Aunt Sarah were like sisters, with Aunt Sarah going out at night as often as my mother. Forty years later, when a visit with Aunt Sarah had become a relentless barrage of insults from which there was no protection, still would come a blessed moment of calm, when Aunt Sarah, suddenly sweet, would lean forward and say, "Remember that winter, Jackie, when we stayed home one night a week to wash our hair and eat milk toast in front of the fire? The cook simply couldn't understand us."

Chaperoning my mother was Aunt Sarah's last gasp of freedom. When she was married in a brief civil ceremony after her father's death, Uncle Cot took her back to the houses he had owned with his glamorous first wife, Constance Binney. "Throw out that perfectly hideous lamp," Aunt Sarah instructed Helen, the upstairs maid, going through the attic at Manchester as the new lady of the house. "But Mrs. Cotting," Helen said, "you gave that to the *first* Mrs. Cotting."

After her daughters' season, Alice gave them a piece of their capital, which yielded $125 each, four times a year, and told them, "Now, don't ever come to me for money." Jackie and Allie were ecstatic. They moved into an apartment on East Sixty-fifth, where they spent seven dollars a week on food and "enjoyed being strapped." Although Allie had won awards for her artwork at Concord Academy, her mother had bragged about them so much that Allie eventually rebelled and decided to study singing. My mother chose acting. Alice might have been against college for girls, but she very much wanted my mother to be a famous actress. (It was clear by now that she was not going to be a famous pianist.) She took my mother to England to meet her distant cousin Dame Sybil Thorndike. Dame Sybil said, "She's an American, why doesn't she study in America?" which disappointed Alice, who had rather fancied her daughter in England, out of the way. My mother enrolled at the Neighborhood Playhouse in New York, a rigorous acting school where each day began with two hours of dance with Martha Graham. My mother was the lead in the plays, one time playing the "American Woman" opposite Lorne Greene's "American Man" in the dance-drama *Ameri-*

cana, and causing Martha Graham to fume through a particularly arduous rehearsal that my mother "couldn't fall down the stairs right." My mother worked very hard. "It was the only two years of my life I was ever really spoiled," my mother says. "The only time I didn't have to take care of anyone but myself." When it came time to audition for Broadway, though, she had difficulty putting herself forward; selling herself was against all the tenets of her upbringing. After ten months she quit trying.

My mother went up to Labrador to do work for the Grenfell Mission, a charity organization that attracted young society women eager to give up their comfortable lives to help the poor, and my mother loved the work. Her duties were increased, and she planned to stay on another year, but then a telegram arrived from her mother: "Come home immediately. Am getting divorced."

Home was no longer the apartment in New York, but a stone house on the Shenandoah, in Clarke County, Virginia, which Alice had "built in the wilderness" for a lot of money. The original plan had been to build a camp for her and Sommaripa to visit on weekends. The house was a sort of French country peasant house (hardly for peasants—later it was owned by actor Tab Hunter and Senator Lloyd Bentsen, although not concurrently). I "live like a peasant," Alice would rhapsodize. "I go down to the cornfield in the morning and pick corn . . . ." She had a full-time maid and a full-time farming family, and mostly her work consisted of filling in the crosswords during cocktail hour.

Alice had moved to Virginia, she said, "in order to become an ancestor, not just a descendant." She wanted to establish "a new family hierarchy." Beaupère came to Virginia to ride horses on the weekends, and his seductive charm swept through Clarke County. He had an affair with two sisters, transplanted Bostonians, who would greet my mother and her sisters at the train station with great hugs and kisses. Alice discussed all her husband's affairs in great tearful length at dinner—even the gentle Polly urged her to divorce "the s.o.b."—but Alice didn't make a move until her father died. The elder Thorndikes, who had once been so vehemently opposed to him, had become very fond of Sommaripa.

The marriage, which had lasted fifteen years, ended in a fight in front of ten-year-old Amory. Amory was not surprised when he heard his parents were divorcing. Aside from the frequent arguments, he was also aware of the other women—he even knew who the women were. The interesting part, he realized later, was that all of them were very unattractive, bespectacled, dowdy Boston types, as if Sommaripa, unable to gain acceptance in proper Boston society, had found it improperly, in its bedrooms. Amory was surprised when his mother asked which parent he would like to live with; it seemed an extraordinarily liberal thing for her to do. Later, however, when his father began arriving at the house begging to be taken back, Alice grew afraid that he would kidnap Amory and installed a man to live in the house to protect him.

Amory no longer needed protection, however, because after the divorce, his father completely changed. He became gentler and more forgiving and spent more time with his son than he had in the ten years he lived with him. Sommaripa confided in Amory that he had never been happy because he had grown up unloved; his parents had favored another son (the one for whom Amory had originally been named). Alice had been a mother figure, warmer and kinder than his own, who was rather terrible. Sommaripa was far more analytical than Alice, who lacked insight into psychological matters and operated on instinct. Amory had had no trouble choosing his caressing mother as the parent with whom he had wished to live; yet in the end it was his Russian father, not his New England mother, who left the lasting impression—because it was his father who had told him it was all right for a man to cry. His mother had said, Never cry.

When my mother arrived home from Labrador, she found the house streaming with people, as if there had been a death. "My husband lifted his hand to me!" Alice breathlessly greeted the milling mob. She was desperate for comfort, and Clarke County was the place to find it, particularly in liquid form. The summers were hot, and the rich glided through the day in slow motion, drinking on the porches of their lavish (but never air-conditioned) houses and swimming in their pools. Money was not something to hide as it was in New England. There were parties nearly every night, *Gone With the Wind* staircases, stables, and men who made no pretense of going to work.

Alice had been bored with New England, glad to escape its moralism, but still she was a New Englander. She hid her money from her lawyer in various banks and considered herself an excellent businesswoman, because, though her farm lost money every year, she paid her bills the day they arrived. She was running a farm, she said, and waxed endlessly about the difficulties of a farmer's lot.

In the meantime her children were having problems. At Chatham Hall, in Virginia, her youngest daughter, Polly, had begun fainting. After Polly left school, she tried to live in New York as her sisters had, but found herself in tears all the time. Polly moved down to Clarke County, to live with her mother and work as assistant county nurse, beloved by all she met. Some of those who loved her loved her desperately, being desperate themselves. One ex-fiancé killed himself. Later Polly married Bill, a charmer who could play a great game of tennis on three martinis, and they smoked and drank long after their suburban contemporaries gave it up. Once Aunt Polly shared my room when I was a child and woke twice in the night to light a cigarette. Maybe she didn't quit because life wasn't worth it.

As an adult Polly had severe depressions and several hospitalizations that she tried to keep secret, especially from her mother. I certainly hadn't known. Something about Aunt Polly and Uncle Bill represented all that was safe when I was growing up. I always longed to be with them, Uncle Bill with his corny jokes and raspy laughter, Aunt Polly with her low soothing voice, and to live in their house and be like their daughters, who seemed so sit-com happy (and who later had so many terrible things happen to them). Bobby felt the same way about Polly and Bill, my mother told me, calling them when he was teaching at Harvard to invite himself out for a weekend at their house in Connecticut.

My mother also had emotional disturbances in her early twenties: periods when she couldn't stop crying. When she went to the doctor, he said to her mother, "What Jackie needs is to get married."

Then my father appeared and filled the doctor's prescription.

At eighty-seven my father still plays indoor tennis on a weekly basis and Dixieland banjo at his Williams College reunions. Within five minutes of entering a room, he can be found charming the youngest female present. A few years ago he began whistling his favorite tunes in his sleep. My father's happiness has shone on me all my life. He is the least neurotic person I know.

I always thought my father was normal while the rest of us, torn by conflict, were abnormal. Then, in the *New York Times*, I read about a study in which 70 percent of those sampled were found to carry a short gene indicating neurosis, while 30 percent carried a long gene indicating a lack of neurosis, bringing up the interesting theory that it is abnormal to be nonneurotic, because man was meant to worry as a means of survival. So now I cannot say who is stronger—my mother, fighting worry and depression on a regular basis, or my father, breezing through life on a wink and a song. But certainly the attraction he and my mother have for each other says a lot for nature's desire to continue the species.

My father had never heard the word "psychotic" used in a sentence until he met my mother. He came from a long line of doctors (but not of the medically insane) from Winchester, Virginia. His family never had much money (before the advent of my mother, my father thought trusts were illegal), yet, though more approachable than my mother's family, they were, in fact, more snobbish. My father's mother referred to so-called tacky people as "Tacks."

Even my father, who votes liberal Democrat, uses the word "aristocratic" a lot. "I knew I was going to marry an aristocrat," he says in his amiable way. "It's in my genes and always will be." He was thirty-one when he met my mother, and behind him were a trail of society girls with whom he fell in love and the nonsociety girls who fell in love with him.

It was a slow romance. The Winslow girls were all very pretty, and my father first dated Allie a few times. From time to time, either in New York or in Clarke County, he would call my mother up and take her out to dinner or a baseball game. He thought she was awfully beautiful, but rather strait-laced and stiff—"Boston," he guessed, though my father didn't know much about Boston. From Williams College he'd visited New York and Vassar; later he'd worked in Chicago. Boston and Harvard people were sort of a joke to the rest of the world, my father said, considered dull and intellectual. Once he went to a Harvard football game and remembers thinking how behind in the styles the girls were. After they were married, he opened my mother's closet and threw out a ruffly dress. "I won you in that dress," my mother cried out. "No," my father said, "you won me *in spite* of that dress."

My father was seeing a number of other women at the time he was seeing my mother, and he would bring out their pictures to show to her on their dates. On one date he actually brought one of his other girls along. "You have no milk of human kindness," my father would tell my mother when she repeatedly refused to kiss him.

He didn't fall for my mother until one weekend about a year after he'd started seeing her. My mother must have sensed the change, because soon afterward she let my father kiss her goodnight. "She thought she had sinned," my father said, but that kiss seemed to do it, for within a couple of weeks they were beginning to talk about marriage. It was 1942, and my father was a marine captain, slated to go overseas. When he proposed and my mother accepted, my father excused himself and said, "I have to call Daisy," leaving my mother standing there as he went to a phone booth and spoke consolingly to someone who was obviously weeping.

Within a week they were married. (When my mother had her first child ten months later, her mother arrived, fanning herself with relief. "Dahling," she said, "I was *counting* the months on my fingers.") There was no time to send out invitations. The best man was my father's friend, George Smathers, who later became a U.S. senator and great friend of JFK and my godfather, and who previously (and pivotally) had pronounced my mother "F.F.V.-enough" (first family of Virginia-enough) for my father. Both my mother and father were drop-dead good looking, but while my father was blond, lanky, and small-featured, his face boyishly cute, my mother was dark haired, curvaceous, and statuesque, her facial features as pronounced and classically cut as one's image of Helen of Troy. She *was* aristocratic looking; it was as if many years ago the rich men had elected to marry the strongest and best-looking women. And nobody appreciated her looks more than my father.

My parents had known very little about each other before they got married—my mother hadn't even known that my father played the banjo—but their first six months of marriage, stationed at Laguna Beach, California, were wonderful. Then my father left to go overseas. My mother was pregnant with her first child, Billy, and the girl she had intended to room with was having an affair with a married man, so my parents decided she should go to live with my father's mother.

My mother and father had planned to say good-bye on the dock in San Diego, but when my mother arrived, she was told to drop off my father and just drive on. She didn't see him again for eighteen months. My father's mother loved having my mother to stay, though she was not demonstrative. "Mrs. Payne," asked my mother, "what shall I call you?" "Mrs. Payne would be fine," answered my grandmother.

My mother adored babies, and she was determined to be the perfect mother. After Billy was born she rigidly followed the pre–Doctor Spock theory at the time, which was only to pick up your baby every three hours no matter how hard he cried. This was very hard on my mother, but she stuck with it. Forty-five years later her son called her to discuss his "early emotional neglect."

Returning home after eighteen months away was strange for my father. Billy, nearly a year and a half old, was suddenly confronted by a stranger who was stealing his mother. He took one look at my father and said, "Dada," then reconsidered and said, "Mama." "No," my father said, "Dada." "*Mama*," insisted Billy. My father tried to play with him, to no avail. His first Sunday morning home he took him on a promenade in a baby carriage to get the newspaper in town, and Billy cried all the way up and down the street.

■   ■   ■

Around this time Sommaripa was killed in the war. By the time Alice received the telegram, he had already been dead six weeks. Sommaripa, who knew five languages, had been a spy in the OSS, known for his risk taking. He would pick up a rifle at night and go out and hunt Germans, a fellow soldier told Amory. "The Mad Russian," he was called in an article in the *Saturday Evening Post*, glamorizing him and his commanding officer, Colonel Creighton Abrams, who later became famous as a general in Vietnam. Abrams wrote Amory how he had lifted Sommaripa's body from the tank in which he had been killed. He came to spend the weekend with Amory in Virginia and orchestrated various ceremonies in honor of his dead father. He couldn't seem to do enough for Amory or the memory of his father. Only later did Amory realize that Abrams had probably felt guilty, because Sommaripa, who had been so brave, had died for no reason, killed accidentally by American forces.

After my mother accepted my father's proposal, he excused himself and said, "I have to call Daisy."

"Why doesn't Bobby write about the sea?" Aunt Sarah said. "It's so pretty."
The Arthur Winslows at the beach.

12

WHY DOESN'T BOBBY WRITE ABOUT THE SEA?" AUNT SARAH SAID TO ME one day as we sat sipping tomato soup on the deck of Uncle Cot's yacht. "It's so pretty." I was twenty-two at the time and had dutifully dragged myself away from the comfort of my hot, smoke-filled apartment in Cambridge out to Manchester-by-the-Sea, even though I knew it meant I would be required to go out on "the boat." The boat was fifty feet long and so fancy it had a living room and a captain who lived on it year-round and did all the cooking, so that going sailing did not exactly mean "roughing it." "Look how helpful Sally is with the dishes!" Aunt Sarah would cry out when I took my empty lemonade glass down to the captain in the kitchen. Every weekend every summer their whole lives Aunt Sarah and Uncle Cot went out on the boat, motoring to where it sat moored off their land to take the prescribed trip to Gloucester, then motoring back again. ("Mr. Cotting has been navigating these same waters for eighty years," the captain said once, and for a moment I thought I had misheard, but then I realized Uncle Cot had started sailing at age ten.)

Of course Bobby did write about the sea, though not quite in a manner Aunt Sarah would have chosen:

A brackish reach of shoal off Madaket—
The sea was still breaking violently and night
Had steamed into our North Atlantic Fleet,
When the drowned sailor clutched the drag-net. Light
Flashed from his matted head and marble feet,
He grappled at the net
With the coiled, hurdling muscles of his thighs:
The corpse was bloodless, a botch of reds and whites,
Its open, staring eyes
Were lustreless deadlights . . .

Whereas what Aunt Sarah would have had in mind was more like: "as the glittering blue wave floated gently toward the attractive couple, it reminded them of a blue sky in June," or something along those lines.

Certainly no one could accuse Bobby of trying to be decorative. You won't see his lines quoted on ceramic frying pans to hang on a nail in the kitchen, like the one my parents presented me with when they came back from France: *Chacun à son gout.* Even Robert Frost might make it onto some pillows with "Good fences make good neighbors." But I doubt there are any "The Lord survives the rainbow of His will" potholders on the market, and that's about as comforting as Bobby gets, not that I have a clue what he means.

The above quotation is from "The Quaker Graveyard in Nantucket," a long, grand, violent poem in *Lord Weary's Castle,* which has something to do with God, and nature, and the Quakers killing a whale, and the death at sea of my cousin Warren Winslow (whose daughter came out with my mother). I can't even tell you if the dead body floating in the sea is meant to be my cousin or someone else. I don't mean to be snide, but snide is what comes out, because sometimes it's all I seem to have to offer. Bobby was the first to spot snideness in me—not, of course, that he meant it as a compliment. He wasn't a big fan of sarcasm; he called his mother's sarcasm "the opposite of funny to a son" ("To Mother").

Recently I read that Bobby told Frank Bidart that if he wrote about him, let it be serious, which threw me into paroxysms of guilt for weeks. I wish I could express myself seriously, but I cannot. Whenever I try it is terrible. It's not that I don't wish to be serious. All I ever wanted was to be serious, especially when I was young—before, of course, there was anything to be serious about. Now that I am older, I realize that life is sad and terrible, but I do not have the gift of expressing it. I know despair, but even my despair can suddenly vanish when the slipcovers arrive from Bloomingdale's.

Really, you see, I am not too far removed from Aunt Sarah, who is not too far from Mary Chilton, signing her name with an M. I graduated in English from Harvard and am semi-illiterate still, at least next to Bobby, who could chat about Aeneas as if he'd just had a ham-and-cheese sandwich with him.

I will never know Greek; for that matter I will never know a second language because I went to public school where thirty kids day after day chanted, "Le garçon est dans le jardin." I actually used this phrase a few years ago over the phone to a French au pair who didn't know English, to be answered by a torrent of laughter. ("Let me take it," said my friend Patty Marx in an exasperated voice, grabbing the phone. "Je m'apelle Patty," she said crisply, but with an abrupt finality, this being the sum total of her knowledge, as she too went to public school.) I cannot even blame public school. After Intensive German at Harvard, I could only at best defend myself against the Nazis with: "Wir bleiben heute zu Hause" (We're staying at home today). The truth is, Bobby was at ease in the classical languages, while I will never read about Achilles even in English.

Partly I am lazy intellectually, but mainly it is that I just do not have the knack. For me, trying to understand most of the poems in *Lord Weary* is like hitting my head against the wall. I had read everything I could about the Winslows when I sat down to read "At the Indian Killer's Grave." After two days studying the poem, the only glimmer of understanding I had was the sharp realization, like a shot of cool sunshine piercing the clouds, that the poem had been written at graveside, a revelation that lost its earth-shattering quality when I realized that a mere glance at the title might have cleared up the same point. I went back to the poem, continuing my search for Josiah Winslow, who I assumed was the Indian killer in the title, but could only find mention of poor Mary Chilton and her husband John Winslow, who if anything would have been pals with the Indians, and who, for that matter, were in the wrong generation for King Philip's War.

Even in the later poems, which move me with the depth of their pain—the nonsymbolic ones, the ones about the family, the ones about depression, the ones Bobby said could be understood in one reading (well, not quite)—even then, when for a moment I understand what Bobby is talking about, as I read a line about him in Maine hearing the ocean, my brain cannot stay up there with him but instead plummets to the real-estateish thought, *Did Bobby and Elizabeth's house in Maine have an ocean view?*

I spent many days rereading *Lord Weary's Castle*, and while I can feel the power of the poems, for me the door remains shut. I sit staring at the wall with nothing, nothing, nothing to say. How can I have anything to say when Bobby writes about God and man versus nature and Acheron—which I had to look up. I have never, outside of English class, given a single thought to man versus nature, unless you count the time I crushed to death with my bare hand a huge bumblebee hovering near my daughter, Emily, in her crib.

So I closed the book and cooked up a big roast chicken with mashed potatoes and corn bread. "Gee, Mom," my son Teddy said, with dripping scorn, "what are you, some kind of mother from the 1950s?"

As it turns out, even Bobby was baffled by *Lord Weary's Castle*, or at least by its public reception. "I can't really explain why that much attention has been paid to me," Bobby said later to Stanley Kunitz. "Looking back . . . I see it out of the mainstream, a rather repellent, odd, symbolic Catholic piece of work."

When Bobby won the Pulitzer Prize for *Lord Weary's Castle*, my mother was surprised, finding it amazing that he won it for something that was not understandable to the public. It didn't bother Charlotte that nobody could understand *Lord Weary's Castle*; its incomprehensibility only proved its intellectual merit. Charlotte's view, Nell told me, was that "it was a book written for the intelligentsia to which Charlotte had elevated herself, though she was too much of a lady to allow herself to understand the poetry."

Bobby may have loathed himself, his writing driven by the need, as he wrote in "Symptoms," to examine and examine "what I really have against myself," but he also had to have had great self-confidence to have kept writing so furiously for the twelve years before his first success.

Winning the Pulitzer took the heat off him in the family. Prizes are great in terms of getting your family's respect and, it would also seem, in blinding the eye. I had always been told that Bobby was in the doghouse when he wrote about the family in *Life Studies*, but actually he had been writing about the family from the beginning. Everything is obscure in *Lord Weary's Castle, except* the poems blasting the family. How much clearer could "In Memory of Arthur Winslow" be, a poem that condemns to hell the man he thought of as his father?

> . . . the ghost
> of risen Jesus walks the waves to run
> Arthur upon a trumpeting black swan
> Beyond Charles River to Acheron
> Where the wide waters and their voyager are one.

Well, certainly "risen Jesus" is not a phrase employed by my family, not even at Easter. "I was born a nonbelieving Protestant New Englander," Bobby once said to Ian Hamilton. "My parents and everyone I saw were nonbelieving Protestant New Englanders." And yet I'm sure Arthur, Charlotte, Sarah—the whole lot—had no doubt about their belief in God, or, better put, God's belief in them. How could they not believe when clearly God was on their side, or else how'd they get all the servants? In fact they were so certain of their election, they felt they didn't need the forms. I'm sure Aunt Sarah considered herself a pillar of the Episcopal Church, except of course she never could *go* because they had to be at the farm on the weekends. Once, in deep adolescence, I was taken to Trinity Church in downtown Boston by Aunt Sarah. As I got on my knees wrenched by indecision about whether I was being hypocritical when I read along with the prayers, I peeked over to see Aunt Sarah not even holding a prayer book but pulling at her skirt and glancing around to see who was there and what they were wearing.

The poems in *Lord Weary's Castle* (who *is* Lord Weary, and how about "lambkin"?) are deeply religious, which is part of the reason they're obscure, especially to me. My formal religious education consisted of coloring pictures of flowers in Sunday school and, in a desperate moment, reading Monarch Notes on the Bible before a Harvard exam. The nearest I have come to imparting any religious training to my children was gathering them together to watch the video of *Ben-Hur*, during which I gently explained about John the Baptist and Pontius Pilate, being moved to tears when Charlton Heston, seeing Jesus trudging up the hill with the cross to his death, pushed his way through the crowd and rushed toward him. "Oh, don't tell me hero boy thinks he's going to save Jesus," remarked my son Hunter, aged twelve.

When Bobby dramatically changed religion, he picked the religion his family despised, the Roman Catholicism of their Irish maids, although, as almost every writer who writes about Bobby says, he pursued it not with an accepting faith but a Puritan guilt. In my own way I am the same lost (or is it last) Puritan, with the same self-loathing guilt. We were never taught any of this self-judgment in a religious way, but it is there in the underlying belief in my family that if you do a bad thing or have a bad thought, you are bad—that's it, damned to hell, no redress.

I'm not sure of the source of Bobby's self-loathing, but I know I get mine from my mother, whose mother taught her that bad thoughts made her bad. But my mother's mother, Alice, is not related by blood to Bobby (it's her husband Devereux who is related), so my mother's self-loathing and Bobby's actually come from different sources—just as, it turns out, to my utter surprise, that their manic depression is not related. I always assumed that the manic depression in my family traveled on the same gene as Bobby's, until my mother happened to mention recently that the Winslows aren't crazy at all—they just have a tremendous attraction to crazy people.

Devereux, not crazy, married my grandmother, a member of the Thorndikes, filled with manic depressives; Charlotte married into the Lowells, similarly afflicted. The Winslows who settled in England after the Revolution were so attracted to crazy people that they founded insane asylums, bringing up their children among the inmates. Dr. Forbes Winslow, became the most famous "alienist" of his time (he is even *in* the novel, *The Alienist*), founding the *Psychological Journal*, as well as the concept of insanity as a legal ground of acquittal. Forbes Winslow's nephew, Henry Forbes Winslow, also became a famous treater of the insane. He claimed his epiphany came when as a young physician he was called urgently to a house only to find a naked woman in the front bedroom brandishing a knife. As he jumped out the window and ran for help, Henry decided that this was a lot more fun than general practice. He converted two mansions into asylums for lunatics from the fashionable world and spent a happy life. Henry Forbes Winslow's children "never knew a world without lunatics."

Whatever the source, basically, as a family, we're into self-punishment. And so it doesn't surprise me that Bobby didn't have his first clinical breakdown until after he won the Pulitzer Prize. After that the breakdowns began in earnest nearly every year for the rest of his life. "I thought that civilization was going to break down," Bobby later said to A. Alvarez about *Lord Weary's Castle*, "and instead *I* did."

Aunt Sarah and Uncle Cot's, Harbor Street, Manchester-by-the-Sea.

Billy, Sally, Johnny, Hunter (Larchmont).

13

In depression, one wakes, is happy for about two minutes, probably
less, and fades into dread of the day. Nothing will happen, but you
know twelve hours will pass before you are back in bed and shelter-
ing your consciousness in dreams, or nothing. It isn't danger; it's
not an accomplishment. I don't think it's a visitation of the angels
but a weakening in the blood . . . .

—ROBERT LOWELL
(FROM "A CONVERSATION WITH IAN HAMILTON")

Don't you think Jackie's a little inky-binky?
—UNCLE GUS

BOBBY'S FIRST BREAKDOWN BEGAN IN EARLY 1949 AT YADDO, THE WRITER'S
colony in upstate New York. It was a long, protracted collapse, but
somehow Charlotte and Bob senior managed to keep it from the fam-
ily. Even my mother knew nothing about it until the first biography
of Bobby was published.

At Yaddo Bobby was struggling with "The Mills of the Kava-
naughs," writing hopefully in a letter that Virgil only wrote a line a
day. Even years after it was published, my mother remembers him

still working on it, in McLean's during another breakdown, surrounded by reams of paper, rewriting the same sentence over and over.

Bobby had been drinking steadily since arriving at Yaddo in the fall of 1948—so much so that even the drinkers were worried about him. Of course, they were all heavy drinkers in those days; they drank to write, whereas my generation jogs to write. It was during the fall that Bobby had become enamored of the novelist and critic Elizabeth Hardwick (just finishing up a stay at the colony), inviting her to return after Christmas. Elizabeth returned. But by January, Bobby's illness was settling in—though no one quite recognized it as such. He was excited, "blissfully high," and prone to speechifying against Communism. By the end of February, he had accused the woman who ran Yaddo, Mrs. Ames, of being a Communist spy.

Mrs. Ames couldn't have been nicer to Bobby. She had let him stay on as long as he wanted at Yaddo and invite anyone there he pleased. In an earlier letter Bobby had once described her as benign, but in his excited state he connected her with Agnes Smedley, another inhabitant of Yaddo whom the FBI had denounced as a spy in the *New York Times*. Though the *Times* immediately thereafter ran a story in which the FBI apologized to Smedley and admitted it did not have such evidence, nevertheless several FBI agents showed up at Yaddo to interview people. If you've ever been around someone in a manic state, in which the manic person feels that he alone possesses the power to save the world from a giant conspiracy, you can imagine what effect FBI agents suddenly appearing in the wilderness would have had on Bobby. Not helping matters were the FBI agents, who let it be known that Yaddo had been under investigation for five years—in particular, Mrs. Ames—and that it was filled with Communists. Convinced that Smedley and Mrs. Ames were co-conspirators, Bobby demanded that Ames be fired. He called her poisonous and bragged in a letter that he would call on a long list of "important writers" (whom he actually listed) if the Yaddo board did not fire her.

He began sending telegrams to friends to come and help him in The Fight Against Communism. He was also in love with Elizabeth.

Bobby always fell in love in his manic states, and it was always the real thing, because, well, it *had* to be the real thing—he was a Puritan. "Anyone brought up among Puritans knew that sex was sin," Bobby wrote, quoting Henry Adams. (As I read the *New York Times Book Review* once again about some great man's thousand meaningful affairs, I take a quick glance at my husband to be reassured that *no* one could be a great man and wear a baseball cap with a picture of a chain saw on it.)

When Bobby fell in love with Elizabeth he happened to be single—they both were—but then he rigged it otherwise. Having unceremoniously dumped Jean Stafford three years before, Bobby, now in love with Elizabeth, decided that he was still married to Jean—and reconverted to the Catholicism he had shed along with Stafford.

Bobby got higher and higher that spring, traveling down to Washington, D.C., to attend a world peace conference on the same day that the Yaddo board, after reinstating Mrs. Ames, formally reprimanded Bobby. At the peace conference, convened to promote goodwill between the USSR and the United States, Bobby rather unhelpfully addressed the group as "a poet and Roman Catholic" (and therefore, the point was, an anti-Communist). Then he rushed off to visit the Tates in Chicago, who found him pathetic but endearing—until, as a joke, Bobby handed Caroline Tate a list of all the women her husband had slept with during their marriage and then, reciting "Ode to the Confederate Dead," dangled Tate out a second-story window. Taken to the hospital by four policemen, Bobby managed to extricate himself in order to fly to see Peter Taylor in Bloomington, Indiana. There Bobby claimed he smelled the devil's brimstone and wandered the streets declaiming against homosexuals.

Taylor called Merrill Moore, who called Charlotte, and they arrived and hospitalized Bobby. Charlotte and Bob insisted that Bobby pay for his own treatment, which galled Elizabeth Hardwick, herself openhanded. Non–New Englanders are always amazed when rich New Englanders are penurious with their children, making them pay rent when they return to live at home and 8 percent when they borrow, but it is all part of the Puritan ethic—although I have never fig-

ured out what is ethical about it, unless that it is wrong to be gener-
ous (or, rather, "extravagant").

After Bobby left the hospital, he wanted to marry Elizabeth, but
Bob senior advised him to wait, adding that if he should marry, his
new wife would be financially responsible for him. His father had
already deducted money from Bobby's account to pay the hospital
bill, leaving Bobby with six hundred dollars in the bank. I'm sure Bob
and Charlotte thought they were doing the right thing, but I do not
like them.

Charlotte and Bob senior disapproved of Bobby's marrying so
soon, but they did not disapprove of Elizabeth, and the two were
married that July in the Lowells' house. (By then, after Bob senior's
second heart attack, Charlotte had moved them into a small house
in Beverly Farms.) Everyone in the family loved Elizabeth. "She was
the love of Bobby's life, there's absolutely no doubt about it," my
mother said. Even Charlotte liked her. By then Charlotte had done
a lot of work with Moore's recovering alcoholics and had broad-
ened her outlook. Elizabeth may not have come from the kind of
"aristocratic" family Charlotte would have recognized, but she
wasn't "common." She was opinionated, yet she had manners. And
as my mother said, Charlotte knew Elizabeth would take care of
Bobby.

But Bobby was still so sick when he got married, so depressed,
that by September he was in Payne Whitney (the same mental hospi-
tal where Jean Stafford had gone), where he was diagnosed a manic
depressive. Even this diagnosis was better than what Carl Jung had
told Charlotte years earlier: "If your son is as you have described
him,/he is an incurable schizophrenic" ("Unwanted"). But I don't
know how reassuring this was to Elizabeth. Bobby kept his second
hospitalization a secret from his parents for more than two months,
writing them in November that he'd been "ashamed" to write earlier.
Get rid of these parents, I keep thinking, but instead Bobby took Eliza-
beth to his parents' house for Thanksgiving.

Nine months later, on the day of Bobby and Elizabeth's pro-
posed departure for Europe, where they planned to spend the year,
Bobby's father died at age sixty. It was his third heart attack. It was

after his first heart attack that my cousin Nell realized how deeply selfish Charlotte was, how she cared more about the order of her house than life itself. Bob senior's nurse did not get on with Charlotte's cook. Rather than risk losing her Irish cook, Charlotte sent her convalescing husband to live at the country club. "It was an impossible situation," Charlotte explained to Nell. "So *inconvenient* having Bob at home and so much nicer at the country club because friends can drop by." When Bobby writes years later, in "Symptoms," "I have no mother to lift me in her arms," I think, *Did he* ever *have a mother?*

Three days after Bob senior died, Bobby found in his den "the pitilessly complete and clear records of Father's interests since 1945. Here was the twenty-page booklet of scaled diagrams executed in inks of five colors, a page to each room at Beverly Farms. The position and measurements of each sofa, bed, table, chair, etc., were given. Father had spent a cheerful month devising and correcting this booklet; it had proved a godsend to the movers" (from "Near the Unbalanced Aquarium").

My mother visited the Lowells in Beverly Farms in 1950, the summer Bob senior died. Charlotte had done over the house in period detail; it was absolutely beautiful, my mother said, though like a museum. Bob senior was in bed when my mother arrived and she sat in his room and talked to him. Even dying, Uncle Bob had little to say. Aunt Charlotte was her usual self—nervous, tense, amusing, and very pretty.

Poor Uncle Bob. In all his life he only complained once, right before he died. In his poem, "Terminal Days at Beverly Farms," Bobby wrote:

> After a morning of anxious, repetitive smiling,
> his last words to Mother were:
> "I feel awful."

Two years after Bobby's first breakdown, my mother broke down. She also was diagnosed as a manic depressive, though, unlike Bobby, she did not experience a euphoric high. Instead, she had felt uncomfortably drunk for several weeks, a reeling sort of out-of-control high, and then plunged into a more than yearlong depression. Nor did she ever have another breakdown, only chronic depressions. For weeks she would push her way through the day as a mother and a housewife, wishing she were dead every second. We children never noticed.

My mother jokes that she was gypped of the genius part of her manic depression, so that she can suffer as much over the flower arrangement with a movie theme for the Seeds and Weeds Garden Club as Bobby did over "The Mills of the Kavanaughs." The truth is, though, my mother never gave herself a chance. She had real talent as an actress—she even had ambition—but she didn't have the confidence to continue at her work. When she gave up acting and married my father, she channeled her energy into a different dream.

While Bobby's drive was to be a great writer, to be exceptional, my mother's was to be a great mother, to be normal. With an iron will, she took up the role of middle-class housewife, a role her aunt Charlotte would have sniffed at: the mother at home in the kitchen after school planning nutritious dinners of meat, peas, and starch, followed by a Del Monte Fruit Cocktail. There was Sunday school on Sunday, Cub Scouts in the living room, regular bedtimes, and three unruly boys to be dressed in fresh shorts and Sunday caps. She wanted eleven children, for whom she dreamed of providing the security she had been deprived of as a child. She was stopped at four, when she got very sick and was forced to do the one thing she had vowed never to do: leave her children. It did not matter that she had been given no choice, that she was completely blameless. In her heart forever would be the belief that she had abandoned her children.

Sometimes when a family member is depressed, my father grumbles, "You know, sometimes I get depressed too, I'm not *always* happy," but no one believes him. "Yes, dear," says my mother. "I'm sure you were quite blue in 1932 when Beatrice Wells told you she didn't love you anymore." Surely my mother's breakdown was the worst thing that ever happened to my father. But God loves my father, and while my mother's illness was a terrible time for him, the eternal sunshine of his soul kept him from the abyss.

There had been very little trouble up to that point in my family's life. The older boys, Billy and Johnny, aged seven and five, were getting top marks in school, and Hunter, aged two, provided a great deal of entertainment. My father was doing well at the Simmons Mattress Company. He'd just gotten Long Island, which was booming, as a sales territory. "I was as driven as I'll ever be," my father says, "which was not too very driven." He had been a straight gentleman's B at Williams. When he'd first arrived and seen the students taking notes in class, he thought they were writing letters to their girls. The only trophy he ever received in his life was a silver cup for being the first baby born to a member of his father's class at the University of Virginia.

They were happy, my father said, and I believe him, or rather, I believe that my father was happy and that he thought my mother was, too. Of course, something was deeply troubling her, though she didn't know what; all she knew was that she was horribly, oppressively exhausted every second of the day. Still she drove herself forward, keeping her feelings from my father, who, like most husbands, was pretty easy to keep things from. "'Laugh and the whole world laughs with you, cry and you cry alone,'" my mother said to me the other day about a recent depression I'd known nothing about, and I was struck with the awful thought that this has been the basic tenet of her life.

At any rate, my father was happy in 1951, and his children were happy, and his wife seemed happy. He liked his job because it was easy. They bought a little white house in Larchmont, New York, and joined the Manursing Country Club. My mother was pregnant with me, her fourth child, and had three boys under eight, but it didn't stop her. They were always rushing into New York City on Saturdays, taking the two older boys by subway to King Coit's, the arts school where my mother and her sister had gone in their youth. My mother was determined to give her children "culture," the one good thing her mother had given her. The problem was, she also had to give her children meals and clean clothes, and she didn't have her mother's cooks and maids.

Then they had the baby, and it was a girl, and they couldn't believe it. "Are you sure?" my mother asked the doctor when he'd announced my gender. It was a dream come true; even the delivery had been easy. My mother had been so busy reading romance magazines while she was in labor that she'd waved the nurses away and the next thing she knew there I was, eight pounds, by natural childbirth, at a time when most women in America were being put under. "You were so beautiful, all pink and white," my mother told me. "I was so happy." For about a day.

First she got sick physically. She had a blood clot, a thrombosis, and they had to operate immediately. No one mentioned a word about postpartum depression to my father. After my mother's operation she was acting a bit strange, talking about God, my father said, but he didn't think much about it until Uncle Gus arrived for a visit and said, in his matter-of-fact way, "Don't you think Jackie's a little inky-binky?"

The next thing my father knew, he was taking my mother home from the hospital, accompanied by her doctor and a psychiatrist. Also in the house were the two women my father had hired to help him with the children—Mrs. Carper, an elderly white woman who had recently arrived, and Margaret, a young, taciturn black woman who had been helping my mother since Hunter's birth. There they were, ten altogether, in the tiny little house, hovering around my distraught mother. It was an awful night, my father said. He still hadn't realized my mother was off her rocker. Her first night home should have been festive, but instead the doctors were conferring ominously with each other and making phone calls as my father stood in their midst, listening but not comprehending.

Then all of a sudden an ambulance pulled up to the house, its sirens whirring and blaring, and out stepped a nurse to take my mother away to someplace up the Hudson River. My father rode along in the back of the ambulance, his only reference point being the movie *The Snake Pit* (with its white-johnnied, screaming women and strong-arming matrons, *The Snake Pit* seems to be a part of everyone's memory from this time; even I have a traumatic memory of watching it on television as a little girl on a sunny Sunday afternoon).

In the ambulance my father started imagining his wife being forced into a straitjacket. He glared at the nurse riding with them, sitting so vigilantly near my mother. When they arrived at the hospital and two more nurses came striding toward the ambulance, he was seized by the horrible thought that the nurses were cruel and that they were going to get his wife alone and whip her. But before he could think of anything to do, more nurses were upon them, leading my mother away.

It was daylight by the time my father returned to Larchmont, feeling more dead than alive. Mrs. Carper put him to bed, and he took the next day off; it was a Friday, he remembered, though the rest of what transpired over that weekend is a fog. On Monday my mother was moved to New York Hospital in White Plains, a mental hospital that had, oddly enough, once been called Bloomingdale's. Nobody had liked to admit they had gone to Bloomingdale's because everyone knew it was a mental hospital. When New York Hospital took it over, they kept the word "mental" out of the name.

My father had no idea what was going to happen. The following morning, Alice was on the doorstep, later wailing, "It's all my fault!" when she was brought to see her daughter. She gave my parents five thousand dollars. Her youngest brother, who had given my mother and her sister their coming-out party, gave them another five thousand, and my aunt Sarah gave them five thousand, and my father's family gave them three thousand—various sections of the family financed the whole hospitalization, which lasted a year and a half. "They didn't push you out the door," my mother said of New York Hospital, in the understatement of the year.

For six months my mother wasn't allowed to see her children. My father would drive to see her on Saturdays, though sometimes he would be told, "Mrs. Payne is unable to see you today," and be sent away until the following week. For some reason visitors were not allowed on Sundays. In the beginning when my father did get in to see her, she *was* inky-binky. She'd say, "See that lamp over there? That's *very* significant." And my father would accept it, unlikely as it sounds, hoping maybe they'd taught her something about the lamp that he didn't understand.

At home my father kept Margaret and Mrs. Carper on, again paid for by the various relatives; the women and all four children slept crowded on the second floor, while my father, as man of the house, had the first floor to himself, though he was often not at home till late. He was invited to people's houses for dinner quite often and played his tenor guitar; on the weekends he took the two older boys to Sunday school, where they were first in their class, my father said, though I have never heard of anyone being first in their class at Sunday school.

Billy and Johnny continued to do well in public school; once, however, Billy threatened to throw an eraser at a teacher. The principal summoned my father, who explained about his wife and broke down a little in the office, and the principal comforted him. The next week my father took Billy, in the dead of night, or so it seemed to him—it was probably nine P.M.—to a psychiatrist in White Plains, who tested Billy and said, "There's nothing wrong," and asked how the other sons were doing. The other sons were doing fine. Johnny had no problems; in fact since my mother had left he'd rather remarkably begun to take care of himself. And, Hunter, the youngest, was happily in love with the new baby.

Six months after my mother went to the hospital, my father's mother died. From the beginning of my mother's breakdown, she had urged my father to "get Jackie home to see the children," but she was dead before my mother was allowed out for a Saturday afternoon. My mother was upset by her mother-in-law's death, and the visit home was not deemed a success by the hospital; it was further decided that it would be too painful for my mother to go home that Christmas, even for the day. It was nine months since my mother had gone away.

When she'd first arrived at the hospital my mother had been not blissfully high but consciously, miserably crazy. One roommate, committed because she was terrified of sex, asked my mother to talk to her about the subject, and my mother obliged, possibly at rather great length and with greater enthusiasm than the woman could handle; the next day she was removed from my mother's room. Most of the women there were afraid of sex. Terrible scenes would ensue when their husbands came to pick them up. My mother's situation was most healthily the reverse: Early on, the hospital had to convene a special board meeting, which resulted in my father being allowed to come and take my mother to a motel for conjugal visits.

No psychotropic drugs were used then at New York Hospital; instead, even when they were manic, patients were treated with a regimen of activities: therapy almost every day, steam baths, sewing classes, massage, gym, long walks and marches—so much physical exercise that my mother's limbs were swollen her first few days. "New York Hospital taught me about the importance of schedules and activities," my mother said, who had nothing but good to say about the hospital. It was on beautiful grounds, like McLean's (the family asylum near Boston) and only cost twenty-five dollars a day with food, as well as free visits to shrinks after you were discharged.

The idea that her daughter was mentally ill was hard for Alice to accept, despite the facts that the illness was in her family and her favorite, youngest brother had only recently broken down. It was a stigma to her, and she kept trying to think about it in different terms. Later she pulled strings and got in to see the well-known astrologer Jeanne Dixon, reporting excitedly back to my mother that *Jeanne Dixon* had told her not to worry—her daughter was going to get well! But before she had the assurance of this famous expert, Alice was less than confident. She talked and talked with my mother, pouring her heart out. "I think it helped *her* a lot," my mother said, but for several months nothing seemed to help my mother. She was still horribly depressed; she couldn't sleep. In fact, during the whole eighteen months in the hospital, my mother would never get a decent night's sleep—except the night after she got the electroshock therapy. After the shock treatment, she wasn't inky-binky anymore, but it left her very absentminded for a while and, for a long time, for the remainder of her stay, deeply depressed.

When the doctors began to talk of discharging her, they worried about the ball-and-chain of home. "It's going to be hard, it's going to be painful," the doctors warned her, and when my mother finally did go home to visit, it was very painful. She felt so sorry for her children, so guilty that she was not there with them.

But home was part of the problem or, more specifically, the *baby* at home was part of the problem. My mother's therapists had concluded that my mother's breakdown had come about because, though she had always dreamed of having a girl, deep down she had feared it. Throughout her pregnancy she had believed that this fourth child would be a girl, and she had grown terrified at the thought of raising her because of what had happened to her during her own childhood.

During the second year of her hospitalization, my mother came home weekends to four kids scrambling for her attention. By Sunday night the hospital must have looked almost good. It was awful for her to have those kids clinging onto her, my father said, but she seemed almost too miserable to notice. He remembered looking at her one weekend as she played with the children on the floor: she was drawn and thin, wearing a black cocktail dress, and though he could see her suffering, with her white skin glowing against her dark hair, she had been breathtaking, nevertheless.

Finally, the fall before the second Christmas, my mother came home for good. Instead of bursting with joy, as my father had hoped, she was quiet, subdued.

Soon after, my father got a promotion and plans were made for the family to move to New Haven, Connecticut. One day my parents drove in a downpour to take a look at the new house they were building. The rain was coming in and streaming down the windows of the half-finished structure, and suddenly the neighborhood didn't look so nice anymore. My mother began to sob. Desperate to make her happy, my father had to buy their way out of the deal for three thousand dollars, a small fortune for them at the time.

In another neighborhood they bought a picture-book house with a brook behind it and a mortgage they couldn't afford and joined a country club. It is in New Haven that my memories begin; my brothers were not so lucky.

Hunter creates a better world by kissing Johnny's girlfriend.

14

My brothers have almost no memory of my mother being away. And yet, clearly, they were deeply affected by her absence. When my mother left, Margaret (with Mrs. Carper subbing on her days off), took over the running of the house—the cooking, the cleaning, the shopping, and the bringing up of three little boys and a newborn baby. Even when Margaret came to help after Hunter's birth, my mother had always been the primary caregiver: the discipliner, the cuddler, the confidante. Margaret had never hugged my brothers, and this didn't change after my mother left. My mother later said that Margaret was "not demonstrative," that as a servant she felt it was not her place to hug her charges. But possibly Margaret had other reasons for her reticence about touching anyone. Her body was covered with scars from stab wounds; she had suffered in a way none of us would ever comprehend, and her suffering was not over. Her ex-boyfriend was in jail in Florida, and in a few years he would be released.

Margaret gave my brothers no indication that she loved them, nor did they love her. It is quite possible that they wrong Margaret here, though understandably: My brothers were unable to accept Margaret's love because they resented her for taking my mother's place. What is amazing is that Billy and Johnny have no negative memory of

Margaret, no accusations of her losing her temper or even being unfair, when such accusations are often the very breath of childhood. I have seen the sweetest, most whispering of mothers being told by her child, usually in a public place, "Stop yelling at me!" I myself was so overly gentle with Emily that when asked on a preschool form how I disciplined my child, I had to answer: "Have never disciplined child." Yet at age four still from Emily came the piteous wail: "I cry in bed every night to hear you be mean to the boys!" because, it turned out, every night I asked them if they had brushed their teeth. Whether Margaret loved my brothers I will never know, but she pitied them and worked hard for them and was never mean.

As for my father—he loved us, to our salvation, but he was not what you call a nineties father. It was the 1950s, and my father was no diaper changer. He was the man of the house, the breadwinner; my mother would not have wanted it any different. In earlier years he came home to children fed and bathed and soon to bed, followed by a quiet dinner with his freshly lipsticked wife. After my mother got sick, my father played with his children whenever he was home; he paid the bills and negotiated the peace between Margaret and Mrs. Carper, who didn't get along; he worked at his job and visited his wife at the mental hospital and survived his own despair by his natural gregariousness—but he could not take my mother's place.

My eldest brother Billy has almost a photographic memory of his life's events. He was seven when my mother broke down, and he is the only one of my brothers with any recollection of my mother going away, though his emotions about it were detached at the time.

Billy remembers that a few days after my mother went to the hospital to have a baby, he and Johnny were taken out of school and sent down to our relatives in Virginia, for what seemed like a very long time. It was at least four weeks, because I was born in early March, and the cherry blossoms were out the day Grandmother Payne told the two boys, "Your mother has had a breakdown." Billy can still picture her straightening out the beds in the glassed-in porch after his nap as she told him, but he hadn't the slightest idea what a breakdown was, and it never occurred to him to ask. When he and Johnny returned to the little house in Larchmont, Billy could not help but notice that my mother was gone and that Margaret and Mrs. Carper had taken her place. Mrs. Carper had gray hair in a bun and glasses; in the one picture of her in the family albums she stands near me in my crib, in a white uniform. Unlike Margaret, Mrs. Carper was affectionate, but Billy didn't like to kiss Mrs. Carper because she had facial hair. He had no particular emotions toward the women taking care of him. This didn't matter to Billy, or anyway he didn't think it mattered, because his affections were firmly planted elsewhere, on his third-grade teacher, the divine, soft-spoken Miss Stack.

Miss Stack was a first-year teacher. She was young and pretty with freckles and curly red hair, and Billy loved her. It is easy to see in retrospect that Miss Stack had replaced my mother, and her classroom had replaced our home, but of course Billy was not the slightest bit aware of it at the time, and of course, it was not to last. He needed Miss Stack too much, and in the sad way life has, because he felt loved and safe in her presence, it was in her class that Billy "acted out." One day, after being particularly fresh, he was asked to stay after school to write ten times a statement promising never to commit his offense again. But instead of writing the sentence ten times, Billy kept putting ditto marks under the first line, despite Miss Stack's gentle pleadings to stop and be a good boy. Then suddenly before him appeared Miss Hirschbeck, the principal, and he was suspended.

Soon, to his horror, he was changed to another third-grade class—Mrs. Plowman's—and taken away from the beloved Miss Stack. He was dragged, kicking and screaming, down the hall. Sometime later—a few days, a few weeks, Billy doesn't remember—he was sitting in the auditorium with Mrs. Plowman's class when he glimpsed Miss Stack—she had the exact same hairdo as my mother, Billy suddenly recalled recently, at age fifty-one—leading her students in, and he got a lump in his throat that wouldn't go away.

Then one day Grandmother Payne died, and Billy felt responsible for her death. Margaret called for the older boys to give them the news. Billy remembered Johnny's mouth making an O and that he, Billy, turned away and walked down the stairs to draw on the chalkboard, and that Margaret followed him. This is the only time he remembers her putting her arms around him.

Billy felt guilty because of something that had happened the previous summer when he and Johnny were visiting their Payne grandparents. Grandmother Payne had a bad heart, she was very thin, and Billy remembers how every night Grandfather Payne would sweep her up in his arms to carry her upstairs. One summer evening Billy and Johnny had been playing down the street, and when Grandmother Payne called them, Billy had pretended not to hear, causing his grandmother to stride down the street to fetch them. For years Billy was sure that this extra exertion had led to her death. Billy remembers little about the visit my mother made home the first year she was away, after my grandmother's death, except that it was in October, his birthday month, and that the visit made him so intensely happy—as all her later visits would make him—that he told about it the following day in show-and-tell.

Billy and my brother Johnny, two years younger, were a team, while my brother Hunter, turning three, spent his time with Margaret and me. Whatever Margaret felt about the boys, she loved me and held me and gave me my chance for happiness. Hunter also loved me, and it is not an accident that I named my first child for him. I suppose in a way I replaced my mother as a receptacle for his affection. "Who's that?" someone would ask, pointing to me in the cradle. "That's my baby," Hunter would answer. Hunter survived my mother's leaving, as he would survive his whole life, by creating a better world. He even invented his own words for things, with a serene confidence that brooked no doubt. "My car was red sepin I painted it blue," Hunter told Margaret one day. "What does 'sepin' mean?" asked Margaret. "Bosom," said Hunter firmly, in the only possible reference to my mother that anyone can remember him making in the time that she was away.

Billy and Johnny would later become fierce rivals, but this did not begin until after my mother returned. The year my mother left, Billy felt solicitous of Johnny, not competitive. Later Billy was told how worried mother had been about his troubles in school while she was in the hospital. "I'd worry about that other son if I were you," her shrink had said, "the one who is doing so well."

■   ■   ■

Johnny was five when my mother got sick—that age when boys want to shoot bad people and sleep in their mother's beds—and he was still in the midst of the intense, fuzzy, dependent love that often recurs at age eighteen (usually disastrously) and is called first love, though really it is a mimicry of the true first love, mother love. The feeling he experienced must have been one of bereavement, of the rug being pulled out from under him. But Johnny has no memory of our mother's leaving nor of her return. Years of traditional and nontraditional therapy have never succeeded in bringing it back.

My mother was away from the second half of Johnny's kindergarten through the whole of his first grade. Johnny had tested "genius" in the fall of kindergarten and been moved to High Kindergarten, a smaller class he didn't like as much. The only other kindergarten memory he had was of sitting at a picnic table in the yard after school and feeling horribly lonely. Then, in the first grade, he remembered Valentine's Day.

Valentine's Day, as every mother knows, is the key moment for heartbreak in the elementary school year, particularly in first grade. Johnny had only just turned six, young for his class, when Valentine's Day was presented to him as a concept. The filling out of the correct amount of Valentines with the proper names is a rather complex operation for six-year-olds to undertake, and one that requires the clear guidance of a parent. But Johnny took the terrible task upon himself. Someone at home gave Johnny a batch of Valentines—he doesn't remember who—and Johnny counted out the right amount and carefully wrote "Johnny" on the back of each heart. When he arrived at school and learned that the Valentines were to be delivered not by him personally but by a "postman," he dutifully handed them over to the designated boy without a word, though he knew what the disastrous result would be. Sunkenly he watched as every one of the Valentines he had made for his classmates was delivered back to him. When several children came up to ask why they hadn't received a Valentine, Johnny didn't answer—he felt mortified, as if he'd done something horribly wrong. When he got home, he cried alone in his room, wishing that his mother were there. This is the only time

Johnny remembers consciously missing his mother the whole time she was away.

Though Johnny says he has no memory of my mother going away, he does remember one weekend having a vague feeling that she was coming home to visit. He was playing outside with Billy in the backyard. They were playing Space Monster, and Johnny was sitting on a stack of logs, which was supposed to represent the spaceship. Billy was pretending to be a monster from another planet, and he had picked up a log and was going "Ugrrrhhhh" and was about to throw it. Johnny knew Billy had no intention of hitting him—they were playing—but just before Billy threw it, Johnny says it came to him like a prophecy from God: *If I move my hand and put it on this log, Billy's log will hit my hand.* And then Johnny placed his hand so that Billy's log came smashing down on it.

Johnny was wearing a glove, and when he took it off, his whole hand was bloody. Billy was more upset than Johnny, who had to be taken to the hospital, but Johnny didn't care. His mother was coming home, and he apparently wanted her to stay so much he was willing to have his hand crushed to keep her there.

Finally my mother came back for good, and Johnny was filled with happiness. We moved to New Haven the year Johnny was going into the second grade, and he felt no sadness at leaving the house in Larchmont; he was glad to move, glad to get to New Haven, even though we moved in the summer and he had no friends and nothing to do. It was a new beginning.

Billy also remembered New Haven as a happy time, with everything in place. Great care was given to fairness. Family conferences were convened to settle disputes, which soon after my mother returned began to get intense between Johnny and Billy. In the mornings Billy got up to set the table and cook the bacon. Johnny and Billy made their own lunches and the little kids' beds. Even five-year-old Hunter had a chore, which was to go around the house every day and collect the trash from each wastebasket, which would later be burned in the incinerator in the yard. I remember envying Hunter his chore, which I placed on the lofty par of a mailman rather than a trashman. When I was two and a half, I proudly presented my mother for her birthday a big paper bag filled with carefully collected trash from her desk wastebasket. "What in the world is this?" my mother said, and my heart broke as the old, torn envelopes spilled all around her.

In my memory there was never a time when my mother was not there. I have a picture from the period she was away of me with a white bow affixed miraculously by Margaret to my nearly bald head, and one of my father holding my baby face next to his to show that we looked exactly alike. I'm told when my mother came back I sat upright in her lap while she rocked me. When we moved to New Haven I clung to my mother's legs everywhere she went (and once, by mistake in the supermarket, to a strange woman's legs). Mostly what I remember is feeling happy and secure. Even when my mother went away to the hospital when I was five to have her varicose veins removed, I took it in stride, simply telling myself that she was off to have a baby. I greeted her happily when she returned, it never occurring to me to wonder where the baby was.

My mother recovered so fully and threw herself back into motherhood with such force that none of us children could ever imagine it otherwise. And she pulled it off: From 1954 to 1964 we were the perfect family, and then it ended, as perfect families always do.

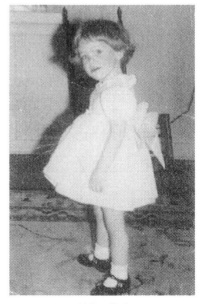

Me at my (delayed) christening.

Charlotte & Bobby

Chardira – Summer 1930

"*. . . will mother go on cleaning house
for eternity, and making it unlivable?*"
("*Unwanted*")

15

*When Mother died, I began to feel tireless, madly sanguine, men-
aced, and menacing. I entered the Payne-Whitney Clinic for "all
those afflicted in mind."*

—"Near the Unbalanced Aquarium"

In 1954, shortly after my family moved to New Haven, Charlotte
Lowell died at age sixty in Rapallo, Italy, where she had been spending
the winter. No one seemed to know why Charlotte had gone to Italy,
not even Charlotte herself. Merrill Moore had been against the trip,
thinking it aimless—that what Charlotte really needed to do at this
pivotal point in her life was to achieve something meaningful. This is
what most women from her background needed to do, but they
seldom did it. When I look at the pictures in the Chilton Club news-
letter of Aunt Sarah and a horde of energetic, well-meaning, well-
heeled Boston matrons wearing the contraptions they'd spent days
creating for funny-hat night, I cannot help but wonder: *How did these
women stand their lives?* They had been brought up with a Puritan
work ethic and then given servants to do all the work. They prided
themselves on their busyness (I always began letters to Aunt Sarah
with "I know you are very busy . . . "), but the very purpose of this

frenzy was to show the world that they weren't required to do any-thing. Seen in this light, funny-hat night *was* an achievement.

Charlotte was very bright, but she could not escape her first and foremost duty: to be a lady. So when Moore offered her a full-time job after Bob senior died, she refused it. When he came up with the alto-gether implausible suggestion that she collaborate with Elizabeth Hardwick in writing a history of Bobby's childhood, she dismissed it out of hand. The only proper thing for a lady—widowed and at a loss—was to go to Europe, and Charlotte took Italian lessons the sum-mer of 1953 to give her decision weight. She left for Italy in October.

Aunt Sarah said later that Charlotte had gone to Italy to flee Moore's advances, "but that was just Sarah's fancy," Elizabeth Hard-wick told my cousin Nell. The wishful suggestion that Moore, nearly twenty years into his relationship with Charlotte, had waited until the death of Bob senior to make his move was Aunt Sarah at her revision-ist best. Whatever the relationship between Moore and her sister had been, the time for advances was long past. What Charlotte *was* fleeing, more likely, was Moore's concept of her making something of herself.

When Charlotte died, my mother, recovered from her nervous breakdown, was reengaging herself with her four children in the idyl-lic house in Connecticut. Her impression at the time, from conversa-tions with Aunt Sarah, was that Charlotte had been thinking of moving to Italy for good, that the trip had been a kind of trial run, that she no longer had Bob senior to look after, and that she was very fed up with Bobby. Bobby, on the other hand, felt that his visit with his mother that September, the month before she left for Italy, had been the best ever. He had stayed with her for two weeks in her house on Marlborough Street and, in the middle of a heat wave, talked on and on about Charlotte's upcoming trip to Italy and also about Freud, whom Bobby had just read and become obsessed with. More to my mother's point, however, is the fact Charlotte had decided to leave Boston at the same moment that her son, after nearly twenty years' absence, was in the process of returning home. While visiting his mother, Bobby had signed papers on a house in Duxbury, Massachusetts. He was ready to settle down, after two years traveling in Europe with Elizabeth and several months teaching in the

Midwest, and, for all his battles with his mother, he chose to settle down near her. My mother believed that Charlotte had thought of the trip to Italy as her last chance to have her own life. Instead Charlotte had a stroke and died ten days later, alone in a hospital in Rapallo.

Bobby was deeply tied to his mother; she may not have been nurturing, but he was the center of her life. Yet when Bobby got the news that his mother was dying, after rushing to Europe he perversely stopped just short of rushing to her bedside, staying up drinking in Neuilly with Blair Clark instead. By the time Bobby finally arrived at the hospital, shortly after midnight on Valentine's Day, she had been dead a half hour.

Much of the prose autobiography Bobby drafted in the mid-1950s became *Life Studies*, but the story of his mother's death and his subsequent breakdown, "Near the Unbalanced Aquarium," wasn't published until after his death. For an hour and a half in the hospital room where his mother lay dead, Bobby wrote, the nurse and he "stood with tears running down our faces," as she told Bobby about his mother's final days, how "she thought she was still at her hotel and wanted to go walking, and said she was only suffering from a little indigestion . . . and how she kept trying to heal the hemorrhage in her brain by calling for her twenty little jars and bottles with their pink plastic covers, and kept dabbing her temples with creams and washes, and felt guilty because she wasn't allowed to take her quick cold bath in the morning and her hot aromatic bath before dinner. She kept asking about Bob and Bobby . . . ."

Afterward Bobby did everything that his father could have wished. "I met the Rapallo English colony, Mother's brief acquaintances. I made arrangements at the simple red-brick English chapel, and engaged a sober Church of England clergyman. Then I went to Genoa and bought Mother a black-and-gold baroque casket that would have been suitable for burying her hero Napoleon at Les Invalides." The Italians misspelled Charlotte's last name on the coffin—"Lovell." Bobby wrote: "I could almost hear her voice correcting the workmen. 'I am Mrs. Robert Lowell of One Seventy Marlborough Street, Boston, L, O, W, E, *double L*.'"

Two days after the Rapallo funeral, Bobby sailed back home with his mother's body, arriving in New York on March 1, then traveling up to Boston. In Boston he had lunch with Aunt Sarah, Uncle Cot, Elizabeth, and my mother at the Chilton Club.

The lunch at the Chilton Club was right before Charlotte's Boston funeral, and it was the first time my mother had ever met Elizabeth. At lunch Bobby was full of jokes; he couldn't seem to stop talking, and my mother thought that he was acting rather excited, probably too excited, and she, so recently released from New York Hospital, was acutely aware of the signs. But nobody remarked on it, if they noticed it at all. Even my mother's attention was diverted by Elizabeth, who she thought was very pretty but quiet, a little mouse.

The funeral was very correct, my mother remembered, "very Episcopalian." Afterward my mother, Aunt Sarah and Uncle Cot, Bobby and Elizabeth, and a variety of Winslow relatives were chauffeured up to Dunbarton, two hours away. It seemed odd to my mother then, and this would be true in the years to come, that Aunt Sarah never seemed the least upset when people died, but totally in control, bossing everyone around, without even a quiver of the lip. My mother didn't cry either, but then my mother had never been close to Charlotte. Bobby, my mother said, was in a controlled manic state, much quieter than he had been at lunch; he seemed quite happy up there with all the Winslows, dead and alive—not in mourning at all.

Bobby's initial reaction to his mother's death was great relief and pleasure at doubling his income, feelings that were immediately swallowed up by great guilt. It is hard not to be glad when you inherit money, and harder not to be guilty that you are glad. I used to think, rather stupidly, that being a poet meant that Bobby didn't think about money, but then a friend reminded me of the poem in which Bobby details exactly how much money his father lost in the stock market. I don't imagine Bobby ever sat around balancing his checkbook, but he certainly thought about money in the larger sense. How could he not, with a mother who, as he himself wrote in "91 Revere Street," would "return frozen and thrilled from her property disputes" with a cousin over an ancestral estate.

By mid-March, Bobby and Elizabeth were back in Cincinnati, where he had agreed, before Charlotte's death, to deliver a series of poetry lectures. By now Bobby was very high, announcing to friends and colleagues (but not to the family) that he was going to divorce Elizabeth and marry an Italian girl with whom he had fallen in love eighteen months earlier, when he and Elizabeth were living in Salzburg. He had been high then, too, but the attack had been relatively mild. This attack, his fourth in the four years he had been with Elizabeth, was different. This time Elizabeth had to obtain a court order to commit him. Bobby was so high that even after electroshock therapy his mania returned. At the end of April he was transferred from the Jewish Hospital in Cincinnati to Payne Whitney in New York, but even there he was confined to a locked ward for three weeks. Bobby's descriptions of this stay in "Near the Unbalanced Aquarium" are the funniest, most chilling, and, I believe, most accurate I have ever read.

At Payne Whitney, Bobby was put on the new drug thorazine, which had an immediate effect, and his diagnosis was changed from its initial one of schizophrenia to manic depression. He was released from Payne Whitney in September of 1954.

After this breakdown Bobby and Elizabeth moved to Back Bay Boston, purchasing, in 1955, a town house at 239 Marlborough Street, one block away from where Bobby had lived with his parents. For four years they lived a fairly proper life. They entertained and had a maid and linens in the linen closets, and in 1957 they had a baby. Elizabeth was a good cook and a great housekeeper, my mother said, someone who made places pretty and comfortable. Elizabeth was a devoted mother, and Bobby would joke about becoming a father so late, at age forty, and how for so many years they had been trying everything to have a baby, seeking help from innumerable doctors, until finally they had given up—only to go off on vacation where a few hasty embraces had resulted in Harriet. After Harriet was born, Bobby had come to visit us in New Haven and insisted on taking my mother's baby gift back to Elizabeth to open. Three days later a letter came from Elizabeth: "Dear Jackie, I'm sure your gift to Harriet was absolutely marvelous and I want to thank you so much, but I have to tell you that your cousin left the present on the train." What my mother remembered most about Bobby and Elizabeth as a couple was how funny they were together. As she sat in their cozy parlor, she thought, *What a nice, warm, happy family.* As opposed to Jean Stafford, who always seemed to gripe when Bobby read a poem, my mother would see tears in Elizabeth's eyes. "Darling," Elizabeth would say, "that's beautiful."

It may have looked like a nice life, but Bobby's mental state was always precarious. (He went two years without a breakdown during this time in Boston, the longest time off he would have for the rest of his life, due to thorazine.) The family always referred to Bobby's stays in McLean's as lasting a few weeks, but I notice that the poem about returning to his baby daughter from McLean's (and more electroshock treatment) is called "Home After Three Months Away."

Despite his problems, I think that for a long while it made Bobby intensely happy to have a house on Marlborough Street. He read the boring family books, and he even officially went back to the Protestant faith, though his denomination was more High Church than his family's Low Church. Nestled in Back Bay Boston, he was living as a proper Protestant trust-funded father. It was a life that fitted the picture of what Arthur Winslow had wanted for him; for once he might even have had his grandfather's approval. It was too late, of course—they were all dead, his grandparents and his parents, by the time he was able to please them. Still, when Bobby moved back to Boston, he found enough peace to write the book that would bring him universal fame. It was *Life Studies*, a brutal look at the New England world he was trying to embrace, and a particularly brutal look at his parents. He had moved back to Boston to find his roots, but instead he nearly dug them up.

Right before *Life Studies* was published in the spring of 1959, Aunt Sarah met my mother, who had been invited to lunch, in front of her house on Beacon Street. "I've just read what Bobby wrote about Charlotte and Bob, and it's just awful, " Aunt Sarah announced. With that she marched my mother, without benefit of the usual two glasses of prelunch sherry, around the corner to Bobby and Elizabeth's on Marlborough Street to tell them, as she stood in their foyer refusing to sit down, that what Bobby had written was all dreadful lies. "I'm sorry you didn't like it," Bobby answered in his soft voice. "I thought it was rather good." Then he added that he never wrote about anyone unless they were dead. But what my mother remembered most about that stormy day (for Aunt Sarah would also get mad at her later, over lunch at the Chilton Club) was Elizabeth saying in a very quiet way as they were about to leave, "Aunt Sarah, you want Bobby to write about the way he thinks and feels, don't you? You don't just want him to write about nothing, do you?"

Well, preferably, yes, would have been the answer. It was one thing to write all sorts of gobbledygook with classical allusions that nobody could understand, but to write about how you felt listening through the walls as your mother yelled shrilly at your father was beyond comprehension. Even though Aunt Sarah had shown no emotion when Charlotte died, five years later let Bobby dare to imply that Bob senior and Charlotte's marriage had not been ideal, and the emotion came out in an uproar. "They *loved* each other *very* much!" Aunt Sarah insisted again and again forever after *Life Studies* was published. She would eventually forgive Bobby, but she never got over *Life Studies*.

Life Studies is said to be the book that launched the confessional style of poetry, but to me it isn't really confession because confession implies that a person is seeking forgiveness. When Bobby writes of bringing his classmates over to the park day after day to ridicule his best friend, a little German boy quarantined for whooping cough, because doing so made him popular, he isn't asking the reader for sympathy, he is merely stating, *This is the person I am.* He was always searching for what is true (even if he had to "invent the facts," as he put it), and that's why he had to make *Life Studies* nonfiction, why he had to use the real names—this I finally understand. He gave up trying to be fictional, which had gotten in the way, and wrote straight about himself.

The problem was, the family didn't want to know. Negative emotions were to be conquered, not expressed. ("Shy means thinking about yourself," was how one New England family admonished sensitive children.) Bobby had bared his soul and been rejected; not by the world, of course, but what does it matter if the world applauds you if your family does not? Shortly after his encounter with Aunt Sarah, Bobby checked himself into McLean's.

■   ■   ■

The same year *Life Studies* came out, Elizabeth published an incisive essay in *Harper's* excoriating Boston, called "Boston: A Lost Ideal." ("Elizabeth never understood about Boston," my mother said, but Elizabeth *did* understand Boston; she just didn't like it. She was "not Boston," a condemnation she mocks in her essay, a phrase that echoes in Concord to this day, dating back to Marmee Alcott, who, on taking a look at her daughter Amy's stylish portrait done in Paris, had sniffed, "Not Concord.") Years later Bobby would refer to his famous great-granduncle James Russell Lowell as a "poet pedestaled for oblivion" ("A Conversation with Ian Hamilton"). He didn't think much of fat Amy either; in fact the only Lowell ancestor he admired was the enthusiastic (if a touch masochistic) Civil War soldier Charles Russell Lowell, his first cousin several times removed. Hell-bent on fighting the Confederates, he had his badly wounded body strapped onto his horse to ride into battle.

In all of 1959 Bobby finished only one poem, and it was in a state of emptiness and self-loathing that he wrote "For the Union Dead" in January 1960. He had been asked to read a new poem for the Boston Arts Festival, which was taking place in the Public Garden, where Bobby had played in his youth (and from which he had once been formally expelled). By the time he delivered the poem that June, Bobby had accepted a fellowship that would allow Elizabeth and him to move to New York. The poem was greeted with great applause, though I doubt that the festival organizers got quite what they had bargained for.

Bobby's poem is about the demise of Boston and the demise of the Fifty-fourth Massachusetts, an all-black regiment in the Civil War, which was led into battle by Col. Robert Gould Shaw. Shaw was twenty-five years old, from a proper, upper-class Boston family of strong Abolitionist sentiment. In the bronze Saint-Gaudens monument erected in memory of the Fifty-fourth, he has the lean, driven look of a true New Englander:

> He has an angry wrenlike vigilance,
> a greyhound's gentle tautness;
> he seems to wince at pleasure,
> and suffocate for privacy.

Two months after Shaw marched the Fifty-fourth gloriously through Boston, half of them were dead. The Saint-Gaudens monument, dedicated by William James in the Boston Public Garden, now "sticks like a fishbone/in the city's throat." Boston has become a city of parking lots, of steam shovels excavating the Boston Common "to gouge their underworld garage." The old aquarium that Bobby visited as a child is gone:

> . . . Everywhere,
> giant finned cars nose forward like fish;
> a savage servility
> slides by on grease.

"For the Union Dead" is Bobby's counterrejection of Boston, which, in the form of Aunt Sarah, had rejected him, but it also draws a close parallel to Bobby's own life and the situation in his family. Colonel Shaw's sister had married Charles Russell Lowell two years before his death-bent horse ride, making Colonel Shaw a kind of relative of Bobby's. And so the poem is also about a family member suffering for his ideals. In Colonel Shaw's case he is sacrificed by his family for them; in Bobby's case he is rejected. The feeling of rejection is so strong in the poem that if you did not know the history, as I did not when I first read it, you would think Shaw had been rejected by his family for leading the Fifty-fourth:

> Shaw's father wanted no monument
> except the ditch,
> where his son's body was thrown
> and lost with his "niggers . . . ."

The reality was that Shaw's Abolitionist father felt that his son, as a soldier, should be buried in the field alongside his black soldiers; the word "niggers" quoted in the poem comes from the Confederate general who insisted that the colonel be thrown into the same ditch as his men. And yet, in a sense, Shaw *was* rejected by his family, who were more than willing to give him up to fulfill their long-held beliefs.

Though Shaw made his own decision to lead the black troops, the pressure of his moralistic parents was overbearing. His father traveled through the night to deliver the governor's letter asking him to take command of the black regiment. When at first the younger Shaw declined—doubting his ability to command, as well as loving his current regiment and loving even more his new bride, whom he was loath to subject to ridicule—his mother wrote the governor it was "the bitterest disappointment" of her life, and then proceeded, gratuitously, to blame her son's weakness on her husband. Shaw was not a fanatic like his mother, but he was an idealist and though he dearly loved his life, which from the beginning of the enterprise he had a premonition he would lose, he soon decided to accept the command. His mother then happily wrote that she now would gladly die, forgetting for a moment whose life was in jeopardy. Like all zealots, she cared more for her own ideals than for human life, even her own son's.

"For the Union Dead" is Bobby's most beautiful poem but also his saddest, for me anyway, laced as it is with his feelings of our family's rejection of him. A few years ago I went into Boston to visit the Saint-Gaudens monument, allowing an hour before I had to pick up my daughter, Emily, from school. It was early spring and drizzling, and a terrible feeling of desolation descended on me as I walked across Commonwealth Avenue, across Marlborough Street, across Beacon Street—all places where once my family lived, and will never live again, where Bobby wished to live, as I too have wished, but in the end could not. There I thought of the boyish Colonel Shaw and his regiment, and how for the black soldiers it had been worth dying for that one chance of dignity, and worth it also for Colonel Shaw, who led his men cheerfully and proudly into the slaughter at Fort Wagner.

I walked into the Public Garden and saw the duck statue commemorating *Make Way for Ducklings*, the children's book more famous by far than *Life Studies*, and the statue of Edward Everett, famous for what I will never know, and the same "yellow dinosaur steamshovels" that Bobby wrote about grinding loudly away. It seemed impossible that they would still be working on the same underground garage, but before me was a sign that read: ENLARGEMENT OF BOSTON COMMON UNDERGROUND GARAGE. The noise was deafening, and I could not find the Saint-Gaudens statue, so I wandered down to the swan boat rides, where Aunt Sarah used to take me, and where, despite the name, there were never any swans, and where even at age eight, with my sweet chattering aunt beside me, I felt uncomfortable, out of place, phony, knowing I did not belong in this world of chauffeurs and sunny thoughts.

"Where is the monument to Colonel Shaw and the black soldiers?" I asked the guy at the swan boats. He answered, "Oh, you can't see it now, they've moved it, to work on the garage." And though the whole purpose of my visit was lost, my heart also leaped, for by now all I wanted was to get away from the Public Garden and the specter of my vanished family, and I dashed through the puddles to my car, thankful to drive home, away from Boston.

Aunt Sarah in a funny hat, 1964.

16

Manic depression was never explained to us in our youths; it was just something that ran in the family, like diabetes, accepted in the most casual way. Our mother was a manic depressive and Bobby was a manic depressive, that much we knew, but in my mother's case her very normality made her breakdown ultimately seem irrelevant, and in Bobby's case it was as incomprehensible and in some senses as enviable as the genius we were unable to grasp. We knew little about Bobby's life in New York in the 1960s, had no idea that he was drinking and getting high and sometimes violent; all that came out later. We were simply told that Bobby checked himself into McLean's whenever he needed a rest.

Bobby may have banished himself to New York, where he and Elizabeth bought a duplex apartment on West Sixty-seventh Street, but he always flew back every November for Aunt Sarah's Thanksgiving. If public acclaim had not quite vanquished family reservations about *Life Studies*, it had vanquished all reservations about Bobby. At Thanksgiving he was received as a hero. There was always a great bustle when he, Elizabeth, and young Harriet arrived at the farm: Elizabeth charged with humor; Bobby vague, bashfully smiling, embracing Aunt Sarah; my father and mother and the gray group of

Winslow cousins rushing forward; my brothers and I standing back, on the periphery of the laughing crowd.

One would expect my brother Billy to have had the clearest memory of Bobby at Thanksgiving. It was Billy who, sent away to boarding school against his will, craved being with the family; Billy who knew the names of the amorphous Winslow cousins; Billy who actually enjoyed the long, giftless, bleak-skied holiday of finger bowls and adult conversation. Billy had even read some of Bobby's poetry, and yet Billy's main memory of him is of the older relatives saying at some point during those long Thanksgiving afternoons, "Shhh, shhh, Bobby's upstairs taking a nap."

My brother Johnny, whose high school teachers—like those he had in kindergarten—believed he was a genius, had the same preoccupied expression as Bobby; he even looked like Bobby, with his large frame, handsome, regular features, and protruding chin. Johnny was the only true intellectual in our immediate family. He should have had the most to say to Bobby as the years went on, and yet, of us children, it was he who would have the least relationship with him.

My youngest brother, Hunter, had the best disposition in the family, meaning he wasn't as loud as the rest of us. The bigger the crowd, the more anxious Hunter got, and yet it is he who remembers Bobby most vividly at those Thanksgivings of the 1960s. The hush that fell when Bobby spoke at dinner was a different hush from the one that fell when our Great Uncle Cot rose in his checkered vest to make a toast; it was the hush of, *My god, he's a genius.* Bobby seemed distracted, tickled inside, as if something were secretly amusing him, and would not sit down for long anywhere. At dinner Hunter also had glimpses of Bobby saying things that didn't make any sense. Later, on the way home, he remembered my mother and father saying that Bobby was "high."

For me, from the time when I was six, Bobby's arrival meant the arrival of Harriet, younger and cuter than I, the erstwhile baby of the crowd. And yet somehow Harriet was never delivered up to us children to be played with, but sheltered between her parents in the grown-up throng. She was dark haired and blue eyed and looked a great deal like Aunt Sarah had at that age, but she barely said a word. "How could she," my mother joked later, "surrounded by those brilliant parents?" I was twelve the Thanksgiving when Bobby, manic, was quietly informing friends that Johnson had chosen him to be a member of his cabinet, but all I remember is sitting with my brothers in Uncle Cot's dark den with the football game on the black-and-white TV, wishing it were time to go home.

We were a happy, wholesome family from Concord, Massachusetts, in 1963. My parents were popular in the country club set, even though they didn't have "any money"; my father played his banjo at parties and taught my Brownie troop how to march like marines in the Patriot's Day parade. My mother attended meetings of the Seeds and Weeds Garden Club, and cooked us balanced but economical meals—margarine instead of butter and ice cream only on Sundays. Billy was attending my father's alma mater, Williams, and Johnny was off to Harvard, having won half the awards at Concord High. Hunter was a dapper high school sophomore, a favorite with the senior girls. I had my last lead in a school play and still believed I was pretty and, for the first (and only) time in my life, was popular. We were in our golden period, but of course we didn't know it.

We had moved to Concord six years earlier, when Simmons transferred my father, to a shabby, peeling Victorian on Main Street, where the train ran hourly behind the backyard. We children had cried when we first saw our new home, late one night, looming over us like a haunted house in the glare of the streetlight, across from the large green sign for Route 62, but the house was spacious and cheap enough to require no mortgage, and the neighborhood was filled with children. My mother allowed us a crabgrassed side yard for our own, which we ground joyously to dirt that summer and every summer after, playing baseball and kick-the-can with the wild herd of children we ran with. Concord became home to all of us, except for Billy, who that fall was sent away to school.

Billy was the oldest, but my father had been away during the war after Billy was born, and it was Johnny who was his favorite. "Big John Special," my father called him, after the title of an old jazz song, even before he began playing Dixieland clarinet. Whether it was this favoritism, or my mother's breakdown, or simply the fact that Cain slew Abel, Johnny and Billy's fights had steadily escalated over the years, so that I used to dread returning home after school to the sound of screaming and yelling and breaking light bulbs. One time Billy ran away from home in the middle of a family excursion to Boston and had to come home in a taxi, at his own expense. (We were always being taught responsibility by having to pay for our mistakes.)

Billy was in the ninth grade when he was sent away to school, partly to separate him from Johnny, but mainly because sending sons to private preparatory school was what had always been done in our family. He was taken around to see a select number: to Noble and Greenough, because my mother's father, Devereux, had gone there; to Milton Academy (where my mother had gone), though for a less discernible reason, since he was told before they visited that my parents couldn't afford the tuition; to Phillips Andover; and to Episcopal High in Virginia, which Billy chose because he liked the smell of the box bushes there.

At Episcopal High, Billy was hazed mercilessly for one year and so homesick that he wrote letters to my parents threatening to run away. They were careful not to respond to the threats. "Stick to the original plan," was the unofficial creed of my family, and possibly one that is not always wrong, for by the end of the year Billy was first in his class. (Later, however, Billy maintained that overachievement was a sign of abuse. "All I know is that I was never first in anything again after Episcopal High," he said.) He was awarded a five-hundred-dollar scholarship for his achievements. "Now we can paint the house," my mother said.

The one advantage of Episcopal High was that my grandmother, Alice Sommaripa, lived nearby. We called her Yammy, derived from the Y.A.M. she signed at the end of letters to her daughters, short for "Your Adoring Mother," and though she was not the typical indulgent, cookie-baking grandmother, we all adored her. Even her enduring cheapness became a family joke, though not always so funny at the moment when the Christmas wrapping rolled off to expose the batch of clear plastic pens that didn't write, or instead of the promised toaster, a metal rack for the stove, its $1.49 sticker still attached.

One year my grandmother presented my mother with a pearl necklace. "Your father, Devereux, gave you this when you were christened, and I just wanted to give it to you for your birthday," she gushed. My mother allowed that it was an awfully nice present but one which, technically speaking, had already been bestowed on her. "Oh, Dahling, of course it was!" said my grandmother, giving my mother no argument whatsoever, but no other birthday present either.

She paid little attention to us grandchildren until we turned adolescent and became "interesting," but we didn't care. We loved her "dahling's" and the soft-creased cheeks she gave us to kiss under her ridiculous hats, and the coy way she stood quietly next to her car door waiting for my brothers to open it for her. She was utterly charming, but she was also lonely; my mother had received phone calls from my grandmother's friends claiming that she had been drinking too much.

After Billy went to Episcopal, my mother warned Alice that if her son reported back that she was drinking, he could never be allowed to stay with her again. The threat must have worked because Billy never remembered Yammy drunk. Instead she regaled him with stories about her childhood and how once, locked in a closet for punishment, she had spat on her mother's dresses and ruined them. "I was a terrible child," she said. Other times she would declare, "Oh, Billy, you look just like Devereux, you're just like him," and then she would tell the story again about their courtship and how the trip to Europe when Devereux was dying had been the most wonderful time of her life. But mostly she talked about her second husband, Beaupère, Alexis Sommaripa. Maybe because he was killed so shortly after, my grandmother still felt guilty about divorcing him, still seemed to be in love with him.

Each of my brothers spent a summer with Yammy. Johnny—who was so driven and successful at everything, to the worship of us all— remembered working long hours painting fences and pitching hay in the hot sun, at no one's particular behest (neither my grandmother nor her farmer had expected—or even wished for—such zeal), he realized later, making even a summer on the farm a prison.

Hunter remembered my grandmother sitting in state at the head of the long Italian dinner table, ringing the bell for Matilda, the black maid who lived in another part of town in a dirt-floored shack (later replaced by a son with a prefab house on the same spot), and who once, when my grandmother complained of the houses popping up on the mountain that was her view, said she sure wished she had Miz Sommaripa's troubles. My grandmother was always up early in morning, at 5:30 A.M., looking like a million bucks, even though Hunter had left her the night before asleep in front of the TV to the sign-off strains of "The Star-Spangled Banner." Hunter was fourteen the summer he stayed with my grandmother, and every night he played Scrabble with her as she drank spiked lemonade. As the evening wore on, my grandmother would say, "Don't tell your mother," and then, to Hunter's horror and pleasure, she would put down the letters for "fuck."

In the spring of 1964 my grandmother traveled to her daughter Polly's house to die of pancreatic cancer. "Oh, doctor," she'd flirted when he lifted her frail body from the bed, "you're so strong." Bobby was an usher at Yammy's funeral; she had been his uncle Devereux's wife. My grandmother loved anyone famous, and had proudly kept the copy of *Life Studies* inscribed to her in 1959: "To Alice, love Bobby."

At the time of my grandmother's death, Bobby was recovering from yet another breakdown, one that had begun in November 1963, after John Kennedy's assassination, and one that had seemed to come out of the blue, after Bobby had struggled through a year of sobriety and strict adherence to his doctor's orders. Now to Bobby's despair it seemed that nothing he did would make any difference, that the breakdowns would continue to come upon him every year, inescapably— that they were as much a part of him as the poetry he wrote.

In this depressive state Bobby was preparing a book for publication, named for his poem "For the Union Dead." The book would not be published until the fall of 1964, and, with Robert Frost recently dead, some reviewers would start calling Bobby the greatest living American poet. But six months earlier, at the time of my grandmother's funeral, Bobby was experiencing terrible doubts about himself and the book he had written.

My grandmother's funeral was in March, on a sunny, bitter cold day. It was my first funeral. I had just turned thirteen and had hoped to fling myself, weeping, on the kneeling pad in a drama of catharsis, as I had once seen Mandy Banks do, so incongruously in the well-mannered crowd, one bright Sunday morning at Concord's Trinity

Church. But I was a New England Protestant, and my emotions fled at the church door, where I was confronted by row after row of my dry-eyed relatives, their grief expressed only by the effort to suppress it.

I have only a vague memory of Bobby hovering at the entrance, dressed conservatively like the other male members of the family (except that Bobby always looked as if he had just emerged from a long nonstop car trip), in a suit, narrow tie, and white shirt. My cousin, Polly's fifteen-year-old daughter, remembers walking down the aisle and bursting into sobs at the sight of the three strong backs of her mother, my mother, and our Aunt Allie, rigid in the front pew, and that it was Bobby who came over and put his arm around her.

It turned out that my grandmother had died with a million dollars, quite a lot of money in 1964. Even her estate lawyer was surprised at the sum, uncovering it bit by bit in various investment firms around the country. My parents' share came just in time, because it was shortly after my grandmother died that my brothers' troubles began. "All I know," my mother said later, "is that we never had any trouble until we inherited mother's money."

Yammy.

The last Christmas card.

17

MY GRANDMOTHER'S FUNERAL WAS MY FAMILY'S LAST DAY IN THE SUN.
For, by the spring of 1964, something terrible was happening to my
brother Johnny—the star around whom all of us revolved—though
we would not know about it until months later.

My family's brief golden era is immortalized in a framed series of
Christmas cards in my parents' present apartment. In the card from
1964, we all sparkle in clean-cut beauty, my three brothers in crew
cuts and sports jackets, me in a shirtwaist dress and perfect bubble
cut, all gathered around my parents in their Sunday best. It was the
last Christmas card ever to be adorned with a photograph of the fam-
ily. In the winter of 1965, Johnny was taken from Harvard College by
ambulance to McLean Mental Hospital, and nothing was ever the
same again. "Jackie and Bill are all right," my aunt Sarah began to say
when introducing my parents to her friends, "but their children are
just *terrible*."

Bobby had been a "difficult child," but my brother Johnny had been
the perfect child after my mother's breakdown, considerate of his
parents and hardworking in school. His third-grade New Year's reso-
lution, printed beneath a drawing of my mother with her feet up, had

been to help her more so that she wouldn't have to work so hard. In the eighth grade he was selected for the Honor Division, where he excelled with a seriousness that set him apart from the other high achievers. By then Johnny had established a routine. He would come straight home from school and eat an enormous snack—he was still growing into his height of six feet, six and a half inches—four bowls of cereal and maybe a couple of jars of custard pudding or peach baby food (a favorite at our house), while reading U.S. News & World Report, or Time or Life magazines; then he would go upstairs and spend the rest of the afternoon in his tidy room studying, with stunning concentration, his papers and books neatly organized on the desk beside him.

I, five years younger, would sometimes lie next to our mutt, Scout, in the sunny spot beneath the skylight outside Johnny's door, with the perfectly printed KNOCK BEFORE ENTERING sign placed exactly in its center. Seldom did I knock. But years later Johnny was the one person who ever confided to me the precise progression of his breakdown, blow by terrible blow, and I saw in the details maybe a way to understand what had happened to the rest of the family.

In high school Johnny was awarded the lead in the school play and first place in the state math fair two years running. To our deep embarrassment no one in the family understood a single word when Johnny hotly debated his theorems about "congruent planar and spherical polygons"; then the announcement came that he had won first prize. It was obvious to us that Johnny was someone special, out of our league.

Johnny won the Harvard Book Prize, awarded to the outstanding junior and, his senior year, early acceptance to the college. Best of all, he was in love with Robin, an exotic beauty for Concord, who in 1962, when the other girls wore bows in their flips, wore her thick black hair streaming down her back. Warm and gentle, Robin loved her driven, achievement-oriented boyfriend. In the high school play their senior year, she played a glowing Anastasia to Johnny's dark, scheming Prince Bounine.

It was perhaps the happiest moment of our collective lives, that warm June day when my family sat in the stands at Concord-Carlisle

High School and watched Johnny win award after award at his graduation: my father, of the gentleman's B; my mother, who had yearned for but been denied college; my Aunt Sarah, stylish and erect, chattering through the ceremony; my grandmother, Alice, oozing charm, in a hideous rayon dress; Billy, a college man; Hunter, fifteen, in a seersucker suit, winking at the girls in the stands; and I, still happy, still living in a straight little girl's body, in a new fifty-dollar dress from Kussin's—the expensive shop in town where we never shopped—bought by my grandmother for me the day before. ("Oh, Mother," my mother had said in tearful gratitude, though as it turned out, my grandmother had charged it to my father.)

"To someone we can really look up to," Mr. Donovan the principal had said as he awarded the American Flag Award to Johnny, who, returning to his seat, had blithely placed the flag on the ground neatly under his chair—an action denounced in the irate letters that flooded the *Concord Journal* the next week concerning Johnny's graduation speech, which stated that socialism was possibly not such a dirty idea.

"He has a fine patrician voice," my aunt Sarah had remarked during the speech, "like all the Winslows."

It had never occurred to Johnny that he would have trouble adjusting to Harvard. One of the reasons that he had wanted to go to Harvard was because it was the toughest place there was, and there he would push himself harder.

Johnny studied fervently his freshman year. The problem was he had a 9 A.M. class and his roommates joked around late at night. He liked his roommates: They were smart and funny and they weren't preppy. The preppy people put him off, the guys who had been to Andover and Exeter and were so cool. The first semester Johnny was given one of the three top marks out of a class of three hundred on one of his exams, but no one noticed. The lecture halls were huge, and no one knew who you were. In high school each success had signified to him that someone was out there listening.

That fall Johnny began to feel odd and fuzzy, kind of nauseated; one night he had gone to Lamont Library and hadn't been able to concentrate, and this worried him. He grew depressed. His roommates would try to be quiet at night, but frequently their laughter would wake Johnny. He was often exhausted and freaked out that there were times he couldn't make himself study.

All his anxiety left the weekend Robin came down to visit from Bennington; he felt better than he had all fall. But when he rode with Robin on the subway to the stop where she was catching a ride back to school, he was suddenly overcome and started to cry. He couldn't stop. He felt as if it were the end of the world. When he started back alone to Harvard Square, a new kind of desolation settled on him: an indescribably horrible feeling of the bottom dropping out, that everything was lost.

The feeling was not human—it was not fear, not agitation, not even terror. He had never felt this way—when he was little and felt sad, he'd been able to shut it off, protected by God or Mother Nature—but now it seemed he could no longer be protected.

For days the feeling wouldn't leave. He forced himself to go to classes, willing himself through each minute, calling Robin at night for comfort. Finally, after a few days, he walked into Stillman, the college infirmary, and made an appointment with a psychiatrist, who told him that the only thing that might help was long-term psychotherapy. He cautioned that it didn't always work and that often you felt worse before you felt better—and that to get it, you had to go outside the university health services.

The terrible feeling lasted until that Friday, a total of five days. Rehearsing with his clarinet in the pit for the Harvard production of *The Gondoliers*, Johnny felt that he couldn't stand it for another second, and he wanted to run from the room screaming. He decided he would borrow the parents' car and visit Robin. That afternoon he walked up the stairs of Sever Hall to go to class and heard the professor saying that Kennedy had been shot. The teacher, a typical jaded Harvard academic who had never shown any emotion, was completely choked up by the news. Johnny went back to his room to find his roommates similarly devastated—as opposed to Johnny. When he learned about Kennedy, he had immediately felt better. He had felt so disconnected before, but now he felt connected to everyone. He went out into Harvard Yard, where the bells were tolling and everyone was just standing there, aimlessly, in a daze. But all that time Johnny wasn't feeling anything but *I'm all right now, I'm out of it, it's over.* It *was* over, the terror of those long five days.

The terror vanished, but not the depression, which lasted through that spring, when Robin broke up with him on Freshman Weekend, and throughout the summer. That summer he went to Europe—my mother had suggested it after he'd broken up with Robin, Europe always having been the panacea for broken hearts in the family. Johnny would always feel that my mother understood him best; later, when he was institutionalized, he felt worst for my mother because he knew she, of everyone, knew what it was like. Johnny had loved his first European trip with our cousins three years before, not realizing that much of what he had loved was being with the cousins. This time he hadn't brought the womb with him. He was alone: hitchhiking, playing his clarinet in the cafés, and passing the hat, counting the days until he could go home.

That second fall at Harvard, Johnny could not make himself work. He went to the shrink he'd seen at Stillman and described how miserable he had been in Europe, and the shrink told him that he needed to go into private psychotherapy—which meant my parents would have to pay for it.

The weekend Johnny came home to ask my parents to pay for therapy was the weekend we were having our last Christmas-card picture taken. He was nervous, jittery, as we posed for the camera. How happy he looks in that picture, taken minutes before he went into the living room with my parents and closed the double mahogany doors. He tried to make light of his problems, saying he was having some trouble and had been told he should see a psychotherapist, and that it wasn't that serious, that he would be fine. My mother reassured him that he would be okay and that money, so often an issue, would not be one.

Twice a week Johnny went to see Doctor Leeman in Boston. To complicate matters, Johnny had been prescribed dexadrine by the regular health services when he'd complained of lethargy. This was before anyone knew that speed was dangerous, of course. Soon

Johnny had taken himself off the drug, which was not difficult, since the dex had never given him any energy. Nevertheless he had kept a stash around and began taking it again in December. For a day or two Johnny felt good, felt he had solved everything, that he was cured, that life was wonderful. He figured that at the end of their next session, Leeman would volunteer that Johnny was done with therapy. But instead, all Leeman said was, "See you next time."

The new semester began in February, and Johnny signed up for Abnormal Psychology, despite the fact Dr. Leeman had vehemently opposed his taking the course. He'd had a cough for several weeks, but it seemed to be getting better. Then, one afternoon, a couple of weeks into the semester, he came home after a visit to the Isabella Gardner Museum and found suddenly he couldn't move. He had to lie down; he was totally exhausted and running a fever, and finally he managed to drag himself over to Stillman Infirmary.

It turned out Johnny had pneumonia, and for one blissful week, he lived in Stillman in a double room that he had to himself most of the time, surrounded by flirtatious, attentive nurses. He was able to keep up with his courses in the infirmary; he was particularly riveted by his textbook on Abnormal Psychology. Gradually he began to piece together what had happened to him when my mother had broken down: that at age five he had been closely tied to her and bereft when she had suddenly left, feelings that had been stimulated by his breakup with Robin; and that, years ago, when my father had tried to explain the breakdown by saying my mother had been run down by all the children, Johnny had felt that it was he who had been responsible.

When my mother came to visit at Stillman, Johnny reassured her that it wasn't her fault, that he had figured out why he was depressed and that everything would be fine now. He even started going to classes while he was living at Stillman, and in class, he felt everything was effortless and fascinating—well, for that matter, all of life was fascinating now. He'd done it, he'd solved the problem of his life—the mind was king, and any troubling emotion could be figured out.

Somehow he started going up the pole; it was a gradual thing, says Johnny, and where the line between sanity and insanity is he doesn't know. But the way he felt right before he went manic, "hypomanic," they call it—well, if he could feel that way again, he would never want anything else in the world.

Dexedrine, pneumonia, genes, his conflicts over Robin and our mother—Johnny cannot say which one caused what would happen next. But suddenly he was no longer calm, talking a little compulsively, overenergetic. One night he noticed his heart pounding—his pulse was 180—and he woke up one of his roommates and said, "I'm scared."

He saw the shrink the next day, which was Friday, and told him about the pulse, returning the bottle of Librium pills Leeman had prescribed earlier in the week. By Saturday night he was holding court in the dorm living room with his roommates and talking about how he suspected he was Jesus. Then Robin arrived.

After their breakup, they'd had an on-again, off-again relationship. When it was off there would be no communication between them, and then suddenly Robin would surface by letter or in person, and they'd be together, almost like before, in the way first love often connects, with the intensity of close family feeling. Johnny and she went into the bedroom to be alone. Johnny was calm—very rational, he thought—but Robin must have sensed some undercurrent, because after several minutes she said he was scaring her and left.

After Robin left, Johnny returned to the living room to continue his show for his roommates, but he noticed they weren't laughing. They brought him to Stillman, and a doctor ushered Johnny upstairs to the floor of his happy pneumonia days. He felt he was back in the cozy womb, this time in a truly private room, a single room with no other bed, and he called our father collect, Mr. Payne for Mr. Payne.

Johnny felt himself getting higher, but at the same time lower—a mixed state of depression and elation—and he was really scared. Whether the lows were brought on by the thorazine the nurses had given him, or were just the natural course of events, he doesn't know. He called his philosophy tutor to come visit, and when he arrived they discussed the *Bhagavad-Gita*, but Johnny noticed that the tutor was nervous. "Why are you fiddling with the zipper on your jacket?" Johnny demanded, and though the tutor denied it, Johnny noticed him licking his lips nervously, and Johnny shouted, "Don't go, don't go!" and then he just screamed the tutor's first name, but when he looked next the tutor was gone.

Soon after Johnny turned on the radio by his bed and instructed it to go faster or slower, and he found the radio *would* go faster or slower at his command, and he became frightened of his power. "Don't crucify me!" he shouted, at the same time pleading that Mary O'Hara, a pretty blond in his tutorial whom he barely knew, be sent to see him.

"I came here searching for truth, *veritas*, and Harvard doesn't know what *veritas* is!" Johnny raved, and then he loudly called out for people to put money into the pay telephones to call Harvard to complain—or, if they preferred, they could call Mary O'Hara; either one would do. Then he began to hallucinate the sounds of dozens, then hundreds, of dimes going into the phones as everyone called up Harvard and/or Mary O'Hara.

Johnny was screaming and ranting until the hospital aides strapped him to a gurney and told him he was being transferred. Then he became completely quiet, though he felt much worse. The mental pain was so bad that all Johnny wanted was to die; he couldn't understand how anyone could take this much pain, or why he was still alive. An ambulance drove him to Glenside Hospital in Jamaica Plain, where my father met him. Johnny had never felt worse in his life, but when my father asked, how are you? he responded with the automatic WASP reply: "Fine." For a few seconds the power of this hypocritical custom asserted itself, and Johnny *was* fine. It felt incredibly good to see someone he loved. But then he was back in his misery, and by the time his shrink arrived, he was ranting again.

Johnny remembers that he couldn't bear to look at Doctor Leeman and sat, bent over, in his chair. It was as if the shrink were God. Leeman said, "I like you just as much when you sit up," and Johnny raised a finger as if trying to say something, but he couldn't say it; he couldn't speak. Here he had been toying seriously with the idea that he was God, and then the God above him in the hierarchy had come in, and all Johnny could say was "I-I-I-I." After Leeman left Johnny reascended into his position of celestial authority, calling out to the other patients when told he was being transferred yet again, "Don't have shock treatment; feel good about yourself!" Then a couple of burly aides jumped him and took him to a padded cell, where they locked him up after injecting his butt with thorazine.

"I just want to go home to my mother!" Johnny screamed for about an hour, and then a woman came calmly into the room with a long letter from Robin, which said, essentially, "I love you, hang on," and suddenly Johnny was saved, no longer in terror. When the aides came to transfer him to McLean's, they let him sit up in the ambulance and inside, to his surprise, was our mother.

It was mid-March, the dreariest time in New England, but to Johnny everything suddenly looked gorgeous; the bare trees were bright with beauty. "I love you, Mom, I love you, Mom," Johnny said, though since adolescence he had called her "Mother."

"I know," my mother said, looking away, trying not to cry.

"Just take me home, Mom," Johnny said, "I'll be a good boy, I'll behave. Please just take me home."

July 1924

Bobby~Mattapoisett

18

*For holding up my trousers, I invented an inefficient, stringless
method which I considered picturesque and called Malayan. Each
morning before breakfast, I lay naked to the waist in my knotted
Malayan pajamas and received the first of my round-the-clock injec-
tions of chloropromazene: left shoulder, right shoulder, right but-
tock, left buttock. My blood become like melted lead. I could hardly
swallow my breakfast, because I so dreaded the weighted bending
down that would be necessary for making my bed . . .*
                                    —"NEAR THE UNBALANCED AQUARIUM"

NEAR THE UNBALANCED AQUARIUM" WAS WRITTEN ABOUT BOBBY'S BREAK-
down at Payne Whitney in 1954, but many of his subsequent breakdowns
were spent at McLean's. McLean's is a fancy mental hospital in Belmont,
Massachusetts, which has been around almost as long as my mother's
family has been needing it. Sometimes two members of the family are
there simultaneously, staring blankly at a wall without the other knowing
it. Bobby went there when he was living in Boston with Elizabeth, and
later when he came to Boston to teach, sometimes taking a cab from
McLean's to his classes. Bobby was a tortured, romantic figure to many of
the students he taught, and McLean's was a tortured, romantic place.

McLean's is set on rolling hills off the road of one of the short-cuts from Concord to Boston that I learned from my father. I get a cozy feeling whenever I pass McLean's. I learned to drive on the long, hilly drive around the buildings, careening off the pavement toward the wandering, wondering patients. There is a traffic light near the entrance to McLean's, and sometimes when it is red, I get an extra minute to sit there remembering.

I first drove through the gates of McLean's and up the long drive-way on the afternoon of my fourteenth birthday. That day I was wearing a lemon yellow shirtwaist dress with a matching yellow cardigan, and South Pacific tan stockings and white shoe-polished sneakers, following the vogue at Emerson Junior High. My father had taken me out for our annual father-daughter lunch in Boston, and he decided to swing by and visit Johnny on the way home.

My father remembers the day he was called to the phone on the floor of Jordan Marsh, the department store where he was selling mattresses to his least favorite buyer, and instantly knowing, with a sudden weight in his heart, that Johnny had broken down. After what he had been through with my mother, it was a terrible moment to realize he was to see it happen again with his son.

At thirteen I had known none of this. Johnny had been my idol. I had bragged about his accomplishments, undeterred by the glazed disinterest of my friends, ever since I could remember, but I seldom dared to interrupt him in the midst of his pursuits with my childish questions. I asked no questions when he came home from Harvard for Sunday dinner and sat at the table morose and withdrawn. I asked no questions when he stopped coming home for Sunday dinner. I don't even remember what we were told about Johnny's "nervous breakdown," but I do remember it was the last time for a long time I could enter a room without a crippling self-consciousness enveloping me. Suddenly my nose was too big; I had no idea where to put my arms when I walked. My confidence had been a reflection of Johnny's, the moon to his sun, and now I was lost in the dark sky.

On that overcast afternoon of my fourteenth birthday, I waited in the parking lot while my father went in to visit Johnny, wishing with all my might I could get a pair of knee-high leather boots like Halle Watson's. Forty-five minutes later my father reappeared, striding toward the car with a distracted look, his mouth pursed, then soon relaxing into the whistle that was his second nature. On the way home he told me once again about Beatrice Wells, the Chicago socialite who had loved him for a week in his senior year in college. Despite all that has happened in his life, when my father speaks of sadness, it is of the week after his graduation from college when he received the letter from Beatrice Wells saying she had changed her mind.

McLean's is where rich people go when they go crazy, and when you drive around the beautiful grounds it is easy to imagine all the lovely trust-funded people inside getting "rests," even when you know better. You think, *Well, if I have to be crazy, let it be here where it is quiet and the sun shines so warmly on the clean, glinting windows.* My brother Hunter was sixteen in 1965, and to him McLean's was like a rich kid's camp, a beautiful hotel, where you went if you were brilliant, where you might go to write, like Bobby Lowell.

The reality was somewhat different. Bobby didn't write at McLean's, he unwrote what he had already written. One time in the late 1950s my mother showed up at McLean's to find Bobby surrounded by sheets of paper. "I am just rewriting all my poetry!" he said, but when my mother looked, he had simply replaced each word with a synonym. "Oh, Bobby," my mother pleaded, "don't do this!" When she returned a few weeks later, Bobby had narrowed down the field to one poem. "I'm rewriting 'The Mills of the Kavanaughs' and it's going to be entirely different!" he said. By then he had descended from mania to depression and looked miserable, my mother said.

My mother's family provided the manic-depressive genes, but at least—for a while, anyway—it also provided the money for their proper care. My mother's inheritance from my grandmother allowed my parents to send Johnny to McLean's that first time in 1965, although later the well ran dry. In 1965 McLean's was still full of what Bobby called "Mayflower screwballs," former Harvard clubmen and all-American athletes wasting their lives and their trust funds year after year at McLean's.

McLean's not only looked like a country club, it even had a golf course. In 1965 the basic charge was forty dollars a day, Johnny remembered, which didn't include the cost of medication or therapy sessions. The cost went up to ninety dollars a day if you were on "Specials" ("Specials" meaning you had a nurse or aide with you twenty-four hours a day, as Johnny was his first three days, constantly referring to Jesus and his Dartmouth Bible).

The nurses at McLean's were warm and bubbly, giving Johnny his "Mommy fix." He was relieved that he was no longer at Harvard. He had a room to himself because his roommate was off skiing for a month while his parents continued to pay for the room. When the roommate finally returned, Johnny couldn't figure out why he was at McLean's. Most of the patients in fact seemed quite normal; you had no clue why half of them were incarcerated. Another example was Hernando, a South American with rich parents, who taught Johnny how to play pool. Hernando had a girlfriend on another ward, a crazier ward, who was on five-minute checks—meaning a nurse had to check on her every five minutes—and Hernando's claim to fame was that he managed to have sex with her between checks. Everyone thought that was so cool. You could figure out why some people were there, of course, like the lady they called the spacewoman who went up to Johnny and said, "You're very tall, but you're not a ladder," and then pulled up her dress to show she wasn't wearing underpants.

After three days Johnny was introduced to Dr. Mark W. Walter, the head of the ward, who took Johnny off Specials. For the next few weeks, Johnny played on the McLean's basketball team and felt pretty good, although he was nervous about the conference the doctors held three weeks after a patient's admission in which they pronounced their diagnosis. Johnny believed he was fine—although when another Harvard boy was admitted, maintaining he was Jesus, Johnny tried valiantly to calm him down, knowing in his heart that if anyone was Jesus, it was Johnny. Ultimately the McLean staff came to the conclusion that Johnny was a paranoid schizophrenic.

Not that anyone came to Johnny and delivered the news. At the time he was still seeing Doctor Leeman, and Johnny kept asking about his diagnosis. When Leeman reluctantly told him, he stressed that there had been a disagreement, that Leeman himself was convinced that Johnny was in no way schizophrenic, but rather manic depressive. (Leeman was right, it would turn out, but he had been overruled by the McLean staff.) To be judged a paranoid schizophrenic was a terrible sentence, but oddly, Johnny, who had been so agitated before, found that after he learned the diagnosis he no longer cared.

In a way the diagnosis confirmed Johnny's feeling that a real split existed within him. He found that he could act completely sane at the same time that he was in a crushing depression. He was very sociable with others in the hospital; he even gave a concert one night in the cafeteria. But then he would go to a softball game and think, *I can't stand this anymore.*

Johnny still had no clear idea as to the source of his depression, aside from the insight he'd had at Stillman concerning the repercussions from my mother's breakdown. Then one day, when he was talking to Doctor Walter about being in so much pain, Doctor Walter had looked at him and said, "Life *is* painful." This simple statement came to Johnny as something of a horrifying revelation. *No, it can't be, I don't want it to be!* he thought, but as the days passed he felt somewhat less isolated and alone. In a similar way Bobby had found solace during his breakdown at Payne Whitney in 1954: ". . . 'only man is miserable.' I told my doctor that this summed up my morals and my aesthetics" ("Near the Unbalanced Aquarium").

Bobby had broken down around the same time as Johnny, but instead of McLean's he had gone to the Institute for Living, a psychiatric hospital in Hartford. His mania had begun in November of 1964, following the successes of *For the Union Dead* and *The Old Glory*, an off-Broadway trilogy that would win five Obie Awards. He had held hands with Jean Stafford (with whom he had become friendly again) while watching a production of his translation of *Phèdre*, fallen (according to Jean) for the actress who played Phèdre, to no avail, and finally fallen for a Latvian dancer, Vija Vetra, whom he brought home for Elizabeth to meet (not a success) and then set up in an apartment on West Sixteenth Street. There, once again, he planned to begin a new life, though soon all agreed that this new life needed to commence at the Institute for Living, where he was driven in late January, sitting between Blair Clark and Vetra, holding hands with both, in a hired limousine.

When Bobby broke down the following December, he was driven from New York up to McLean's. This time he was smitten with Jackie Kennedy. Bobby had gained a certain amount of political fame by 1965: He had accepted Johnson's invitation to read at the White House Arts Festival, then declined in order to protest Johnson's bombing of Vietnam, and sent a copy of his refusal to the *New York Times*. The *Times* not only ran Bobby's letter on the front page, they ran another front-page story the next day about support for Bobby from twenty other famous writers.

Bobby's acquaintance with Jackie Kennedy deepened in 1965 after he dropped off a signed copy of *The Old Glory* at her apartment on the anniversary of her husband's death. Bobby's obsession with Jackie grew as his mania increased, a situation Mrs. Kennedy seemed to have in hand. The journalist Murray Kempton later told my husband a story Jackie had related to him about Bobby. "You know," Bobby had whispered to her one night during the opera, "Lyndon Johnson was responsible for your husband's death."

"That's right, Bobby," Jackie had answered calmly.

On the first day of December, Bobby appeared on the front page of *Woman's Wear Daily* escorting Jackie to a premiere. On December 6 Bobby was admitted to New York Hospital, and the next day to McLean's.

Johnny remembers running into Bobby once at McLean's, although he's not sure when. Johnny remembers saying hello, and thinking to himself, *Uh-oh, this guy is in his own category.* Bobby had the appearance of being completely elsewhere, Johnny said; he had the glow of a mystic. His body was sluggish, but his eyes glittered. "He was incredibly high and incredibly drugged, and even though he was talking to you, he was a million miles away."

The more depressed Johnny got at McLean's, the more privileges he was given. "I felt worse and worse, until I was suicidally depressed, and then they released me," Johnny said. All the time, as his depression worsened, he kept thinking how he wanted to return to Harvard by the next fall.

He was officially released in August; though he had lived the two previous months in an apartment in Cambridge while attending Harvard Summer School—during which time my parents still paid for his room at McLean's. Johnny had never considered suicide until, just before he was released, a patient from the ward killed himself. The man was an M.D. with two young children. He jumped fourteen stories from the hospital, where he was serving his residency. When he heard, Johnny returned for one night at McLean's. It was at this point, as he was about to be released for good, that the thought of suicide became obsessive, the word going around his mind like a mantra.

What kept him from killing himself was what his death would have done to our parents.

Harvard Summer School had not been a success; he had had trouble concentrating. When it came time for final exams, he turned in an almost empty exam book and failed the course. The dean suggested he take some more time off, so again Johnny returned to McLean's, this time as a day patient, but only for a few days. After the flunked exam, he had expected to feel despondent. His goal had always been to get back to Harvard, and now it was not going to happen. And yet, once he realized he was not going back, he felt relieved. The pressure was off him.

He moved home to Concord, where my parents urged him to get a job, believing it would make him feel better. He raked leaves for a friend of my mother's. He picked apples with itinerant workers. Then one day that winter Robin's mother read a classified ad seeking an editor of math textbooks for Houghton Mifflin. Johnny met with a little old lady who asked him about the "Medical leave of absence from Harvard" he had mentioned on the résumé that my parents, always so careful to be truthful, had helped him prepare. Johnny told the truth about his breakdown, certain it would ruin his chances, but to his surprise, he was hired.

When Johnny got sick my mother was told by the psychiatrists that her breakdown had caused Johnny's. Back in the 1960s manic depression wasn't supposed to be hereditary; every week my parents would drive into McLean's to learn what they had done wrong for fifty dollars an hour. But long before medical research confirmed the genetic link, we knew better, because everything in our family was due to heredity. Environment, of course, probably played a role as well, as it must in every case, but what made my mother and my brother's breakdowns tragic was their genetic base—the fact that they were probably inevitable.

I have always believed that genius is related to manic depression, but I no longer believe it is a wonderful gift, that the manic state provides divine inspiration for the artist as compensation for the suffering that will follow. Bobby didn't write poetry when he was high. He told my mother he wrote in depression because it saved him.

Bobby also believed his illness was genetic, a consequence of the interbreeding of his old New England family. His manic states didn't help him write, he told Ian Hamilton, they were just "dust in the blood."

"She wants to be home to share in the suffering of her brothers."

Alice Moulton

19

My brother Johnny had been the center of all our lives, and when he changed, we changed, too. At fourteen Hunter had sported slicked-back short hair and clothes from the Prep Shop; at seventeen, he grew his hair in a bush like Bob Dylan's, smoked unfiltered Camels, and accused the parents of being social climbers for asking him to mow the lawn. We had all burst with pride at Billy and Johnny's high school graduations; at Hunter's, which my parents forced him to attend, we sat miserably in the stands, the realization slowly dawning on us, as Hunter strolled forward to receive his diploma from the sedate Miss Kiplinger, that he was wearing nothing under his crimson gown. "Thankya, baby," Hunter said, leaning into the microphone.

That fall Hunter left for Kenyon College. There was only one reason Hunter had applied to Kenyon—he thought he could get in because he was related to Robert Lowell. He didn't want to go to college; he hadn't wanted to go to first grade. School had always come easily for Billy and Johnny, and later for me, but Hunter hated every minute of it.

Hunter, two years younger, had always been in Johnny's shadow. He would watch in stupefaction as Johnny arrived home from school

and laid out his books and the cereal boxes on the kitchen table and
settled down to read. Even Johnny's music seemed to come to him
with the same focused energy, a gift rather than an effort, as opposed
to the rest of us kids who blundered forth with our various instru-
ments. Hunter's school years would each begin with his teacher
exclaiming, "Oh, you're Johnny Payne's brother!" but the excitement
wouldn't last long.

Johnny's specter followed Hunter throughout those years. Where
Johnny's streak of independence had been seen as an exercise in the
democracy we live in, Hunter's petition for the students' right to do
the twist at dances was seen as an exercise in flippant defiance.
Hunter wasn't a rebel—yet—and defiance was the last thing on his
mind, but increasingly he began to feel like a marked man in the eyes
of his teachers.

One day Hunter's social studies class was given an essay test, the
first question of which was something like, "In the old days pioneers
went out West and tilled the land. What do today's pioneers do?" The
proper answer was supposed to be how we're exploring space, but
Hunter wrote what he thought was a reasonable reply: that modern
machinery had made agriculture very different, different indeed from
the days when pioneers had tilled the land with horse-drawn ploughs.
Hunter knew his response wasn't particularly brilliant, but he
believed he had acquitted himself well, considering the dullness of
the question. He was, in fact, feeling rather sanguine, until class the
following day. He entered the room to see Mr. Atlas—a huge, big-
headed man—looming over the class, holding a stack of tests.

"Here is an essay someone wrote," was his ominous greeting to
the students, and he then proceeded to read Hunter's effort, making
clear by his tone that he considered the writer to be an idiot.

"What is going on in the brain of this person?" Mr. Atlas asked
when he finished. "I'm not going to tell you who wrote it," he contin-
ued, as he deliberately handed the paper to Hunter. Another time Mr.
Atlas asked Hunter to see him after school and for two hours berated
him in the tiny teachers' office. "Why can't you be more like your
brother John who works, who tries, who cares!" demanded Mr. Atlas.
John was God. Well, Hunter knew that.

But then, three years later, God broke down. That summer Hunter, seventeen, was sent on a bicycle trip to Europe, where he became increasingly depressed and homesick. After he returned home, he asked the parents if he could see a psychiatrist.

Seeing a shrink was now in vogue because of Johnny and Bobby; Hunter thought his depression made him deep. *Perhaps I have genius in me after all*, he remembered thinking. My parents found him a shrink recommended by their shrink at McLean's, and twice a week Hunter sat in the guy's basement office not uttering a single word. Hunter didn't like him and he wasn't going to talk to someone he didn't respect, especially an adult. It never occurred to Hunter to tell my parents that he didn't like the shrink, and he continued to see him until he left for Kenyon.

Hunter had majored in girls in high school, the lesser subjects being guitar and smoking. Kenyon was a college of eight hundred men in a town of sixteen hundred, and the closest school with women was more than fifty miles away. Goddard, the coed hippie college where Hunter had also been accepted, would have been a more obvious choice, but, Hunter says, "I was a freight train going down the track, not knowing I was about to go off the side." He went to college because you were supposed to go to college, and Kenyon seemed to satisfy everybody. It also got him away from home.

Hunter remembered Johnny's freshman dorm in Harvard Yard, Wigglesworth, with its hardwood floors and living rooms with fireplaces, steeped in years of history. Williams had looked pretty much the same, and Hunter thought *that* was college. But at Kenyon he was given a twelve-by-twelve-foot room with two metal beds, two metal desks, one overhead light, a linoleum floor, and a nerdy roommate, compared to Hunter, with his long hair, guitar, and work shirts. Just about everyone at Kenyon looked like they came from Belmont Hill, the prep school of my family's best friends in Concord, the Potters, who were better off and better looking than we were, and always would be. But almost before he knew it, Hunter found himself linked up with one student who was different, and who, rather conveniently, was the son of a pharmacist.

The pharmacist's son took one look at Hunter and obviously thought, *Now here's a kid I can work with.* Within three minutes he had introduced Hunter to dexedrine in pure powder form. Hunter took a little on his tongue, and, well, he felt great, invincible, totally brilliant. He guessed it was like being manic, a state he had romanticized and longed to experience. He and the kid kept taking dex all during Orientation Week, which was also Fraternity Rush Week.

Hunter's idea of a fraternity was the beautiful house at Williams where Billy had belonged, but the Kenyon fraternities looked like hell, and the guys coming up to him were like the gung-ho people in high school he hated, not like Bobby Lowell at all. Hunter had imagined Kenyon as sort of a "deep" farm, with little Bobby Lowells sitting around being profound. All the other freshmen were jazzed by the idea of getting into a fraternity, and a small part of Hunter wanted it too. He longed to belong to a group, to be part even of the preppies. (We were almost the only children in the Concord Country Club to have gone to public school; as a result we hated the preppies on the one hand, but wanted them to like us on the other.) As Rush Week went by, the question became academic. Hunter and the pharmacist's son were looking weirder and weirder, and the rushers steered away. It was 1966, and Hunter and the pharmacist's son were the only hippies at Kenyon, pioneers in the field of drugs and dropping out.

For a while Hunter and the pharmacist's son formed their own little camp, staying up until three and sleeping until eleven. Classes began at eight in the morning. Within the first three days, Hunter had used up the maximum number of cuts allowed for the entire semester. He also became aware of the stigma of being seen with the pharmacist's son, because the kid was a real druggie, and the more he learned about him (after five days of speeding, he knew the kid's whole life), the more he didn't like him. Within a week the kid was gone, dropped out, and Hunter found no one else to be with.

By the Wednesday of the first week of classes, Hunter had seen enough of Kenyon. He was also terribly homesick. But when the president refused to refund his full tuition, he decided not to call my parents. He packed his bags and left for Delia Black's, a friend of his in

Philadelphia. Delia Black was a kind of goddess, gorgeous, brilliant, and offbeat, the daughter of family friends. She had been Johnny's girl-friend one summer. On his way to Kenyon, Hunter had stopped at Delia's apartment in Philadelphia, where she was living with a guy, playing house, and getting stoned. Earlier that summer Hunter had been indignant when he'd heard that Johnny had smoked pot, worrying that he would become hooked, but after his visit with Delia, when he had gotten stoned and ended up taking a bath with her, he had seen the light. College had certainly paled next to the perfect life at Delia Black's. After he left Kenyon, Hunter showed up on Delia's doorstep, but instead of welcoming him back, she, clearly nervous, traitorously called our parents from a pay phone down the street.

Hunter flew home the next day in complete disgrace, arriving at the gate at Logan only to hear (his plane had been late, and my parents had panicked) his name being broadcast ignominiously over the loudspeaker.

The following week, I received a postcard from my parents telling me that Hunter had come home from Kenyon. At the time I was living, a woman imprisoned, in a beautiful brick dorm overlooking hills of brilliant foliage at the Northfield School for Girls, where my parents had sent me to save me from my brothers. But the only thing I wanted to be saved from was the Northfield School for Girls. A few weeks later I too arrived home, having been referred by the school to a psychiatrist in Cambridge. "She wants to be home to share in the suffering of her brothers," Doctor King had told my mother. "The family failures," Hunter said as he greeted me on the back porch, putting his arm around me. The next day he drove me to the public high school, on his way to McLean's.

When Hunter had first arrived home from Kenyon, he'd spent his days smoking and watching TV, until my parents, at a loss, sent him to McLean's—where, for a lot of money, he smoked and watched TV. Hunter was a day patient at McLean's—he wasn't crazy as Johnny had been, just depressed he wasn't crazy. Even at McLean's, Hunter said, he couldn't pass muster, flunking the tests for craziness and being relegated to the outpatient group, though for most of the day he hung out with the inpatients, who were young and cool and included singers James and Livingston Taylor, who were just becoming famous in 1967.

On his first day Hunter met with Doctor Hopkins, the only shrink he ever liked, who prescribed him Stelazine, a drug that was meant to smooth a patient's highs and lows. The next day Hopkins asked him how he felt. "Great!" Hunter said, and suddenly realized he had given the wrong answer: They took him right off it.

At McLean's, Hunter remembers, nothing really happened. He made no particular friend among the outpatients, who were mostly older people. He had group therapy once a day and watched *The Fugitive* every day on TV at one o'clock. Besides these commitments, his time was free.

Bobby was admitted to McLean's on Christmas Day. Eight policemen had arrived, guns drawn, to take him away from Frank Parker's house in Cambridge. Bobby had gotten high that fall while teaching at Harvard and hanging around with a young Irish earl and his wife. Bobby had wanted to go to McLean's earlier, but he had been afraid that if he went, Harvard might not give him tenure. And so his mania grew with his drinking—vodka and milk at ten A.M.—and his obsession with Napoleon and making midnight calls to Bobby and Jackie Kennedy. When Bobby's Cambridge friends convened at Frank Parker's that Christmas morning, Bobby agreed to go to McLean's, but he panicked after the police arrived and took a swing at Frank Parker and threw a milk bottle at the police before docilely being led away. Bobby would be released from McLean's that February; in March he would turn fifty, and, for his crowd, that was pretty old. Many of the poets who had been his friends were already dead.

The last time Hunter had seen Bobby was two years before, at Billy's graduation from Williams. Hunter, my parents, and I had gone; Johnny was still in McLean's. It was a significant day for the family, the first of the children to graduate from college, and for all my parents knew it would be the *only* college graduation. The ceremony was held in the auditorium, and we couldn't see who was on the dais, and suddenly Bobby appeared to receive an honorary degree. After the ceremony we went to the president's house, and Billy explained to Bobby that he had just graduated, while Bobby looked at him blankly. Then Bobby turned to Hunter, with whom he had shared Thanksgiving dinner for the last ten years, and said, "Nice meeting you."

"Here we were at the first graduation of one of us from college," Hunter remembered, "and it turns out God is getting a degree and we're connected to God, and then God didn't know who the hell I was." The next day Bobby called my mother and apologized profusely for not having remembered Hunter or that Billy was at Williams.

But at McLean's Bobby sought out Hunter soon after Bobby was admitted. Hunter said Bobby looked much more crazy than Hunter had ever dreamed of being. Bobby was jittery; he had obviously been administered a battery of drugs, but they had failed to subdue his manic energy. Bobby seemed excited, but at the same time very anxious. He urged Hunter to come and talk with him any time he wanted. Hunter figured the chat would be about how Hunter could get better psychologically, and Hunter's reaction was that Bobby was not exactly in a position to advise him. But he felt that Bobby's offer of help was genuine and he was touched by it.

Hunter played on the McLean's basketball team, such as it was, and one day my parents brought Bobby with them to watch a game. Their opponent that day was Belmont Hill, the big jock prep school, the other side of the coin, so to speak, and the McLean's team—all smokers, in bedraggled pants, without uniforms, on every kind of drug known to man, prescription and nonprescription—meandered one by one onto the court.

"We didn't have any drills, we didn't know where to go, we didn't even have regular practices," said Hunter. "We just went out and tried to make the lay-ups look good." They were aging hippies—some of them had been at McLean's as long as seven years—pasty white, crooked, and bent over. "When you're depressed you can't hold your spine up," said Hunter. "The Belmont Hill kids' spines were completely straight."

Out on the court bounced the preps, a streak of color, in perfect warm-up suits, every one of them ten feet tall, the picture of all-

American vigor, with perfectly coiffed short hair (in those days hair told the whole story), and it was the longhairs versus the shorthairs, the crazies versus the have-it-togethers.

The worst part, said Hunter, was that during the game, knowing they were drubbing them, the golden ones held back, to be kind, but also because they were a little scared of the crazies. For Belmont Hill it wasn't a real game; it was a charity event, done as community service.

It was the Potters versus the Paynes all over again—with Hunter on the wrong side. He couldn't cut it as a prep for the parents, and he couldn't cut it as a fellow sufferer for Bobby. "I wanted so much to be as cool as Bobby Lowell; I wanted so much to earn his respect; but here I was playing this dumb game." Hunter had been hoping he was nuts; being nuts relieved you of responsibility because it put you in the genius boat with Bobby and Johnny. But try as he might, Hunter just couldn't seem to measure up. As his ball rounded the hoop and went into the basket, he thought, *I'm just not brilliant enough to be crazy.*

At the end of the game, Hunter said, Bobby for once was at a loss for words, though he did mumble that Hunter had played a good game. Afterward the parents, Hunter, and Bobby walked around the grounds. Bobby seemed down, though better than he'd been the week before when Hunter had run into him again and hadn't been sure that Bobby had recognized him or was even capable of talking. The day of the game he seemed more human. What Hunter didn't realize was that Bobby would have understood his feeling of inadequacy as they were clobbered by Belmont Hill. Later Bobby would write about the golden boys at St. Mark's School who had ridiculed him:

> but who could break them,
> they were so many,
> rich, smooth and loved?
> ("St. Mark's, 1933")

Hunter was at McLean's and going nowhere, and then my father mentioned that my mother needed an operation, that it was not a big deal, the doctors were 98 percent certain she was going to be all right. As a rule Hunter would return from McLean's in the midafternoon to smoke cigarettes in the playroom and eat frozen Sara Lee cakes charged to the parents, and I would sit with him silently, trying to be profound. But one afternoon Hunter was lounging alone in his den of pot and ginger ale, when he looked up from the couch to see my father walk in, in tears, completely broken down. He had never seen his father in tears before. "They had to remove your mother's breast," my father said. "She doesn't even know yet because she's still under the anesthetic."

Somehow the power of the moment shocked Hunter out of his lethargy; for once he could take a look from the outside and say to himself, *What the hell am I doing?* Within minutes he called up a girl-friend's mother who worked at WGBH, the public television station, and before five that day he was in her office, saying that he wanted to be a cameraman and that he would take any job available. The next morning he went into Cambridge to work in the mailroom of WGBH.

Hunter never set foot in McLean's again.

Arthur Winslow and his daughter Sarah.
"My father knew how to bring up his children,"
Aunt Sarah would say, looking pointedly at my mother.

20

Bᴏʙʙʏ ᴍᴀᴅᴇ ǫᴜɪᴛᴇ ᴀ ꜰᴜss ᴏᴠᴇʀ ᴍᴇ ᴀꜰᴛᴇʀ ᴍʏ ᴏᴘᴇʀᴀᴛɪᴏɴ," ᴍʏ ᴍᴏᴛʜᴇʀ said. He came out to Concord a day or two after her mastectomy and sat with her in Emerson Hospital. Three other patients shared my mother's room. When my father visited, he would draw the white curtain around the bed, desperate for even the illusion of privacy, and when Bobby came they couldn't really talk, but it had never mattered to Bobby what he and my mother talked about. "Bobby was never critical," my mother said. "He had a kind of spiritual liaison with you, the rest of what you thought wasn't important."

My mother and Bobby had never had much in common, but in 1968 they shared a similar passion: They were against the war in Vietnam, and they refused to keep this information from the family. "Well, there goes the inheritance," I couldn't help thinking one night, as my mother argued vociferously, if not always logically, with Uncle Cot and Aunt Sarah. The airing of my mother's views to Uncle Cot and Aunt Sarah didn't change their opinions, and it certainly drove the fatal wedge between them and us, but it was the right thing for my mother to have done. Bobby had been independent from the beginning—he had known almost from the cradle that the life he had been born into was unjust—but while my mother's independence came late, it gave her a belief in herself she had never possessed and saved her life at a time when she had nearly lost it.

Nothing bad had happened to Aunt Sarah since 1922 when her brother, Devereux, died, and nothing bad to Uncle Cot since the same period, when he lost his wife and father. From the 1920s on it was as if their purpose had been to insulate themselves from any of the pain that accompanies even the most privileged life. The most fortunate person in the world, the minute his first child is born, opens himself up, forever, to an infinite possibility of suffering. No parent can emerge unscathed, but Uncle Cot and Aunt Sarah had been careful to marry only after it was too late to become parents. Together they had led a life so splendidly regular, so safe from unwanted change, that they could complacently view the struggles of the lives passing below them with an unchallenged supremacy. But the Vietnam War and the protests that grew up around it ended their tranquillity. Their life and everything it was based on was attacked—and attacked at home.

Bobby was out of sight, in New York, and then he had always been "a trial," but my mother's treachery took the Cottings by surprise. She was Aunt Sarah's pet; she even looked like a young Aunt Sarah, though on a higher plane. Even at age seventy-nine, my mother cannot escape the defining impression of her beauty. The power of my mother's looks can never be overemphasized. They were a large part of the reason she had become Uncle Cot's and Aunt Sarah's favorite among the family; but her looks also imprisoned her. They implied a docile femininity and led to the expectation that she would remain as girlish and flirtatiously silly as Aunt Sarah had remained for seventy years. But in the early 1960s my mother began to rebel.

"It was not planned that I become a democrat," my mother said, "but I always had in me this feeling of fairness." Aside from her long political arguments with Aunt Sarah and Uncle Cot—which began with my mother voting for Kennedy in 1960—my mother was growing independent in other ways as well. In 1960 Uncle Cot had not quite given up on our family, had not yet turned to the museums and schools to continue his name. In fact, though over seventy, he began to hunger for the family he had been afraid to have, and he tried to obtain it, pitifully, the only way he knew how: by buying it. When my parents moved to Concord from New Haven, Uncle Cot began offering them houses on his estates. He had already inherited several houses in Manchester, and he wanted to give my mother "the little red house," which had maid's quarters and was not so little, around the corner from the Cottings' sweeping residence on Harbor Street. My parents were supposed to move from Concord to live in the little red house full-time, except for winter weekends when they were invited to inhabit a house on the farm. Even if my parents had wanted to abandon their independence and leave Concord, where they were happier than in any other place they had ever lived, they couldn't have afforded to live in Manchester. They would have been expected to belong to three clubs, which they couldn't afford—just as my mother couldn't afford the Chilton Club in Boston, even after Aunt Sarah offered to pay her initiation fee, because of the cost of the yearly dues. It was a concept Aunt Sarah and Uncle Cot could not understand.

During this time Uncle Cot and Aunt Sarah also came up with the bizarre idea of legally adopting my first cousin Kit. It never seemed to have occurred to them that Kit already had a perfectly good set of parents, who wouldn't have dreamed of giving him up. My mother's sister Allie was so devoted a mother that she once traveled with fifty of her children's pets (some fish) in the car from New York to Maine for a family vacation, and her husband, Uncle Everard, so successful he ran CBS every summer when William Paley went away, was also so devoted a parent that he left network meetings to attend guinea-pig birthday parties. Kit was golden haired, intelligent, and ingenuously charming, and at age twelve he spent a few weeks in Manchester with the Cottings, where he proved to be very knowledgeable about boats. The rest of us were bored and queasy on "the boat," but Kit couldn't get enough of it. His enthusiasm touched Uncle Cot's heart in a way that none of our reactions ever had. Aunt Sarah behaved like Auntie Mame around Kit, we joked, but the real surprise was that it was Uncle Cot, so careful never to show emotion, who came up with the idea of Kit's adoption. (Uncle Cot's feelings were so strong they would survive Kit's transformation at Harvard into a diehard member of SDS. Even after Kit picketed his Harvard graduation, Uncle Cot wrote him a letter offering him a job. And yet the funny thing is, Uncle Cot's faith was well placed: Kit later became just the kind of adventurous businessman Uncle Cot admired—and Kit retained his love for boats.)

Uncle Cot and Aunt Sarah were amazed when Kit's parents categorically refused the honor of giving up their child. "We offered to *adopt* him!" Aunt Sarah and Uncle Cot would gasp, still in shock years later. The theory being, evidently, that while Kit's parents were rich, compared to my family, anyway, the Cottings were far richer. For a short while after the rejected adoption plan, my mother said, the Cottings tried to like my brother Hunter, but it didn't take.

In those days Aunt Sarah was still sweet, though sometimes she would get very cross. The problem was largely physical, it would turn out: a slow-growing dementia had already begun that would get worse over the next thirty years. But not all of Aunt Sarah's anger was rooted in dementia. She had built up a lifetime of silent resentment that had its beginning in her relationship with her controlling father. Even back in 1936, when my mother had stayed with Aunt Sarah during her debutante season, Aunt Sarah would be very, very quiet now and then, and my mother had learned to leave her alone. But never had Aunt Sarah been mean. "She was darling to me during my breakdown," my mother said, and for a long time afterwards she continued to be generous and loving.

The first time my mother noticed meanness in Aunt Sarah was in the late 1950s, when we had moved from New Haven to Concord, and Aunt Sarah had, in front of its previous owner, cast aspersions on our new house, which was in bad repair and not nearly as pretty as our house on the brook in Connecticut. A few years later when Johnny was still in high school, we arrived a few minutes late for Thanksgiving dinner, because we children wanted to see the end of the Concord High game against our Revolutionary rival, Lexington High. My mother was upset even before we got there, caught as she was between Aunt Sarah and her children. When we arrived Aunt Sarah ignored us from her seat at the head of the table, where dinner had been pointedly started without us, referring to my mother only as "she," as Aunt Sarah contrasted my mother with her own father, Arthur Winslow, whom in real life she had hated.

"*My* father knew how to bring up *his* children," Aunt Sarah waxed, in a paroxysm of historical revisionism. "Home life, that's what he believed in. Disciplined home life. Breakfast at 8:00, luncheon at 1:00, dinner at 7:00 sharp. Cook had the food on the table, and if you were late, you went without, that's what you did, he didn't care if you were dead on the highway, he started without you. My father *loved* his children."

In the mid-sixties my mother was still somewhat in favor with Aunt Sarah, who reserved the greater part of her venom for the Ralph Lowells (the richer side of Bobby's greater family.) Ralph Lowell was a prominent philanthropic figure in Boston, known for starting WGBH, the local public television station. "While Uncle Cot did things quietly, Ralph was a public figure," my mother says, "very forward looking, though he never did learn to drive a car." Ralph Lowell was always being honored for everything he did; he always made a splash, as opposed to Uncle Cot, who had given a substantial building to Harvard without causing a ripple. This drove Aunt Sarah crazy, even though Uncle Cot himself hadn't wanted the attention. (The family didn't pay it much mind, either. Kit, the former-adoptee-candidate-turned-Communist, told me Uncle Cot had given the building because he needed a tax deduction.)

Aunt Sarah had been making nasty remarks about the Ralph Lowells for years. By 1964, when my grandmother Alice died, relations with the Lowells were so strained that without my mother's hard-pressed intervention, Aunt Sarah would not have been invited to the reception following the funeral, hosted by my great-uncle Gus and his wife, who happened to be Ralph Lowell's sister. (My family is always marrying Lowells, beefing up the manic-depressive gene.) My aunt Sarah was of course my grandmother's sister-in-law, wife of her beloved Devereux.

A year or so later my mother witnessed a skirmish between Aunt Sarah and Mrs. Ralph Lowell during Harvard commencement. My mother accompanied Aunt Sarah to the ceremony, in which Cot was marching with his class. More to the point for my mother, both

Martha Graham, my mother's dance teacher for two years at the Neighborhood Playhouse, and Bobby were receiving honorary degrees. My mother and Aunt Sarah proceeded to Harvard Yard, where they were ushered to a choice row of seats. As the sections were arranged by Harvard class, Aunt Sarah knew just about everyone who came to be seated. She would turn to each person as she arrived and announce, "You know, Bobby is going to get an honorary degree today." Then my mother saw Mrs. Ralph Lowell sailing down the aisle. (Ralph was in the same class as Uncle Cot, a year ahead of Joe Kennedy.) Mrs. Ralph Lowell was statuesque, still quite pretty, and very well dressed. That day she was wearing a lightweight chiffon hat, with a huge brim, and she took her seat directly in front of my mother and Aunt Sarah. Aunt Sarah leaned forward and said, "Charlotte [Mrs. Lowell's name happened to be the same as Bobby's mother's], Bobby is going to get an honorary degree today," and Mrs. Ralph Lowell replied, haughtily, "You know, Sarah, when Ralph got an honorary degree, *we* kept quiet about it until it was announced," implying that Aunt Sarah's boast was in the very worst of taste. After that, whenever anybody else came to be seated, Aunt Sarah would lean over and say, "Bobby is getting an honorary degree today—he's absolutely *no* relation to Ralph." And each time my mother would see the round brim of Mrs. Ralph Lowell's gossamer hat shimmer just a little.

By 1968 my mother and father were licking envelopes for Eugene McCarthy and switching from the Episcopal church in Concord to the Unitarian church, which was so liberal you didn't have to go. It was wonderful to behold the transformation in my mother, who had always been told she was beautiful but dumb. She read scholarly books and debated politics at cocktail parties and voiced opinions about the world at large. The Vietnam War seemed to give her a confidence in her intellect she had never had before, and the loss of her breast seemed to make her even braver.

By then, too, after Yammy's death, we were relatively affluent. Gone were the margarine years. We ate butter full-time; we even took the European tour—if not quite the breezy trust-funded tour of my great-grandparents' era about which Bobby wrote so wistfully. (As I look at my aunt Sarah's young, disgruntled face as she feeds the pigeons with her parents in St. Mark's Square, however, I cannot help but think of my own indignant refusal to visit Pompeii because I had to blow-dry my hair.)

In response to my parents' liberalism, I announced that I was "a benevolent monarchist." I was a junior in high school in 1967 and 1968, and from that lofty position I looked down on my mother's effort to educate herself; meanwhile Robert Lowell, who was perhaps *a shade* more knowledgeable than I, had no contempt for my mother's intellectual aspirations. ("Jackie," he would insist when my mother voiced her own self-doubt, "you *are* an intellectual.") That fall Bobby traveled the country with Eugene McCarthy, though at Thanksgiving I noticed that it was Robert Kennedy that got his eyes to shine. Bobby liked McCarthy enormously as a person, but it was Kennedy who appealed to him as president, mostly for the toughness of character that McCarthy lacked. "Of course McCarthy could never *be* president," Bobby would say casually over the mock turtle soup that inevitably began each Thanksgiving dinner (and always brought to my mind the softening shells of the poor little turtles I had buried every week in our backyard), as if such an idea were an extraordinary one. (Later I read that McCarthy aides would always groan when he was left alone with Bobby before an appearance, watching in dismay as their candidate emerged from the limousine, liquidly lyrical, wrecked with spirits and Shakespeare.)

"Bobby became quite rabid against the war in Vietnam," my mother said, but while Bobby had bravely protested the war early on to the world at large (and Harvard, his employer, in particular), I don't remember him ever bringing up the subject with Aunt Sarah and Uncle Cot. It was Elizabeth Hardwick who stayed up late arguing with Uncle Cot.

Elizabeth never got in trouble with the family, who always considered her "the real wife," but sometimes her honesty got her in trouble with others. One time Bobby got my mother tickets to a Lillian Hellman play, and my parents drove into Manhattan, dressed to the nines, only to be told flatly at the door that the tickets were not there.

They had been rescinded, it turned out, because Elizabeth had been on the radio the night before and had mentioned, in rather strong language, that Lillian wasn't really a very nice person.

In the 1960s Bobby seemed to get away with just about everything with Aunt Sarah. But my mother, who was living the most regular, exemplary life, was increasingly in the doghouse with her aunt, who had launched her attack when my mother had been at her most vulnerable—when her son's troubles began. Aunt Sarah had been irked by my mother's growing independence, but by the mid-sixties, after Johnny had been at McLean's, she became brutal in a way my mother had never thought possible. And she knew the way to hurt my mother was through her children. "Are you normal yet, are you normal yet?" Aunt Sarah would say, poking her head under Johnny and Hunter's shaggy manes. Then she would talk loudly about the So-and-sos, who, when their children had misbehaved, had simply disowned them.

*As I look at my aunt Sarah's young, disgruntled face as she feeds the pigeons
with her parents in St. Mark's Square, I cannot help but think of
my own indignant refusal to visit Pompeii because I had to blow-dry my hair.*

*"If you were sensible," Aunt Sarah would say to my mother,
"you'd disown your children."*

Scout.

Me, smoking.

21

All our adult lives my parents have hoped and prayed that each of us children would stick to the same job, forever and ever, whether we liked it or not. "We've lived through the depression," they say, "and we know." Sometimes, when Charlie and I are borrowing from the bank to go on vacation so our children won't know we're broke, I think my parents may have had a point. But it's not surprising that we didn't listen.

In 1969, the Simmons Mattress Company transferred my father to Westchester County, New York, in order to give the Boston territory to a younger man. My father had worked for the company for twenty-five years and was nearing retirement, and he did not want to leave Concord. But when he was offered a job teaching at the high school, he turned it down, unable to face a career change at that point in his life. Though they struggled to put a bright face on it, the prospective move was devastating to my parents. My father arrived home one evening with a face swollen with tears after bidding farewell to the man at the liquor store. Nevertheless my father's replacement at the Simmons Company, Mr. Raimondo, was invited to dinner at the house. "It's not *his* fault, after all," my mother said, as we set the table in the dining room that overlooked the little willow tree we always optimistically replaced each spring after it was killed by the cold New England winter.

Still, relatively speaking, the spring of 1969 was a good time for us. Billy, out of graduate school, was to be married that summer to a girl from a lovely family of similar background (meaning there would be liquor at the wedding). Johnny, who had been depressed for four years, was suddenly energized, having recently recorded "Astral Weeks" in New York City with Van Morrison. Hunter had been found unfit for military service, a kind of accomplishment in this era, though one achieved partially by accident. Hunter, remembering a high school textbook that said that a typical heterosexual had a complement of heterosexual and homosexual tendencies, had dutifully checked off "yes" next to the question, "Do you have any homosexual tendencies?" I had been accepted by Harvard, and Johnny, back in Cambridge, had decided to return there with me in the fall. It was going to be wonderful.

Instead, that September, my parents and I drove up from Westchester a day early for my Freshman Orientation to kidnap Johnny and take him to Mass. Mental Health.

One sign of the decline of the WASP ruling class is that they can no longer afford a nice place in which to have their breakdowns. In 1969 my parents could no longer afford McLean's. They had spent thousands of dollars there in 1965, and now the apparent, horrible, but unspoken worry was that Johnny's mental illness was not necessarily ever going to be cured. Mass. Mental Health was a teaching hospital for Harvard Medical School, but it was an inner-city institution and, from my sheltered Concord point of view, within a slum neighborhood. Instead of rolling hills shaded by ancient trees, only a tiny cement courtyard was provided for the patients' exercise. The rest of the time the patients congregated in a brightly lit, overheated room, "the Day Room," that was as seedy as a bus station at midnight. As we glanced with sinking hearts at the fat woman selling candy at the door and the drugged-up patients slowly smoking cigarettes, my mother said maybe being in Mass. Mental instead of McLean's would get Johnny well quicker.

.   .   .

Mass. Mental did not cure Johnny, but it certainly cured the rest of us of any lingering thoughts we might have harbored about the romance of mental illness. Mass. Mental was a no-frills hospital, where people from the street could get a free breakdown, and the drugged despair of its numerous inmates was more horrifying than the frenzy of *The Snakepit*. Instead of quiet young men who seemed troubled, there were lots of truly crazy people of all ages crowded into one common room. After visiting Johnny in Mass. Mental, Hunter remembers every time getting into his Volkswagen Bug and breaking down uncontrollably. I do not know if the patients at McLean's felt the same despair as the people who sat in the Day Room of Mass. Mental Health—Mass. Mental isn't around anymore, and I heard a rumor recently that McLean's was slated to become a condominium complex—but the despair *was* different for the people who visited. I took the Green Line subway a hundred times to Mass. Mental my freshman year at college, and while my memory of it is vivid, the only time I have ever been back was one night at 2:00 A.M. when I was twenty-three, drunk and alone during a flash flood in Boston and hopelessly lost, and I looked up and saw Mass. Mental Health looming over me. Suddenly sober, I got out of there like a bat out of hell.

The fall of my freshman year, Bobby telephoned to ask if I wanted to go to dinner with him at Aunt Sarah's. He was teaching as usual that semester at Harvard, living at Quincy House. He arrived by taxi, and when he saw me in the foyer of my Radcliffe dorm, he smiled as if he'd never seen me before. "You look just like Mary Devereux," he said, referring to my beautiful first cousin, who had grown up in New York City. Everyone knew Bobby and Elizabeth adored Mary Devereux, she was so intellectual, so ethereal and charming, with her milky white heart-shaped face like a character in a Victorian novel, and curling lashes, dark brows, red-brown hair, and a soft, breathy way of talking that was mesmerizing. "Mary Devereux is simply *brilliant*," everybody always said.

Many years later Mary Devereux told me how desperate she had been as a young teenager to live up to Bobby's expectations, showing

him her copy of Camus's *The Rebel*, the significant passages under-
lined with cigarette burns to show him that she was a sophisticated
smoker and therefore a person with whom Bobby could communi-
cate. Bobby was very kind and humble, Mary Devereux said, and
always took her literary endeavors seriously, even when, at age thir-
teen, she was first invited to Bobby and Elizabeth's apartment in New
York to read poetry with him. Before the visit Bobby had asked her if
she had written any poetry, and Mary Devereux, desperate to please,
had replied enthusiastically that she had written quite a lot. Then to
her horror she was asked to bring her poems with her. After a frantic
survey of her oeuvre, consisting of a handful of lines about putting
her dolls in the closet for good and hearing them cry through the
closet door, Mary Devereux grabbed a twenty-five-page manuscript
about despair and industrial waste and teenage romance, written by a
rather advanced girl she had met at the French-speaking camp in Bar
Harbor, Maine, where everybody had spoken English all the time and
learned nothing but how to smoke.

When Mary Devereux arrived at the Lowells' apartment, Eliza-
beth had politely absented herself, and Bobby had read his young
cousin some of his translations of Valéry, Baudelaire, Verlaine, and
Racine. Bobby loved trying out his latest poetry on people and, think-
ing of the French camp, asked Mary Devereux what she thought of
his translation of French idiom. Mary Devereux was full of praises
because, of course, she had understood nothing. Then they moved
on to the subject of Mary Devereux wanting to become a poetess.
Bobby was very encouraging, until Mary Devereux began reading her
friend's run-on haiku about the sun shining above rusted tin cans
spotted with blood, mingled with lost illusions of love. Bringing a
rather quick halt to her awkward reading, Bobby gently probed as to
meaning: how the images related to the subject, why the blood, and
even what it was she particularly wanted to say about love. At thir-
teen Mary Devereux was prepubescent and still very naive—for all
she knew, she realized later, the poem was filled with some kind of
sexual imagery—and had not the least idea what the poem was
about. She sat in stunned silence. Apparently it never occurred to
Bobby that the piece was not her own, Mary Devereux said, though

he did give her the helpful hint that it was a good idea to have some thought about meaning when you wrote a poem. (Walking forlornly home from this visit, Mary Devereux realized that her friend's poetry had not been very good, and vowed to learn to write truly great poetry to win her cousin's favor. A few years later she won an honorable mention in a poetry contest in the *Atlantic Monthly*.)

I looked nothing like Mary Devereux. This fact was finally hammered home during my senior year in college when a boyfriend, who I had once thought was complimenting me when he called me tall and blond, finally informed me that he liked girls short and dark. Taking one look at Mary Devereux he had said, "Now, that's my type." We don't look alike, and yet whenever I see my cousin after an interval of several years, we stare at each other like Hayley Mills in *The Parent Trap*. Maybe that night I looked like Mary Devereux in some way. In those days my looks were constantly changing. The last time I had seen Bobby, he read us his poem about Aunt Sarah in the living room at Concord, and I weighed 112 pounds, with the greenish pallor of the anorexic. Now, ten months later, I was pink and creamy, radiant with apparent health, having piled on ten pounds' worth of doughnuts and ice cream sandwiches in the space of one month.

Whether this overeating was because I was happy or sad it is hard to say. I'd put my brother in the mental hospital my first day of college and then, as a remedy, fallen wildly in love with an intense scrap of a boy I met doing acting exercises at the Loeb Theatre. With great pride a few weeks earlier, I had taken the boy to dinner at Aunt Sarah's, where one dressed for dinner: Uncle Cot in black patent leather pumps, me in some ridiculous concoction dug out of the squalor of my college room, and my new boyfriend in a fifties suit bought at Goodwill for the occasion. There my boyfriend from California had been asked, "Who *does* Sally look like? She doesn't look like a Devereux, and she doesn't look like a Winslow!" to his total stupefaction.

I do not know if Bobby even knew that Johnny was in the hospital; I don't think I said one word about it that night, though clearly I was not reticent on the topic of my new boyfriend. "Young Lochinvar," Bobby called him, greatly interested and amused by the subject. "You must invite Young Lochinvar to Thanksgiving dinner, Aunt Sarah," he said sitting next to her beneath the portrait by John Single-ton Copley (who had married a Winslow) of our ancestor, Sarah Waldo. I still have the creased picture of me at age six, bony and embarrassed in my helmet hair, standing next to Aunt Sarah under the Copley portrait, which had been passed down in the family from a Sarah to a Sarah for generations—until it was decided I didn't have a proper wall to hang it on. Recently I paid seven dollars and fifty cents to view the portrait at the Peabody Essex Museum, where it was donated under Uncle Cot's name.

Aunt Sarah and Bobby bantered flirtatiously that night. He seemed totally at ease with her, as opposed to my mother who would sit with a tightening mouth whenever invited there, as Aunt Sarah swung into the refrain, "If you were sensible, you'd disown your chil-dren." But there was no tension that night; Bobby's garrulity took the heat off me to think of something to say across the years to my great-aunt and uncle. Aunt Sarah told her usual stories charmingly while Bobby listened appreciatively, usually contradicting her, but getting away with it every time. Aunt Sarah did invite Young Lochinvar to Thanksgiving dinner—the first time any boyfriend had been invited—but by then he was in New York with his high school girl-friend. Instead of Thanksgiving at Aunt Sarah's farm, Hunter and I tossed a football around in the asphalt courtyard of Mass. Mental while Johnny stood watching.

From time to time that night Bobby would look at me wonder-ingly, as if surprised that I *wasn't* Mary Devereux. Later my cousin told me how excited she had always been when Bobby came to visit at her family's apartment, which he did regularly when he was living in New York in the 1960s, often at the beginning of a manic phase. Once he had taken her and a favorite high school teacher to meet T. S. Eliot, who had been polite and flattered that someone so young took an interest in his poetry ("Thank goodness he didn't ask me to discourse on *The Waste Land*," Mary Devereux said.) Later, when she reached her twenties, Bobby and Elizabeth started setting her up on dates with intellectuals and writers. "They had such high hopes for me, and I know I disappointed them," Mary Devereux told me, long after—emotionally and financially exhausted—she abandoned her Ph.D. program and took a job in business,

After dinner Bobby took me over to see his suite at Quincy House. It was early; dinners with Aunt Sarah ended by 9:45 A.M. Bobby showed me me around the suite with a bashful pride, though there wasn't much to see, just a kind of disheveled impersonal mess in two hideously modern, cold rooms of cinderblock and bright red paint. I couldn't think of a single interesting thing to say. After a few awkward moments he took me home in another taxi, and at the door he kissed me (chastely) on the mouth.

My parents had been living in Katonah, New York, since the summer, in a large reconverted barn with an enormous playroom on the second floor, though none of us lived at home anymore. When my mother came up from Westchester to visit Johnny that fall, she stayed with Aunt Sarah at 410 Beacon Street, in the third-floor guest room with two single beds and more cold floor than carpet. There, after a grueling dinner, my mother cried herself to sleep.

Besides politics and the state of my mother's children, Aunt Sarah was also mad at my mother about money. Uncle Cot managed the small amount of money left of my mother's inheritance, and as it yielded very little, maybe a few thousand dollars a year, my mother would sometimes have to ask Uncle Cot to sell some stocks to pay a bill. This was shocking in itself to Uncle Cot—the selling of capital was simply incomprehensible to someone who had always had so much money—but even worse, for a short time my mother and father took the money away from Uncle Cot to invest themselves, on the theory that surely they could make more interest than Uncle Cot, who had invested it very conservatively. The experiment was a failure—my parents in fact lost a small amount of money—and the capital was returned to Uncle Cot's safekeeping with due humility. Aunt Sarah never forgot it. One time I arrived for dinner, and she glided down the stairs like a girl of twenty, scornfully remarking, "You know your mother's money is just a tiny *nut* compared to the money Uncle Cot's used to managing."

In this period, my mother says, Aunt Sarah always sat my mother and father next to this "awful couple" who had pushed their way into Aunt Sarah and Uncle Cot's lives, plying them with flattery in order to get them to leave their possessions to a local museum. It was as if the vultures had sniffed the decline in Uncle Cot's affection for the family and begun swooping in. "Aunt Sarah loved compliments and she was not getting them from me at this point," my mother said. The couple were very chummy with Aunt Sarah and Uncle Cot and came to dinner often, but then they got a little *too* familiar. "We've arranged a wonderful trip to Honolulu and Sarah and Cot are going to come with us!" they announced joyfully one night. But Aunt Sarah and Uncle Cot had no intention of going on a trip with anyone; the only trip they ever took outside the forty-five miles that circumscribed their houses was the annual six-week trip to their club in Sarasota, Florida. Aunt Sarah had loved Europe when she had traveled there as a young woman, but after marrying Cot I do not believe she ever went out of the country again. She certainly wasn't going to Hawaii. The invitation marked the end of her relations with the cloying couple.

But in the fall of 1969 those two were very much in their ascendancy, in juxtaposition to my mother, who sank lower and lower as she argued over dinner with Uncle Cot about politics. "I've *never* seen anything like it!" Aunt Sarah said in a loud voice, ostensibly to my father, but really to the assembled company, "I don't see how you can stand her, Bill; no *wonder* she had a nervous breakdown!"

In early 1970 Hunter returned to Cambridge from Colorado, where he had gone with a girl Johnny once had a crush on, though the girl had only liked Johnny as a friend. Hunter and the girl had planned to join the idyllic life the girl's sister was living in the mountains of Colorado, an idyll that consisted of sharing, in the middle of winter, a one-room tarpaper shack with five people, who slept in lofts dug out of the ceiling and did a lot of drugs and drinking: means of survival no longer open to Hunter, who had switched from marijuana to transcendental meditation after my mother's operation. At the end of three months Hunter was back in Cambridge, single again. In those days all his girlfriends seemed to last three months.

Depressed and wanting terribly to pay back the money he had borrowed to get to Colorado, Hunter took a job driving a cab. On his return to Cambridge, he had put himself on a cleansing macrobiotic diet consisting primarily of brown rice, and, having gone to bed with his last cigarette still smoldering in the ashtray, he would get up at 5 A.M. to cook his breakfast, lunch, and dinner of rice, which would simmer quietly while he meditated. Then, dressed entirely in white, he would pack the breakfast and lunch in glass jars and take them with him, along with his Camel cigarettes, to wait for his cab. As a new cab driver he was the last to get a cab, and rarely would he be given a decent automobile.

After several months of driving twelve hours a day and eating brown rice, Hunter was invited to help a fellow meditator make a movie about the Maharishi. Though he worked closely with the Maharishi during the filming, he was never allowed to go to meetings with him. "Why not?" Hunter finally asked the fellow meditator. "Because you look green," the guy said, and that was the end of the macrobiotic diet.

Hunter returned from Colorado to find Johnny still in Mass. Mental and me in bed because Young Lochinvar didn't love me anymore. In the mornings I would lull myself back to sleep with Twinkies and other processed delights foreign to our kitchen while we were growing up. In the afternoons, when I could summon the energy, I would drag myself up to Harvard Square to take the subway over to Park Street, where I changed to the Arborway-Huntington Line, which rattled above ground past rows of dirty brick buildings over to Mass. Mental. There I would bask with Johnny in the pulsating heat of the Day Room, waiting till the large clock read three, when the nurse appeared with the little cups of medications on a tray. I was depressed, but then, that meant I belonged.

Where I did not belong was with Aunt Sarah, who called my dorm one afternoon, interrupting the anesthetized squalor of a twelve-ice-cream-sandwich-induced sleep. "I have an extra ticket for Symphony," my aunt Sarah said—it was always "Symphony," not "the symphony," for the Boston Brahmins. "Oh, how lovely," I croaked, rousing myself lumpenly from my electric-blanketed womb.

As usual I had to pretend to be delighted. In my family it is a sin to hate Symphony. Saying you didn't want to go to the symphony was something no one in the history of our family had ever said, though now that I think of it, I never knew Uncle Cot, whose father had helped build Symphony Hall, to go. (Even the aunt who bequeathed him the third-row seats was deaf.) Of course, no proper Bostonian male would be seen at Symphony in the middle of the day, and then, as Aunt Sarah would mention, Uncle Cot *had* to get out to the farm Friday afternoon. I don't think Uncle Cot cared a fig for music. While he and Aunt Sarah had many modern conveniences, like TVs in the bathroom and watches that changed colors with Aunt Sarah's moods, they somehow managed never to have a record player. Whenever my parents gave them a record one of my brothers had made, they would say, *Thank you so much, but of course they couldn't* listen *to it, they hadn't a phonograph.*

By 1970 Aunt Sarah was putting her gloved fingers in her ears at Symphony and saying in a loud voice that she couldn't stand that modern music. Yet she would go every Friday for nearly eighty years, and when she called with an extra ticket, I always went too. When I was ushered at a snail's pace into the Beacon Street parlor by the world's oldest living maid, there would be Aunt Sarah and Mrs. Howard, a red-haired, widowed, flibbertigibbet of a woman who served no apparent purpose except that she was always available for meals, until, to the consternation of Aunt Sarah and Uncle Cot, she dared to remarry at eighty-three. "Can't imagine why she did it," said Uncle Cot. When I happened to mention her a few years later, he said, "She died," as if it had served her right.

Always when I went to Symphony, I was so wrongly dressed. There would be the girls who went to private schools, with their thick, shiny hair pulled back from their faces, so that their features, whether beautiful or hideous, were always arrogantly displayed, anchored by stubby gold earrings, above a kelly green suit and slightly scuffed but well-heeled navy blue Capezio flats. (When Uncle Cot was asked what relative he thought I looked like, he would always reply, "Wouldn't know. Can't see her face.")

That Friday when I arrived at 410 Beacon Street in a long white cotton skirt and pink sweater, Aunt Sarah said, "How nice you look," and for a moment I felt happy. Then I learned we were to lunch at the imperious Mrs. Eliot's, in whose lavish pool I had swum countless times at Manchester, while she sat in a large flowered hat against the backdrop of her gigantic stone house. "They're *much* richer than us," Aunt Sarah had said to me once as we passed their house on Uncle Cot's yacht. Off we went to Mrs. Eliot's at the top of Beacon Street, across from the Public Garden. The flowers were beautiful in the rain, but I felt that cold, paralyzing fear I felt whenever I went to Aunt Sarah's for lunch before Symphony, trying to please, to do something with my hair, to jury-rig with safety pins and a Scotch-taped hem an outdated skirt that might be nearly right. It seems that whenever I went to Symphony it was early May and dank and wet and cold and beautiful, and I wished I were dead.

Mrs. Eliot's town house was grander by far than Aunt Sarah's, with its two-story marble hallway and liveried butler, and Mrs. Eliot, grander too, dropped the name of her personal friend the Queen Mother, and shot me just a shade of a look when I asked for a Bloody Mary instead of sherry. On the way out the door to Symphony she said to my aunt, "Isn't that raincoat of yours a bit tatty, Sarah?" And then Aunt Sarah, the traitor, as we took our seats of privilege in Symphony Hall among the other women who would never see eighty again, turned to Mrs. Eliot, and said, "Can't imagine what she has in mind wearing a full-length gown in the middle of the day."

It was all downhill from there.

Although Johnny had been the second of our generation to break down, two more first cousins would follow. While this wasn't exactly wonderful, in a dynastic sense the numbers were encouraging. Two out of three of Alice and Devereux's children had broken down, but only four out of ten of their grandchildren followed suit.

Johnny was released from Mass. Mental in the spring of 1970. Earlier that winter he had secretly stopped taking his thorazine, hoarding the pills in case he wanted to commit suicide, but then, to his surprise, he found himself feeling increasingly better. After he was released, he sent his shrink a letter explaining what he had done, and how he had faked psychological epiphanies in therapy in order to avoid having the thorazine forced on him, and that he was telling her this for the sake of future patients. He never received a reply. The following fall, the fall of my sophomore year, Johnny flipped out again. This time we took Johnny to Glenside Hospital in Jamaica Plain, a semiprivate hospital that was moderately less depressing than Mass. Mental. In the end this didn't matter, because Johnny wouldn't sign himself in, and we didn't want to take him to court. Instead he left the hospital and came to live with me at Harvard, in the extra room in my suite in Winthrop House. I was so happy. I thought I could make him better, better than the shrinks and the thorazine had made him.

22

After you are with someone who is really crazy, you never use the word the same way again. When I look at the way I was from age eighteen to twenty-three, before I met Charlie and became normal—or before I started jogging and became normal (I started both at the same time and will never know which made me sane)—I can see why so many of my friends from that earlier time still think of me as crazy. "On *paper*," says a friend, "you look really together, but of course we all know you're crazy." Screwed-up, desperate, immature, maybe: but not crazy.

Crazy is cosmic. Before his first clinical breakdown Bobby quickly reconverted to Catholicism to provide a framework for his mania. Traditional religion only lasted my brother Johnny one breakdown; by his second he had switched over to Scientology, but the idea was the same, just updated a generation later, when experimenting with alternative religions was often a part of growing up. When you are crazy there is a giant conspiracy from which you are going to save the world. In the beginning, in Johnny's case anyway, he seemed not crazy but powerful, brilliant, wonderfully convincing, mesmerizing. The two times we saw him high, none of us noticed, indeed we noticed only how well and happy he seemed. Johnny was powerful, but he was never cruel; even at the precipice he wanted to share the power with you. Once he even got me to start playing my flute again. "Even the tone-deaf can play the flute!" he said, and, convinced, I played better than I ever had or ever would again. There was a generosity in his mania that endeared Johnny to us in a way that might never have happened without it. Other than that I can think of nothing good that came from Johnny's illness.

I was unable to cure Johnny. After my roommates and I stayed up with him in my dorm for several weeks, his mania only worsened, and in December 1970 he was taken by ambulance to Glenside Hospital, where this time he signed himself in. There, early in 1971, Johnny was given a series of six different electroshock treatments. Shortly after, my mother brought Aunt Sarah to see him. Johnny was still groggy and spaced out after the treatment, but this didn't seem to faze Aunt Sarah who had visited relatives in similar states before. She breezed in and sat herself down next to him like an old pro. "So, Johnny," she said matter-of-factly to the ghost of her great-nephew, "you look well. What are you doing with yourself? How are you feeling?" In spite of her awful remarks about my brothers, there were still times when Aunt Sarah's old love for them returned.

After the shock treatments my parents had Johnny moved to a hospital in upstate New York. It was a public hospital, but much nicer than Mass. Mental or Glenside, with leafy grounds and gleaming waxed floors. When I first went to visit, Johnny came down the hallway toward me very slowly, his hair closely shorn. I had left for California in December 1970, abandoning Johnny to my parents and the doctors, in despair that I hadn't saved him. A month later Johnny had written me a letter: "Dear Sister Sally, Thank you for taking care of me when I was sick. Love, Johnny."

"Astral Weeks" had been released by then, and Johnny's name was getting to be known in the music world. Even when Johnny was depressed, he had had real presence. But the electroshock seemed to diminish him. When he was released from the hospital that spring, he was at a loss as to what he would do next. "He was the hollow guy who had always been the big guy," Hunter remembered.

Still, after the shock therapy, Johnny never had another manic episode. Whether this was because of the treatments themselves, or what they signified, or something completely unrelated, Johnny doesn't know. Much as he had feared electroshock, he had also known that my mother had never broken down again after having it, and at Glenside he had actually asked that treatments be administered. Then, too, Johnny had calculated that the total time of his hospitalization since his first breakdown now equaled the year and a half of my mother's own hospitalization, a fact that somehow contributed to his belief that now it would be all over.

Whatever the reason, Johnny rapidly got better and never broke down again. He played with Michael Franks and Tim Hardin, recorded two albums with Bonnie Raitt, and, in 1977, soloed on the Johnny Carson show with Phoebe Snow. To the people he met, he was bearishly lovable, devoid of pretentiousness, but when he got on stage he was transformed and transforming. "Take it, John," the singer would say, and Johnny would take his sax and the audience to places they had never been. But Johnny wanted stability more than he wanted fame, which entailed traveling on the road for much of the year. He got married, started a music school, and had two kids. He even completed his Harvard classes.

"I got my Harvard degree in November of 1972 by walking into an office and giving them a check for sixteen dollars. I gave my diploma to the parents, saying, 'Well, you paid for it, you can have it.' They didn't seem to want it." My parents did take the degree, though they returned it to Johnny in 1975, when my father opted for early retirement and they moved back to Concord.

During my sophomore year at Harvard, Bobby ran off to live with Lady Caroline Blackwood, whom the family called the Countess, even though it turns out she was actually the daughter of a marquess. The story went that Bobby and the Countess drank in the east wing of her castle while her second husband, musician Israel Citkovitz, drank in the west. Though Lady Caroline had once lived in her cousin's castle, she did not have one of her own, I found out later, just a large country house. When my cousin Mary Devereux visited Bobby and her, with some Russian writer she'd met in New York, she said it was a happy, slovenly, overgrown sort of place, where even the gardeners seemed to be drunk.

"I don't care what anyone does as long as it's behind closed doors," Aunt Sarah used to say, but this was the opposite of the way Bobby conducted his affairs, and Caroline Blackwood was certainly the opposite of any woman Aunt Sarah had ever had to tea. Lady Caroline didn't care what people thought of her: an ungraspable concept. She was beautiful, rich, titled, and talented—and she didn't need anyone's approval. But something must have gone wrong somewhere early in her life since the final quote chosen for her obituary was one of her favorite sayings: "if we see a light at the end of the tunnel,/it's the light of an oncoming train" ("Since 1939").

From the beginning Bobby and Caroline's relationship was traumatic, with Bobby breaking down, and Caroline breaking down, and Elizabeth furiously writing letters (letters Bobby later quoted in *The Dolphin*, bringing on more trauma), and a great deal of back and forth between Bobby and the two women.

Before they were married, and right before Lady Caroline became pregnant in 1971, Bobby called up my mother in Westchester County and asked if she would come into New York to meet Caroline. Bobby and she were staying at the Plaza, and my mother and father drove in from Katonah in the Subaru to have breakfast with them. My mother remembered the Countess as being very thin and nervous; she didn't look well. My mother was impressed that she wasn't more chic: She was wearing an ordinary dress. Though she wasn't slovenly, it seemed that she did not care at all about her clothes. Bobby did all the talking as Lady Caroline smoked incessantly, while my mother kept trying to figure out why Bobby liked her better than Elizabeth. Caroline seemed so high-strung, completely dependent on Bobby, whereas Elizabeth had been independent, strong, and supportive. "Elizabeth was one of eleven children from a working-class Kentucky family," my mother said, "and every one of those children went to college."

Bobby was still married to Elizabeth when he sent the telegram from England to Aunt Sarah and Uncle Cot that said: ROBERT JUNIOR BORN TODAY. Aunt Sarah refused to speak to him even after he and the Countess were married in 1972. When we asked her, she would say yes, she would like to see Bobby, but when he called, she wouldn't come to the phone. My mother said the fact that Bobby had named an illegitimate child Lowell was what caused Aunt Sarah to disown him; the illegitimate child itself was not the sin so much as bestowing on him a legitimate surname.

Though the telegram had seemed blithe, Bobby was not blithe about the illegitimacy. Later he wrote that he couldn't sleep:

> thinking of Grandfather in his last poor days.
> Caroline, he had such naked nights,
> and brought his *tortures of the damned* to breakfast—
> when his son died, he made his grandchildren plant trees;
> his blood lives, not his name . . . We have our child,
> our bastard, easily fathered, hard to name . . .
> illegibly bracketed with us . . .
> (*Marriage*, "5. Knowing")

When the telegram came, Uncle Cot, who was always so reserved, turned to Aunt Sarah and said, "That's it for your nephew, Sarah." He was not a forgiving man, and then, he never had liked Bobby.

Around this time Aunt Sarah wrote Bobby out of her will, but none of us knew it. It wasn't until Uncle Cot's death in 1985, when Bobby and Lady Caroline's son's lawyer came sniffing around, that we learned that "only the nieces are mentioned in the will." I remember going to Beacon Street for dinner in 1974 and Aunt Sarah sweeping down the stairs in a cheerful, energetic mood, saying, "Shall I leave you my scrapbooks in my will?" Then she handed me a beautiful miniature clock with *C.W.* engraved on the back. It is the only personal possession Aunt Sarah would ever give me, except of course it wasn't hers but Charlotte's.

When Bobby returned to Harvard the fall of my senior year, he called and asked me to try to persuade Aunt Sarah to see him. By this time I was very much in awe of him, and I kept mouthing to my roommate, "Rob-ert Low-ell is on the phone" while trying to think of something poetic to say. The problem was I couldn't really understand him because of his cultured way of speaking, which had only gotten worse over in England. Finally I figured out that he had invited me to dinner, and managed to get an address, somewhere in Brookline.

The house he and Caroline had rented was Victorian, gloomy, and shabby, and there were all kinds of nannies and children running around. Empty liquor bottles were scattered everywhere on the floors. In Concord we had known a family so sloppy that they left out sticks of margarine all day with bread crumbs stuck to them, but I wasn't prepared for this. Lady Caroline sat elegantly with an empty liquor bottle at her feet that she did not even try to kick under the couch. To me, this made her an aristocrat. I remember a portrait of Lady Caroline hanging behind her, possibly it was *Girl in Bed*, the famous painting by her first husband, Lucien Freud, but at the time all I remember is thinking, *They didn't bring* that *over from England, did they?*

Caroline was stunning and intelligent looking and held an enormous drink in her hand. "Caroline is a writer," Bobby said, and then he handed me an equally enormous drink, which I was thankful to get because they'd invited all these scholarly young men from Harvard, I guess as beaux for me, and they were in the midst of a heated discussion about Tennyson, who might as well have been Longfellow as far as I knew. (Wordsworth I knew because I had seen the movie *Splendor in the Grass*.) I didn't know what to say, but Bobby was very nice and gave me a little smile. He'd given up drinking, he said, indicating his glass. He sat a little off from the group and drank one iced coffee after another while everyone sat around saying Cal-this and Cal-that.

After rather a long time we all stumbled into a dusky—or was it dusty?—dining room and ate something; I was too drunk to figure out what it was. After my third quart-size drink I managed to work the conversation around from Tennyson to what had happened to me on the subway the other day. We were all fairly garbled by then. When I left, Bobby asked me to try Aunt Sarah again, and I promised I would, though with sinking heart I knew I would not succeed, and then somehow I drove back to Cambridge. It took me two days to find out where I had parked my car and when I found it, it was parked so beautifully between two cars that I had to call the police to wedge it out.

That was the last time I saw Bobby. He died four years later. ". . . Never to have lived is best," he'd written thirty years before.

Uncle Cot.
Bobby sent a telegram saying, "Robert Junior born today!"
"That's it for your nephew, Sarah," Uncle Cot said.

———

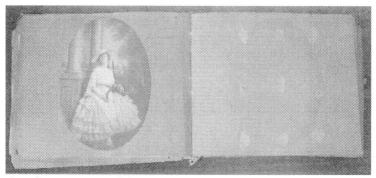

Several years ago I noticed that Bobby's picture had been torn from my aunt Sarah's
scrapbook, and his mother made childless on the family tree.

———

Aug - 1931

Bobby.

23

When I got engaged in 1976, my future mother-in-law frantically started sending her son clippings of Bobby with the wild hair and startled look he wore the year before he died. Her theory on my future pregnancies was that we should stick to raising dogs. In his last few years Bobby's manic attacks became more frequent. "This winter, I thought/I was created to be given away," Bobby wrote in "Thanks-Offering for Recovery," referring to his breakdown in January 1976; eight months later he had broken down again. When I think of my brother, who had only three breakdowns, and what it was like in the overheated Day Room at Mass. Mental, with the girl with the pacifier and the birds chirping in cages and my brother screaming inside but too drugged up to wash his face or light a cigarette, I cannot believe that Bobby lived to be sixty.

Bobby had his first heart attack in January 1977. He had arrived in Cambridge to teach the semester at Harvard and, feeling ill, had been admitted to Phillips House, where his grandfather, Arthur Winslow, had died in a well-appointed room with a view of the Charles River. "Something sinister and comforting/in this return after forty years arrears/to death and Phillips House . . . ," Bobby wrote in "Phillips House Revisited."

When Bobby was in Phillips House, Elizabeth called my aunt Allie and asked if my mother could persuade Aunt Sarah to see Bobby. I don't know where Bobby stood matrimonially at the time. During the last year of his life he went back and forth between two women, two children, and two continents. ("Everyone is tired of my turmoil," Bobby wrote, and nobody seemed more tired than he.) My mother called Aunt Sarah, who had steadily refused to see Bobby for five years. This time she agreed to see him. It was beautiful and sunny the day my mother and Aunt Sarah went to Phillips House. By 1977 Aunt Sarah was refusing to go to the dressmaker's, and sometimes she wore her bedroom slippers with her gown to dinner, but that day she looked presentable. Though her exquisite clothes were getting old, she had on the proper shoes.

When they entered the room they found a disheveled-looking Bobby jumping excitedly out of bed every two minutes to get this or that, obviously disobeying doctor's orders. (I read later that he was smoking in the hospital, and drinking too, though my mother doesn't remember him doing either.) A young admirer was also in the room, a young woman, who didn't leave when Aunt Sarah and my mother arrived, though clearly this was a family visit. Aunt Sarah, brushing past the admirer, sat next to Bobby with a stiff straight back and began making sarcastic remarks. She was just waiting to jump at him, my mother said, waiting "to pierce his heart with an arrow." Years before, when Aunt Sarah had visited Bobby at McLean's, she had greeted him warmly with statements like, "Well, this is a pretty place." Now her small talk took the form of barbs like "So, how are you? You look old," as she fidgeted, crossing and uncrossing her legs, her body poised to depart the chair at any moment. My mother assumed that Aunt Sarah felt guilty because she hadn't told Uncle Cot she was going to see Bobby, but Bobby didn't seem to notice. He was filled with boyish delight to see his aunt again, despite her coldness. After about a half hour, Aunt Sarah rose to her feet and said, "It's time to go," and marched my mother out the door. But Bobby was happy; he thought he had been forgiven.

The liberal politics of my mother's generation and the ragged, radical defiance of my own convinced the older, childless members of our family that their money and possessions might be safer elsewhere. At various times my cousins and I had declared ourselves socialists, communists, or at the very least, dropouts from society, and who can blame them for taking us at our word? Perhaps the grandnephew sitting Indian-style on the floor at 410 Beacon Street wearing what appeared to be a rug was not the perfect inheritor of Uncle Cot's mother's silver tea service.

We lost the money in the 1960s, but it was not until the 1970s that we learned we had lost it. Only then did it become clear that wills had been changed, so that money and possessions that had always been passed down in the family were now being passed to certain museums and schools. The institutions that were getting the money then began soliciting us, who were no longer getting the money, for *more* money. My mother's generation was often solicited personally with a visit to the house; my generation was approached by letter. Most of us complied in some manner, however meager, inheriting the guilt begotten by the money, if not the money itself. In college I remember sending a much-needed (by me) twenty-five dollars toward the building of a library given by a childless great-aunt and uncle, and an additional twenty-five dollars when the library burned down as it was being built. My mother not only felt obligated to give to the various institutions of which her family were benefactors, but for years she served on the Ladies' Committee of one, working with disabled children on a semiweekly basis.

As one's children approach college age and one sees the trust funds and portraits of my family fading into the sunset, one longs to cry out, "We were just kidding, we didn't mean it," but the truth is, we asked for such treatment, though we didn't like it when we got it.

Bobby died in September 1977. He had been married to Elizabeth for more than twenty years when he ran off with Lady Caroline, and it was to Elizabeth he finally returned. Or almost returned. After spending the summer in Maine, followed by a ten-day visit to Ireland, he was on his way back to Elizabeth's in New York when he died of a heart attack in the backseat of a cab outside her door. In his arms was a large brown paper parcel found to contain *Girl in Bed*, the portrait of Lady Caroline, which she had asked him to get appraised.

Bobby's funeral was held at the Church of the Advent in Boston, a much higher church than the family's socially correct Trinity Church, with swinging balls of incense and chiming bells. My husband, Charlie, said it put the Catholic Church to shame. Charlie is very smart but he is not what you would call literary. He had never even heard of Robert Lowell until he met me, and by then Bobby was living in England. But he did meet Elizabeth. I have a picture of the two of them at our wedding. Elizabeth is looking very intense and gesticulating with both arms, and Charlie is looking her straight in the eye. He said he was dead drunk and had not the slightest idea what they were discussing.

There were thousands of people in attendance. Actually there were probably only hundreds. By 1977 my tendency to exaggerate had become notable. Charlie was in the television news business and liked to keep things factual. Anyway, there were lots of people there—relatives, students, reporters, and all sorts of famous people from the writing world. It was pretty flashy for the Church of the Advent, and my Boston relatives sat stiffly in the pews, careful not to be too comfortable. Everything was bustling when we arrived—my parents, Charlie, me, and my brother Billy.

I do not remember much about the funeral itself on account of watching Lady Caroline the entire time. We were seated in the second pew, right behind Elizabeth and Harriet and Lady Caroline and her entourage. She must have brought fifty people over from England with her or, anyway, ten. Some were her daughters, I guess, and governesses, and I know one was another titled Englishwoman. They were all dressed in black—Lady Caroline wore a chic black hat, that looked like a little top hat, though later I heard they had arrived from England for the funeral with nothing but old clothes, and that Elizabeth had had to take them out to buy new ones. They were all gathered around Lady Caroline, who looked like a character out of a Greek tragedy, black eye make-up running down her ravaged face. She shook and shuddered throughout the entire service while the rest of us simply stared. Even Elizabeth and Harriet tried to comfort her, but to no avail.

Aunt Sarah and Uncle Cot sat behind us in the third pew like two sticks of iron, built to last. Aunt Sarah and Bobby had been reconciled in Phillips House, we thought, or why else would she and Uncle Cot appear at his funeral? We were wrong. Several years later I noticed that Bobby's picture had been torn from Aunt Sarah's scrapbook and his mother made childless on the family tree. When Aunt Sarah did this spiteful act I do not know. "You're nothing but middle-class trash," she told me shortly before she died at age ninety-nine. She was only in her eighties when Bobby died, though, and not so cranky. "Who are all the women in the first row?" Uncle Cot shouted in her ear at the funeral. "Those are the wives," Aunt Sarah answered in a clarion voice.

The service was very long. I didn't think they'd ever get Lady Caroline up to the communion rail. Peter Taylor read a poem of Bobby's, which I didn't listen to as I was too busy explaining to Charlie, who didn't care, how this particular writer had taught me at Harvard and given me an A only because I was Bobby's cousin. It was a rather grisly poem, with images of skulls and swarming locusts. "Very pretty, isn't it?" Aunt Sarah commented in the middle.

Bobby had wanted to be buried at the family burial grounds in Dunbarton, two hours away, and somehow my parents were made responsible for getting everyone up there. "Someone has to be in charge," my father had said with a sigh, "and it might as well be someone who knows directions." Charlie had to go back to work after the service, so it was Billy and I and my parents in their mustard-colored Subaru who led the procession of limousines up Route 93. My father had stuck a piece of shirt cardboard in the windshield wiper with "Lowell Funeral" carefully printed on it, which no one could see but the people driving in the opposite direction. My mother had made sandwiches. "Everyone gets a tuna, a peanut butter, and a little bottle of sherry," my mother said, "except for the Countess. She gets a Diet 7Up." "What bothers me," my father said, "is where are we going to go to the damn bathroom?" "It's got to be nice," my mother said. My father thought he remembered one of those rest areas with the brick bathrooms, which was only a little out of the way.

How we all ended up at the rest area I do not know, as my father is the worst person to follow in the world. He's always racing through yellow lights and changing lanes and taking shortcuts that turn out to be long cuts. (The funny thing is, my father's family's whole life is directions. Whenever they visit one another they spend the first half of the time discussing how they got there and the second half how they're going back.) But somehow we all got there. Everyone got out of the limousines—the wives had ridden up together—and my mother passed out the brown paper bags, and soon everyone was chatting and drinking sherry out of paper cups. There were all these young men whom nobody knew who kept running up to Harriet and saying, "He loved you *so* much!" Lady Caroline was evidently still upset, still shaking like crazy; there was a large group gathered around her limousine. One of them, the pretty English noblewoman with the white, white skin, came up to my father and said in the loveliest voice that really you see Lady Caroline was a bit upset and sherry really was not the *thing*, and did we have anything rather stronger?

No one knew what to do, but my father was determined to do something, and the next thing we knew he was striding across the grass and introducing himself to a group of people eating at one of the picnic tables. It turned out that they were on their way up to the Dartmouth-Princeton game. Well, my father said, wasn't that interesting, he had a son-in-law went to Dartmouth, although he himself had gone to Williams, and then they discussed how long they thought it would take them to get to Hanover, and then my father mentioned that they were on their way to Dunbarton, New Hampshire, to bury his wife's first cousin, Robert Lowell, the poet, had they heard of him? No? Well, it seemed his third wife, who was a countess from England, didn't like sherry, etc., etc. From a distance you could see that they really hit it off. My father returned with two little airplane bottles of vodka, to the profuse thanks of the English lady. Soon a tremulous but smiling countess was being taken around and introduced by Elizabeth. "This is Lady Caroline," said Elizabeth to everyone, "Cal's wife."

It was late afternoon, damp and chilly, by the time we reached Dunbarton. My grandmother had always said she didn't want to be buried in Dunbarton because it was too cold. Somehow, though, it seems just right for my ancestors, with names like Moody, Savage, and Stark. The body of Gen. John Stark had long since been moved to the state capital; on the way they must have opened up the casket for some reason, because among Aunt Sarah's letters is the dubious treasure of a lock of the great general's hair. Once we found a tacky china "John Stark" decanter in a junk antique shop in New Hampshire, and my mother gave it to Aunt Sarah at Thanksgiving while we read a little poem as my father strummed the banjo. I can't imagine now how we dared recite little poems in front of Bobby, poems along the lines of: "Yessir, he's our relation,/Nossir, he's not in our generation," although Bobby never seemed to mind.

The graveyard is in a clearing of pines in the forest and is deep green and thick with shadows. It is snug and fenced in, and outside the fence lie smaller tombstones marking the graves of the servants.

I've actually been to Dunbarton a number of times because my parents' cabin is nearby, and Aunt Sarah and Uncle Cot used to drive up every summer just to look at the graves and then turn around and drive back again. As I get older, and death seems nearer, I begin to see their point.

The wives and Harriet threw flowers in the grave as the coffin was lowered, and then someone threw in a spade of dirt. Bobby was buried next to his mother, Charlotte, who died at the same age as Bobby. Next to her lies her husband Bob senior, the only nonblood relation buried in the cemetery.

Dunbarton is just about all that's left of the Winslows; everything else is in storage at the Peabody Essex Museum under Uncle Cot's name, even the silver frame torn from my wedding picture. It never occurred to me after all the fuss that Aunt Sarah wouldn't be buried in Dunbarton; but when she died the instructions were to bury her next to Uncle Cot, in the cemetery across from the Star Super Market in Cambridge.

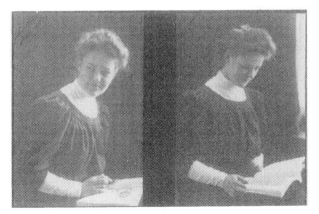

Charlotte Lowell at fifteen.
"It has taken me the time since you died/
to discover you are as human as I am . . . /If I am."
—Robert Lowell ("To Mother")

John Singleton Copley portrait of Sarah Waldo.

Me next to Aunt Sarah under the Copley portrait, passed down from a Sarah to a Sarah for generations—until it was decided that I didn't have a proper wall to hang it on.

24

. . . but it is murder to pity the rich,
even when they are as gone
as Hector, tamer of horses—
always doomed to return,
to be with us always like the poor.
      —"Bright Day in Boston"

In the spring of 1978 Charlie and I bought a town house on Marlborough Street in Boston, near where Bobby had lived with Elizabeth. The first time I went in the house, I had stood at the second floor window gazing out at Marlborough Street with a full heart: I was in Back Bay Boston, where my ancestors had lived, and the glow from the gas-lit lanterns on the street was the glow of the safe, happy, privileged lives I imagined them to have had. Now, I could live where they had lived (though in order to do it we needed to rent out two floors and three parking places and bring in two salaries), around the corner from Aunt Sarah and Uncle Cot's, where everything was stifling, where never once had I said a true thing, but where everything was certain, down to the chicken they ate every Wednesday, year after year.

The move to Marlborough Street did not turn out exactly as I had envisioned it, considering that three days following the signing of the purchase and sale agreement, Charlie walked out after a year and a half of marriage. I was left as landlady, renting out two floors to a guy whose air conditioner fell four stories into the greenhouse, and living on my own, and writing bank ads for NOW accounts instead of *Life Studies*. That autumn came the additional problem of informing Aunt Sarah that Charlie would not be coming to Thanksgiving dinner. In 1978 Aunt Sarah was still the grande dame, performing the same daily rituals, though she had been losing her mind for ten years. "Save the paper!" she had cried out at a large charity fund-raiser, when Uncle Cot was on the podium receiving a wrapped gift.

Charlie had, in fact, asked me for a divorce, and in order to break the news more easily to Aunt Sarah, who knew nothing of our breakup, I went to lunch with Uncle Cot at one of his downtown clubs, a surprisingly modern, high-rise affair with a panoramic view of the financial district. Even during the summer, when he lived in Manchester, Uncle Cot commuted to work promptly each morning. Once, he told me, he had tried to make an exception. It was a beautiful summer morning, and he had been sitting in his seaside dining room with the hand-painted 1890s wallpaper from England (depicting its vision of America, with large groups of African-Americans, in the most stylish Victorian costume, standing by a river), and he had said to himself, *Well, I'm nearly ninety years old; maybe I'll just linger a little this morning.* Then round the corner came my great-aunt Sarah. "What? You still here?" she'd said, and Uncle Cot had hurried off to work.

Sometimes being a WASP can be helpful, and it was helpful at that lunch, when I had to tell Uncle Cot about Charlie, because the last thing in the world Uncle Cot wanted to hear were the details. "Charlie and I are getting divorced," was all I said on the subject. And all Uncle Cot said was, "Do you need any money?" When I lied, "Oh, no," he advised me that the simplest way to go about a divorce would be for Charlie to make a large settlement on me, as Uncle Cot had done with Constance Binney.

Since 1977 I had worked in an advertising agency, writing copy like, "Get a free gift with a two-hundred-dollar deposit" or, if I was feeling clever, "It's our anniversary, but you get the gifts!" Advertising was quite hard, though I always got the impression that Bluma thought it was beneath me. Bluma was the family shrink, at least for the ones who were not manic-depressive. Elizabeth had introduced her to the family. Bluma—we've always called her by her first name—is warm with big brown eyes. She says things like "Sally, darling, you're neurotic, but neurotic is good!"—I guess as opposed to psychotic.

That winter I wrote an ad campaign for an old dingy hotel in the Back Bay that had recently been refurbished to a fake-brass-fixtured grandeur. I realized when I got the assignment that the hotel had once been owned by my great-grandfather, Arthur Winslow, before he lost his money. In "Phillips House Revisited," Bobby wrote:

> But these forty years grandfather would insist
> have turned the world on its head—
> their point was
> to extinguish him like a stranded crab.

Well, that shiny hotel lobby may have extinguished my great grandfather, but it was I who was left stranded, having to write that ad campaign.

My bosses at the ad agency were an Irish boys' club, and I was kind of an experiment as the only woman copywriter. The biggest prejudice I encountered in Aunt Sarah and Uncle Cot's set was against the Irish: The women make good servants but the men are all drunks. Not that the WASPS are against being drunk, provided it can be accomplished during the six o'clock cocktail hour. At the ad agency I simply started the cocktail hour a bit earlier. My career strategy was to "just be myself" (as I was always told as a child, as if somehow this would make everything come out right), in the hope of being accepted as one of the guys. "Hey, Big Tits," was how the fat art director on the hotel assignment greeted me.

The morning we were to present the ad campaign to the hotel client, there was a blizzard on Newbury Street, and the two vice presidents huddled with the fat art director, while I stood to one side, the snow coming between us in sheets. One of the vice presidents had tried putting his hand up my skirt, slobbering drunk at a Christmas party the night before, and now he ignored me as he tried in vain to hail a cab in the snow. "Hey you, over there, hey you!" he started yelling at a chauffeur across the street who was dusting off his windshield. The chauffeur, an older man in a gray cap, acted as if the vice president didn't exist. Then I saw who the chauffeur was. "Roy?" I said. "Why, Miss Sally," said Roy, hurrying over; the next thing we knew the vice presidents, the fat art director, and I were being ushered into the car, where Roy regaled me with stories about Uncle Cot drinking martinis at his club, while my superiors sat in dead silence. When we got out of the car, I tried to explain to the vice presidents why Roy had refused the twenty-dollar bill they offered, but my clumsy explanation of the duties and loyalties operating in the servant world was met with blank stares.

In the spring of 1979 I was invited to Uncle Cot's ninetieth birthday party, an honor (and a punishment) in that I was the only guest under sixty years of age. I put on a green silk dress that wasn't too short and tried to style my hair into a mother-hairdo. As I stood dwarfed by the tall front door at 410 Beacon, I thought, *How bad can it be?*

"This is Mrs. Stuart," Uncle Cot introduced me, each time. "Or do we call you that anymore?"

In the end it didn't matter, because Charlie came back that June and saved me from my life. My mother still refers to that terrible year as "the time Charlie was unwell," a statement that in our family is pretty much guaranteed to fit the bill. In actuality Charlie was the happiest, sanest person in the world until he married me. "I am so lucky I have you!" Charlie said to me the other day, but the fact is, his life was great before he met me; I wonder why he ever came back.

In *The Boston Cotting Family* (privately published), Uncle Cot is quoted as saying that what he found most rewarding was "leading an honest life and giving others, not fortunate, a leg up." Those not so fortunate included struggling young men at the Harvard Business School, preferably from the area (Uncle Cot's scholarships favor boys from New England), disabled and underprivileged children at certain Boston institutions, and white people employed full-time by Uncle Cot. It did not include struggling grandnephews with beards, nor did it include the migrant workers Uncle Cot imported to pick apples at the farm. One of the reasons Uncle Cot actually made money on his apple orchards, as opposed to most weekend farmers, was because he didn't pay the people who actually did the work very much. (Sometimes I wonder if this is what is meant by "being a genius with money.") By 1980 the migrant workers had begun making demands. "Used to be you could give them a quarter and they'd be happy," Uncle Cot said, "now they want a bathroom."

Uncle Cot died in 1985, lying on the chaise in his bedroom at Manchester on a sparkling July morning, looking out the window at his yacht. I used to think I would be willing to die if I could die with a view such as that. *How could Uncle Cot have feared a God who had given him everything?* I once had thought. Then, last spring, I learned that Uncle Cot's father, who had been so concerned that his only child get a hobby, had hanged himself in his son's bathroom shower—the same bathroom in Manchester that Uncle Cot continued to use for seventy years, the shower simply tiled over. "I have no family," Uncle Cot used to say, in spite of all the people who suddenly appeared at his funeral, introducing themselves to my mother and chatting about Uncle Cot as "Cousin Charles." When the museum to which Uncle Cot left all his personal possessions wished to write up his family history, the message came back through Uncle Cot's agent: These items are only gifts of decorative value, not family value. Mr. Cotting has no wish to memorialize his family in any way.

The morning he died, Uncle Cot had dealt with life in his usual unemotional way, the nurse told me, chatting first with Roy about getting rid of some squirrels in the attic. Roy, in his eighties, had been working for Uncle Cot most of his life, and when he died Uncle Cot left him well provided for, but it didn't matter; Roy died two weeks later. That morning Uncle Cot asked that "it" be brought in so that he could see her. He was calling Aunt Sarah "it" by then, and in truth when I had seen her earlier that summer she had been like a zombie, wandering around my parents' cabin in New Hampshire, drugged up and jittery, saying, "I want to take a leak, I want to take a leak." Where she had heard this phrase, a phrase even I do not use, I have no idea. Uncle Cot had become quite harsh with her by then, treating her like a recalcitrant child, exhorting the nurses to use more discipline. When he told me of the nurse who had tied her to her chair when she didn't obey, it took me a long moment to realize that he was applauding the action.

Exactly how long Aunt Sarah had been in this zombie state I didn't know. The last time I had seen her was three years earlier, when Charlie and I had come up for a weekend in Manchester from New York, where we had moved in 1980. It was about this time that my mother informed me that the Copley portrait was no longer willed to me but had been given to the Peabody Essex Museum. "Sally can have it *whenever* she wants it," Aunt Sarah told my mother several times, but when we asked the lawyer after she died we found this wasn't true. In her dementia Aunt Sarah had agreed that her possessions be given to Uncle Cot, so that even the hairbrush on her bureau and the photo album with my family's Christmas cards is now stored in the museum under the Cotting name.

Aunt Sarah's mind was about two-thirds gone by 1982, but sometimes a mood would descend on her and she would be her old self, and so it was that one day, out of the blue, a letter arrived inviting Charlie and me for a country visit. Stupidly I took her up on it.

When we arrived Aunt Sarah waved us away crossly, as if we were a couple of Jehovah's Witnesses selling ten-cent magazines, and I had to beg a maid for a room to put our things in. That weekend I was never quite positive whether she knew who I was—I was always referred to in the third person as "she"—but one thing was clear: Whoever I was, she did not want me around. "She's a picky eater, isn't she?" I was told when I refused a sandwich on the boat. And then: "Greedy, isn't she?" when, cowed, I took one. "She's completely lost her looks," was her greeting as I sat down to dinner in a long dress, my frizzy hair pinned up with barrettes. "Look," Aunt Sarah said. "She's wearing curlers!"

Even Uncle Cot, whose defense for years had been not to notice, took pity. "You should see how she treats me when you're not here," he said at a particularly low point, handing me a piece of his cracker. I learned later that he used to arrive at work with black-and-blue bruises on his shins. The only pleasure I gave Aunt Sarah was on Sunday morning when I gently broke the news that we were leaving. "Oh, you *must* come back soon," Aunt Sarah said, her face suddenly bright with joy, "for a nice *long* visit!"

In his last years Uncle Cot joked that everyone seemed to be after his money. A bevy of pretty fund-raisers was sent to patch up the feud with Harvard about housing students of color in Cotting House. The Industrial School for Crippled Children, founded by Drs. Augustus Thorndike and Edward Bradford, was renamed "Cotting School." A constant stream of mulish infants were dragged into Uncle Cot's office to be viewed as namesakes, his financial adviser told me. I remember once being a bit stunned by a picture on a Christmas card of a young preppy couple with a cute little boy named "Cotting." (When Uncle Cot's adviser appeared one morning with a round of checks to be signed, he said, "Mr. Cotting, is there anything I can do for you?" "Yes," said Uncle Cot. "Get people to stop naming their children after me.") Even his first wife, Constance Binney, appeared nosing around the farm. When Uncle Cot, who had spent years trying to revoke an irrevocable trust given to her, was informed, he simply denied it, saying, "No, she's dead." (Their one-year marriage was to be erased from the record. Later when the curator of the Peabody Essex Museum found, hidden under the bureau paper in a maid's room, a large photograph of Constance Binney in trailing white satin, roses strewn at her feet, standing at the foot of the curving staircase in the house at Manchester with the inscription: "To Rose, love Constance," the picture was swept out of his hands by Uncle Cot's agent.) But it was obviously not true that she had died, just as it was not true that Uncle Cot had no living blood relatives. His adviser employed a team of investigators, only to find a Cotting relative living two blocks away from the adviser's own house.

The only time I ever saw Uncle Cot display any emotion was the night I was invited to dinner after my mother had breast cancer for a second time. "Is your mother all right?" Uncle Cot had asked, before he said hello. If Uncle Cot loved anyone beside Aunt Sarah it was my mother, but when he died with—conservatively estimated—one hundred million dollars he left my mother only ten thousand dollars: My mother, who had honorably rejected offers of houses and club memberships for years; my mother, who had not only sunk to the middle class, she had embraced it—my mother was not rich enough to inherit. For only the rich can care for money; the middle class cannot be trusted: They might spend it.

Aunt Sarah had always told my mother not to let her live on machines; unfortunately in 1985 I was young enough to think life was always worth living. So after Uncle Cot died and Aunt Sarah began refusing to eat, and my mother was away on vacation in Mexico, I rushed up from New York to sit by my aunt Sarah and support my mother's agonized decision to keep her alive by feeding her intravenously. This saved her life, with the result that she spent the next eight years saying over and over, "I feel sick, I want to go back to bed," to the TV in the back rooms of her beautiful houses. Uncle Cot's will stipulated that Aunt Sarah was to live in the manner to which she was accustomed. So the full-time gardener went on growing the vegetables she couldn't eat, and the waitress (an actual job title in Boston Brahmin private houses) waited for someone to wait on at the table, and Aunt Sarah traveled to her various houses with a retinue of servants, including a cook, even though she was being fed through a tube.

My mother and I were the only members of the family guilty enough to keep visiting Aunt Sarah. She did not recognize us, and her remarks never failed to wound, but we felt that we owed her something for all she had once done for us. We went, too, in the vain hope that Aunt Sarah might regress far enough back to remember her old love for us. Aunt Sarah had become so nasty in the last years of Uncle

Cot's life that he had had a hard time keeping servants. The only servant Aunt Sarah had ever been afraid of was Molly, who kept threatening to leave only to be lured back by Uncle Cot. Molly had come over from Ireland as a young girl to work for Uncle Cot's mother and was still alive in a nursing home in 1990 when the curator of the Peabody Essex Museum sought her out to ask her about a particular antique sideboard in the dining room in Manchester. Molly looked at him in shock, "Why, I've never *been* in the dining room," she said. "I was the *cook*."

When we visited Aunt Sarah none of the old servants was left, though this is not to say the servants weren't old. The orange-and-white-haired group that would emerge from the subterranean regions of Aunt Sarah's houses to admit you were as ghostly and eccentrically incoherent with their thick Irish brogues as my Aunt Sarah was in her dementia. "Oh, should of she wananet yesterday, she's a-bob!" one would say as she led you in, laughing at the apparent joke. Aunt Sarah herself could be most articulate. "You're old and ugly, I hate you," Aunt Sarah would greet my mother, her favorite niece, leaping off the satin couch like an athlete, diapered but dressed (by nurses) to the nines. Or, "Thief, thief!" when I arrived with old pictures to look through. The nurses would comfort us by saying that Aunt Sarah was happier when we were not there, counting cars from her window on Beacon Street or watching quiz shows on TV in the dark study in Manchester, the only room that did not face the sea. "Come again soon!" the nurses would say when we beat our retreat.

"What did your aunt *do* all day?" a nurse asked me once, and I tried to explain that despite her money and servants, she never got to laze in bed on a Sunday, but was always up and down to breakfast by 8:30, ready to embark on her regimented schedule of charity and social functions. The dream of my life has been to be rich, but even as a covetous little girl, driving past the grand houses on Main Street or standing in the wide, long entrance hall of Aunt Sarah's house in Manchester, with the sea and sun glittering through the french doors, I knew that it was too high a price, dressing up to go to the beach.

This is not to say that sometimes when there is no money coming in and no immediate prospects, and Miss Sears is calling from BankAmericard, I don't think, *Bring me to that prison of charity functions and ladies' lunches.* Of course, I have never actually lived in that prison.

But sometimes I wonder if in the end Aunt Sarah actually liked being rich. Recently the curator of the Peabody Essex Museum told me about the first time he met the Cottings, out at the farm in 1980. Uncle Cot had invited a group from the museum to come look at the furniture. "We'll have to keep a few sticks of furniture around for the old girl when I die," he had said to the curator. The curator says Aunt Sarah arrived glowingly to greet them in the living room—nobody had told the curator she was out of her mind—and with a big smile she had gone right up to him, the youngest man in the group, taking his hand excitedly and saying conspiratorially, "Come with me!" Back she led him, through the enormous sunny dining room, through the spotless kitchen where Mrs. Ingles seemed to cook without disturbing a single pot, outside to one of the bigger barns, the calving barn, where the farm manager, the man in charge of all of Uncle Cot's prize cows, was working with one of his men. Smiling proudly, Aunt Sarah presented the curator to him. "Here is the man who is going to buy *all* of Cot's cows!" she said joyfully.

In my family you are either crazy or built to stand those who are. The two extremes do not understand each other at all and yet seem to fit together in a larger dynastic sense like a cog and a wheel. They are deeply attracted to each other—the strong nonneurotics and the clinically insane—subconsciously wishing to compensate for traits lacking in themselves.

Bobby was at one extreme; Aunt Sarah, who could sweep into Mass. Mental to visit an incarcerated relative on the way to Symphony, was at the other. Aunt Sarah survived Bobby by fifteen years, dying in 1993. At ninety-nine she was so physically hale that she helped the nurses up when they fell on the ice. Of her husband of fifty years she had not the slightest memory. "Who was I married to?" she would ask. "My father?"

Aunt Sarah died holding a nurse's hand. She had been diagnosed with pancreatic cancer two weeks before, but the only indication that she was sick had been the yellow tint of her skin. She seemed to have suffered no pain. For years my mother and I had consoled each other by agreeing that the real Aunt Sarah had died years ago, when her dementia had made her mean. So I was not prepared for the shock of her death. After I heard, I watched TV for an entire week, biting a facecloth, unable to quell the feeling of desolation and disorientation that engulfed me.

Her funeral was festive, as WASP funerals often are, in a stiff-upper-lip, let's-celebrate-the-life, not-complain-about-the-death sort of way. Neither Elizabeth nor Harriet was there. At the funeral my mother told the story of the time many years ago when Aunt Sarah triple-parked her car in the middle of Boylston Street in downtown Boston and blithely went wandering about Copley Square for two hours. Aunt Sarah was an absolutely terrible driver, except when it came to backing up. When she returned to the car, the other cars had left, and a furious police officer was tapping his foot on her running board. "Oh, officer," Aunt Sarah cried in sincere delight, "thank you *so much* for minding my car!"

Uncle Cot's will had provided for Aunt Sarah only during her life-time, ensuring that none of his money would go to the family when she died; even the proceeds from the sale of their houses went to the institutions Uncle Cot had endowed. But as it turned out Aunt Sarah had a tidy sum of money of her own in the bank, accruing from the $24,000 her father, Arthur Winslow, had left her. Half of this money went to the government when she died, but the other half went to her three nieces. When Arthur Winslow died, he felt that he had failed in his goal to bring the family back to its former glory, but at least none of us is selling matches on the street.

My mother's belief that money was the root of all evil made her anxious when she inherited the money from Aunt Sarah. As she had always feared, with the money came new problems. Now that they could afford it, my parents decided to move into a nice retirement home, though neither of them felt ready. And my mother, having not seemed to worry before, now worried about my father's financial position if she should die first. She planned to save much of her income for this eventuality, but then felt guilty because it would mean that she could not help her children more in their financial struggles. For months my mother didn't even ask the lawyer how much money there actually was. Finally my brother Hunter offered to ask him how much she had inherited. "Oh, I'm so glad you called," the financial adviser said, intensely relieved. "I wanted to tell her, but I didn't think she wanted to know."

One thing the money did for my mother was show her that, twenty years' evidence to the contrary, Aunt Sarah had loved her to the end. Uncle Cot's financial adviser told me that Uncle Cot was surprised that Aunt Sarah wanted to leave the money to her family at all. Aunt Sarah must have wanted very much to give what she had to my mother and her sisters to go against her husband's advice. In the last years of her life, Aunt Sarah (through the adviser) had made ten-thousand-dollar gifts to her family to avoid inheritance taxes. One time someone from the IRS was sent to question Aunt Sarah, who by then, on good days, only recognized generations older than hers ("*You* played with my father when he was a little boy," she would inform Uncle Cot's adviser, who had no other course but to agree), and on bad days recognized no one at all. But, my mother says, when the IRS agent said, "Mrs. Cotting, what do you *really* wish to do with your income?" Aunt Sarah had snapped back: "I want to take care of my nieces."

Uncle Cot's financial adviser first met Aunt Sarah in the 1970s, when he and his wife began being invited once a year to Manchester to go out on the boat for the day and then back to the house for cock-tails and dinner in formal attire. What he remembers most about these visits was that Aunt Sarah would talk incessantly about her nephew Robert Lowell, and what a wonderful person he was, and how he'd written this wonderful poem about her. "Why did she do that?" I asked, surprised. "She had just disinherited him," the adviser said, "and I think she was feeling very guilty about it."

Charlie and I happened to be invited to dinner at Manchester the day Bobby died, and that night Great Aunt-Sarah was without rancor, patting my knee every few minutes and jumping up to refill our drinks. Even when she confused the generations, it was in my favor, mistaking me for my mother and referring to Devereux as my father. Despite everything, Aunt Sarah had loved Bobby, but when he died she acted as if a tremendous burden had been lifted from her. It was as if she felt relief—relief that Bobby had died before her and that therefore, she reasoned, she had never really disinherited him.

Aunt Sarah told many of her familiar stories that evening, but none were the ones she loved to tell about Bobby. She never even mentioned Bobby's name, yet somehow he was there, because she was the same warm, flirtatious person she had always been around Bobby. She hadn't been so nice to me in years; and it was the last time she ever was.

To all of us who remained, Aunt Sarah *was* "the family," an entity that had been creating and re-creating itself since the first self-punishers had landed at Plymouth. Most of us had rebelled against "the family" and its values, but at the same time, we had longed for its approval. Aunt Sarah's death was the end of all that.

Aunt Sarah had survived by thinking the happy thoughts she was supposed to have and, when the thoughts began to sour, her constitution had responded with the loss of her mind, another form of survival. But when Bobby lost his mind, it was not a survival technique; he remembered everything he had done to the people he loved and suffered endlessly for the suffering he had caused. And so, though he led a life as irregular as Aunt Sarah's was regular, he was never free.

One time, when Bobby actually was imprisoned, serving time as a conscientious objector, Aunt Charlotte invited Sarah to go with her to visit him. Aunt Sarah said she would love to; what was Charlotte wearing? They had a long discussion about what one wore to prison. The next morning, dressed to a T, the sisters stood on Beacon Street, and Charlotte hailed a cab with a white-gloved hand. "The prison in Danbury, Connecticut, please," she instructed the driver as they got in. The cabbie turned to her and said, "Lady, why in the world would someone like you want to go all the way to Danbury Prison?" Charlotte turned to him grandly. "My son is *staying* there," she said. When they arrived at the prison, the guard at the desk gave them a queer look. "I would like to see my son, Robert Lo-well," Charlotte said imperiously. "Oh, him!" said the guard with contempt. "He spends whole days in the *library*." When Bobby appeared his face was aglow. `He ran up to his mother and aunt and kissed them. "Oh, Mother," he said, "I'm so happy. It's so peaceful here."

Sarah Chardua - Sept 1927 Bobby

Most of the events described in this book are from my own personal experiences or from remembrances of the members of my family. In addition to quotations from Robert Lowell's own work, I am indebted to Ian Hamilton (*Robert Lowell: A Biography*) and Paul Mariani (*Lost Puritan: A Life of Robert Lowell*) as sources for some aspects of Robert Lowell's life.

Quotations from Robert Lowell are from the following editions of his books:

Robert Lowell: Collected Prose. Edited by Robert Giroux. New York: Farrar, Straus & Giroux, 1987.

Robert Lowell: Selected Poems. Rev. ed. New York: Noonday Press / Farrar, Straus & Giroux, 1977.

Day by Day. New York: Farrar, Straus & Giroux, 1977.

The Dolphin. New York: Farrar, Straus & Giroux, 1973.

For Lizzie and Harriet. New York: Farrar, Straus & Giroux, 1973.

History. New York: Farrar, Straus & Giroux, 1973.

Notebook (1967–68). New York: Farrar, Straus & Giroux, 1969.

Near the Ocean. New York: Farrar, Straus & Giroux, 1967.

Life Studies and *For the Union Dead*. New York: Farrar, Straus & Giroux, New York, 1964.

The Mills of the Kavanaughs. New York: Harcourt, Brace & Company, 1951.

Lord Weary's Castle. New York: Harcourt, Brace & Company, New York, 1946.

HISTORIES AND FAMILY BOOKS

Barck, Oscar Theodore, Jr., and Hugh Talmage Lefler. *Colonial America.* New York: Macmillan, 1958.

Battis, Emery. *Saints and Sectaries: Anne Hutchinson.* Chapel Hill: University of North Carolina Press, 1962.

Bradford, William. *Bradford's History "of Plimoth Plantation."* Boston: Wright & Potter Printing Co., State Printers, 1901.

Burchard, Peter. *One Gallant Rush: Robert Gould Shaw and his Brave Black Regiment,* New York: St. Martin's Press, 1965.

Coons, Quentin, and Cynthia Hagar Krussell. *The Winslows of "Careswell" Before and After the "Mayflower,"* Plymouth, Mass.: Pilgrim Society, 1975.

Devereux, Margaret. *Plantation Sketches.* 1906.

Frederick, A. de B., and Alison Ridley, *The Boston Cotting Family.* Printed by Graphic Arts at Cotting School for the H andicapped.

Heath, Dwight B., ed. *Mourt's Relation: A Journey of the Pilgrims at Plymouth (1622).* Bedford, Mass.: Applewood Books, 1963.

Lahikainen, Dean. "The Charles Cotting Collection: A Window on a Privileged Life," *Peabody Essex Magazine* (1993).

Lepore, Jill. *The Name Of War: King Philip's War and the Origins of American Identity.* New York: Alfred A. Knopf, 1998.

Ober, Frederic A. *In King Philip's War.* New York: A.L. Burt Company, n.d.

Styron, Nell Devereux Joslin. *Fall of the House of Hinsdale,* 1986.

Winslow, D. Kenelm. *Mayflower Heritage: A Family Record of the Growth of Anglo-American Partnership.* London: George G. Harrap & Co. Ltd, 1957.

Winslow, Arthur. "The Land in Ohio", "A Journey in Norway," "The Lure of Mont Blanc" (pamphlets), 1925.

———. *Francis Winslow: His Forebears and Life,* 1935.

Winslow, Edward. *Good News from New England*. 1624. Reprint, Bedford, Mass.: Applewood Books, 1996.

BOOKS RELATING TO ROBERT LOWELL

Axelrod, Steven Gould. *Robert Lowell: Life and Art*. Princeton, N.J.: Princeton University Press, 1978.

Davison, Peter. *The Fading Smile: Poets in Boston, from Robert Frost to Robert Lowell to Sylvia Plath, 1955–1960*. New York: Alfred A. Knopf, 1994.

Fein, Richard J. *Robert Lowell*. Boston: Twayne Publishers, Inc., 1979.

Hamilton, Ian. *Robert Lowell: A Biography*. New York: Random House, New York, 1982.

Hardwick, Elizabeth. *A View of My Own: Essays in Literature and Society*. New York: Farrar, Straus & Cudahy, 1962.

————. *Sleepless Nights*. New York: Random House, 1979.

Heymann, David C. *American Aristocracy: The Lives and Times of James Russell, Amy & Robert Lowell*. New York: Dodd, Mead & Company, 1980.

Hobsbaum, Philip. *A Reader's Guide to Robert Lowell*. London: Thames and Hudson, Ltd, 1988.

London, Michael, and Robert Boyers, eds. *Robert Lowell: A Portrait of the Artist in His Time*. New York: David Lewis Publisher, Inc., 1970.

Mailer, Norman. *The Armies of the Night*. New York: New American Library, 1968.

Mariani, Paul. *Lost Puritan: A Life of Robert Lowell*. New York: W.W. Norton & Company, New York, London, 1994.

Meyers, Jeffrey, ed. *Robert Lowell: Interviews and Memoirs*. Ann Arbor: University of Michigan Press, 1988.

Meyers, Jeffrey. *Manic Power: Robert Lowell and His Circle*. New York: Arbor House, 1987.

Parkinson, Thomas, ed. *Robert Lowell: A Collection of Critical Essays*. Englewood Cliffs, N.J.: Prentice-Hall, Inc., 1968.

Perloff, Marjorie G. *The Poetic Art of Robert Lowell*. Ithaca, N.Y. Cornell University Press, 1973.

Roberts, David. *Jean Stafford: A Biography.* Boston: Little, Brown and Company, 1988.

Rudman, Mark. *Robert Lowell: An Introduction to the Poetry.* New York: Columbia University Press, 1983.

Simpson, Eileen. *Poets in Their Youth.* New York: Random House, 1982.

Taylor, Peter Hillsman. *The Collected Stories of Peter Taylor.* New York: Farrar, Straus & Giroux, New York, 1969.

Made in the USA
Lexington, KY
04 October 2014